Y0-ADY-474

*Mississippian Polity and Politics
on the Gulf Coastal Plain*

Mississippian Polity and Politics on the Gulf Coastal Plain

A View from the Pearl River, Mississippi

Patrick C. Livingood

THE UNIVERSITY OF ALABAMA PRESS
Tuscaloosa

Copyright © 2010
The University of Alabama Press
Tuscaloosa, Alabama 35487-0380
All rights reserved
Manufactured in the United States of America

Typeface: ACaslon

∞

The paper on which this book is printed meets the minimum requirements of American National Standard for Information Sciences-Permanence of Paper for Printed Library Materials, ANSI Z39.48-1984.

Library of Congress Cataloging-in-Publication Data

Livingood, Patrick C.
　Mississippian polity and politics on the Gulf Coastal Plain : a view from the Pearl River, Mississippi / Patrick C. Livingood.
　　　p. cm.
　"A Dan Josselyn memorial publication."
　Includes bibliographical references and index.
　ISBN 978-0-8173-1724-9 (cloth : alk. paper) — ISBN 978-0-8173-5639-2 (pbk. : alk. paper) — ISBN 978-0-8173-8512-5 (electronic)
　　1. Pevey Site (Miss.) 2. Lowe-Steen Site (Miss.) 3. Mississippian culture—Pearl River Valley (Miss. and La.) 4. Mounds—Pearl River Valley (Miss. and La.) 5. Pearl River Valley (Miss. and La.)—Antiquities. 6. Excavations (Archaeology)—Pearl River Valley (Miss. and La.) I. Title.
　E99.M6815L58 2010
　976.2′5—dc22

　　　　　　　　　　　　　　　　　　　　　　　　　　　　　　　　　2010024163

Contents

List of Illustrations   vii

Acknowledgments   xi

1. The Nature of Mississippian Interpolity Competition   1
2. Archaeology of the Middle Pearl River   19
3. Investigation of the Settlement Patterns of the Pevey Polity   55
4. Temper and Culture: Ceramic Analysis   67
5. Analyses of Foodways and of Other Artifact Classes   106
6. Interpretations of the Middle Pearl Mississippian   124
7. Regional Analysis and Interpolity Competition   135

Appendix 1. Ceramic Types and Counts   155

Appendix 2. Macrofaunal Analysis from Two Units at the Pevey Site   183

References Cited   193

Index   221

Illustrations

FIGURES
1.1. Location of the primary sites and rivers discussed in the text   2
1.2. Chronological chart showing the timing of different phases for the Middle Pearl and adjacent river valleys   3
1.3. Number of Mississippian mounds occupied during each year of the Mississippian   15
1.4. Histogram of the start date of mound construction for the mound sample   16
2.1. Topography of the Pevey site and surrounding area   24
2.2. Map of the Pevey site (22Lw510) showing locations of the excavation units   25
2.3. Profile map of Unit B, west ½, east wall, 22Lw510   29
2.4. Unit C west and north wall stratigraphy, 22Lw510   30
2.5. Profile map of Unit SE, north wall, 22Lw510   32
2.6. Map of Unit SE unit base floor, 22Lw510   33
2.7. Profile map of Unit M, east ½, west wall, 22Lw510   35
2.8. Map of Unit M, east ½, excavation level 6 floor plan, 22Lw510   36
2.9. Profile map of Unit T, east wall, 22Lw510   37
2.10. Plan drawing of the base of Unit T, 22Lw510   38
2.11. Profile map of Unit G, south wall, 22Lw510   40
2.12. Plan drawing of the base of Unit G, 22Lw510   41
2.13. Profile map of Unit H, east wall, 22Lw510   42
2.14. Profile map of Unit I, east wall, 22Lw510   44
2.15. The environmental and topographic setting of the Lowe-Steen site   46

viii   Illustrations

2.16. Topographic map of the Lowe-Steen site (22Lw511) showing the location of the excavation units   47

2.17. Topographic map of the primary Lowe-Steen mound, Mound A   48

2.18. Profile map of Unit 975R1007, east profile, 22Lw511   49

2.19. Environmental setting of the Phillips Farm site (22Lw593)   52

2.20. Map of the Phillips Farm (22Lw593) excavations   53

3.1. Map of all known Mississippi period sites in Lawrence County   58

3.2. Map of the locations of ceramics found in Survey Blocks 8 and 9   60

4.1. Anna Incised and L'Eau Noire Incised ceramics   72

4.2. Moundville Incised and other decorated ceramics   73

4.3. Carter Engraved and other decorated ceramics   74

4.4. Mound Place Incised and other decorated ceramics   75

4.5. Plane-polarized, cross-polarized, and color-enhanced images and the inclusion map of a thin section   81

4.6. Biplot of grog and shell abundance in the sample, showing the original temper assignments   84

4.7. Biplot of the sherds in the sample showing cluster boundaries   86

4.8. Histogram of temper modes for brushed and interior incised vessels   91

4.9. Histograms showing the number of each vessel shape having each temper mode   92

4.10. Graph showing the proportion of serving and storage vessels for the units of 22Lw510   100

4.11. Graph showing the proportion of serving and storage vessels for the units of 22Lw511   100

4.12. Histograms of rim diameters, all nongeneric bowls   102

4.13. Histograms of rim diameters of jars, excluding generic jars   103

4.14. Box-and-whisker plots of vessel orifice diameter by vessel type and unit for site 22Lw510   104

4.15. Box-and-whisker plots of vessel orifice diameter by vessel type and unit for site 22Lw511   105

5.1. The flow chart used for sorting and analyzing lithics   116

5.2. Plot of debitage from the Pevey units   120
5.3. Photograph of copper foil and beads   122
6.1. Box plots showing the calibrated date ranges of the samples   128
7.1. Map showing mound sites in the regional analysis that were in use at approximately A.D. 1250   136
7.2. Map showing the Hally circles (18 km) around presumed polity centers dating to approximately A.D. 1250   144
7.3. Map of mound sites in the study area that were occupied at approximately A.D. 1250, showing the number of mounds at each site   146
7.4. Map showing distances from the major centers in the study area   150

TABLES

2.1. Percentage of decorated sherds in each excavation unit at Pevey   39
3.1. Summary of all known Mississippi period sites in Lawrence County   57
3.2. Percentage of decorated and undecorated sherds by site   63
3.3. Percentage of decorated and undecorated sherds by site type   64
3.4. Percentage of decorated and undecorated sherds by mound or non-mound sites   64
3.5. Count of sherds by site and temper   65
4.1. Counts of sherds analyzed, by site   72
4.2. Results of the digital petrographic analysis of temper   78
4.3. Summary of clusters identified through digital petrographic analysis   87
4.4. Assignment of sherds to temper modes, by original assignment of temper type   90
4.5. Percentages of temper by vessel category   93
4.6. Decorated sherds found at the Pevey and Lowe-Steen sites that are consistent with a Winstead phase date   96
4.7. Decorated sherds that are associated with Gordon or Crippen Point phases in the Lower Mississippi Valley   96
4.8. Decorated sherds found at the Pevey site that might be indicative of a post–Winstead phase occupation   97
4.9. Total number of sherds representative of vessel shape, by site   99
5.1. Summary of flotation samples from Pevey site   107

5.2. Plants identified among the Pevey samples   108
5.3. Raw taxa counts from Pevey samples   109
5.4. Kernel and cupule counts for the samples, sorted by ratio of kernels to cupules   111
5.5. Corn cupule and hickory counts for the samples, sorted by ratio of cupules to hickory   112
5.6. Percentages of plant food taxa from Pevey and other sites   113
5.7. Counts of lithic types from the Pevey and Lowe-Steen sites classified by debitage, tool, or other   118
5.8. Totals of analyzed lithic types by excavation unit for the Pevey site   119
6.1. Summary of architectural patterns found in excavation   126
6.2. List of radiocarbon samples   130
7.1. Summary of the regions and polities in the study area   147
7.2. Distances between mound sites in the center of the research area and the closest major multi-mound centers   149
7.3. Time required to travel specified distances   151

Acknowledgments

A project of this size takes lots of hands, and I am deeply in debt to many people for their help, suggestions, and support. The first mention must go to Tim Mooney, to whom this volume is dedicated. Tim directed the 1993 and 1994 seasons of fieldwork at Pevey and Lowe-Steen as a part of his doctoral research. He was extremely hard working, and his enthusiasm and dedication were infectious. His untimely death was a real tragedy, and it is doubly tragic that he was unable to see this work to its conclusion.

I must also give special thanks to Vin Steponaitis, who entrusted me with making sure these sites were ultimately analyzed and reported. He has been generous with his time and his thoughts on southeastern archaeology, and I owe much of my outlook on archaeology to his tutelage. This volume owes a great deal to him in many different respects. In particular, he spent numerous hours helping me understand the nuances of Lower Valley pottery types, and for that task alone I am eternally thankful.

I am deeply indebted to Dick Ford. From my very first day at the University of Michigan, he treated me as a colleague. He always went out of his way to help make my graduate career as painless as it could possibly be, and he is an example of what it means to be a colleague and a scholar.

Many people in Lawrence County helped make this research possible. Several landowners were generous with access to the sites, and they have done an excellent job preserving them for posterity. Annie Pevey, John and Barbara Winstead, Ernest Lowe, David Miles, Herman Sauls, Nancy Coin, Jimmy Lowe, Phillip Lowe, and Billy Stephens all made this project possible. Also, Earl and Voncelle Benoit provided lodgings for four seasons of archaeologists and did so with remarkable generosity. Finally, Joan Hartzog and the late Anita Clinton took special interest in the history and prehistory of Lawrence County and assisted Tim and me in many ways.

Archaeological fieldwork always requires lots of people investing their sweat and energy. This project was possible because of the efforts of the 1993 University of North Carolina Field School students: Tatiana Brecht, Cullen Case, Merideth Griffin, Cleve Hicks, Kristen Howard, Jennifer Kolb, Mickey Loughlin, and Nathan Snider; the 1994 University of North Carolina Field School supervisors and students: Marco Brewer, Cindy Brown, Sam Cohen, Rachel Ferguson, Dee Hunt, Caroline Joyce, Wanda Lassiter, Susannah Livingood, Caroline Moore, Frank Plaza, Scott Thomas, and Angie Tromba; and the brave volunteers who joined me for the 1999 and 2000 fieldwork: Jami Bailey, Katharine Gell, Chris Glew, Dan Hartzog, Susannah Livingood, Trent Luse, Joellyn Palomaki, Mark Plane, Melisa Ricketts, Teagan Schweitzer, Sudha Shah, Kenny Sims, and Jill Soubel.

This project also required long hours in the laboratory. In these efforts I was ably assisted by Jami Bailey, Erica Dziedzic, Rachel Lovis, Joellyn Palomaki, and John Sabol. Jami, in particular, deserves thanks for taking a supervisory role in analyzing the artifacts. Emily Moazami helped digitize the plan and profile drawings utilized in this report.

The ideas explored in this work were the product of many hours of discussion with many archaeologists. I owe much in this regard to David Anderson, Duke Beasley, John Blitz, Tony Boudreaux, Ian Brown, Sunday Eiselt, Chris Glew, Scott Hammerstedt, Baxter Mann, Mark Rees, Amanda Regnier, Chris Rodning, Sudha Shah, Vin Steponaitis, Paul Welch, Greg Wilson, and Henry Wright.

This book benefited greatly from the comments of Chris Glew and Susannah Livingood; those of David Allan, Dick Ford, John Speth, and Henry Wright; and those of Jay Johnson and Marvin Smith, who reviewed the book manuscript.

My fieldwork was generously supported by the Griffin Fellowship Fund, Rackham Graduate School at the University of Michigan, the Department of Anthropology of the University of Michigan's Summer Research program, and the Wenner-Gren Foundation for Anthropological Research.

Last, but certainly not least, I owe so much to my wife Susannah and my two children. Susannah and I met during the 1994 field season in Lawrence County so this work has special meaning to us. She has been incredibly supportive in every way possible, and this work would not have been possible without her.

1
The Nature of Mississippian Interpolity Competition

We currently lack an understanding of the regional limits of interpolity influence during the Mississippi period in the southeastern United States. In the Gulf Coastal Plain between the Mississippi and Black Warrior rivers, some studies (Blitz 1993a; Steponaitis 1991) have explored the role that interpolity interactions played in influencing a polity's social and political complexity through time. For example, the developmental trajectories of the largest polities in the region, such as Moundville, Lake George, Winterville, and Bottle Creek, stand in stark contrast to the developmental trajectories of Lubbub Creek, Pocahontas, and Old Hoover, which remained modest sites despite the fact that many of them were founded at approximately the same time as their larger neighbors. Steponaitis (1991) has argued that the larger, more complex polities were able to preempt the development of more complex political structures among the smaller polities. The current study explores the social and political mechanisms by which these polities may have interacted with each other. We expect these processes will be attenuated with distance, and this research finds a geographic limit to the effects of interpolity competition.

This research reports on fieldwork conducted at the Pevey (22Lw510) and Lowe-Steen (22Lw511) mound sites on the Pearl River in Lawrence County, Mississippi (Pevey has gone by the names Mill Creek Mounds and Pearl River Mounds; see Chapter 2 for details). The Pevey site is a nine-mound Mississippian site and Lowe-Steen is a two-mound site located 18 km to the north of Pevey. These sites provide a "missing link" of sorts to explore these questions about interpolity interactions because of their centrality to the study region and their unusual size (Figures 1.1 and 1.2). By filling a void in the regional data set, these sites allow us to better understand the capacity

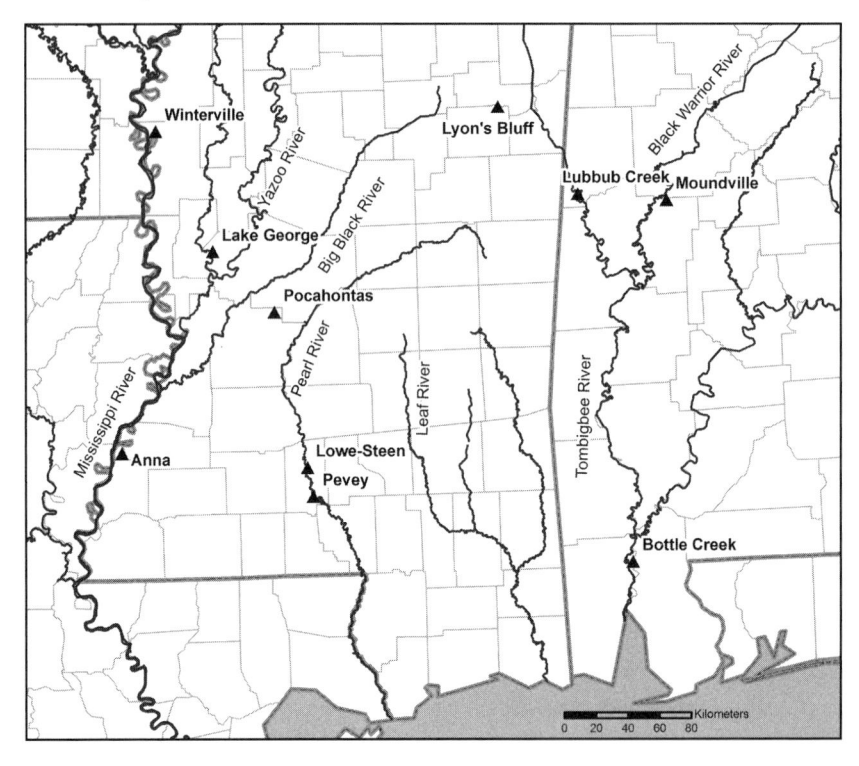

Figure 1.1. Location of the primary sites and rivers discussed in the text and the boundaries of the regional archaeological study area.

of the largest polities to negatively affect the political development of their smaller neighbors.

Mississippian Chiefdoms

Since the chiefdom model (Earle 1978, 1987; Peebles and Kus 1977; Service 1962; Wright 1977, 1984) was applied to our understanding of Mississippian societies, we have learned a great deal about the internal workings of these societies. Specifically, a lot of work has been devoted to improving our understanding of the prestige goods economy (Brown et al. 1990; Marcoux 2007; Welch 1991; Wilson 2001), the organization and economies of farmsteads (Gougeon 2006; Maxham 2000; Mehrer 1995; Prentice 1985; Scarry and Steponaitis 1997), settlement patterns (Pluckhahn and McKivergan 2002; Smith 1978a), the instability of chiefly polities (Anderson 1994a, 1994b, 1996; Blitz 1999), the Mississippian political economy (Cobb 2000; Muller 1997), internal ranking and organization (Beck 2003; Blitz 1993b; Jackson and Scott 1995, 2003; King 2003; Pauketat 1994; Pauketat and Emerson 1999; Welch

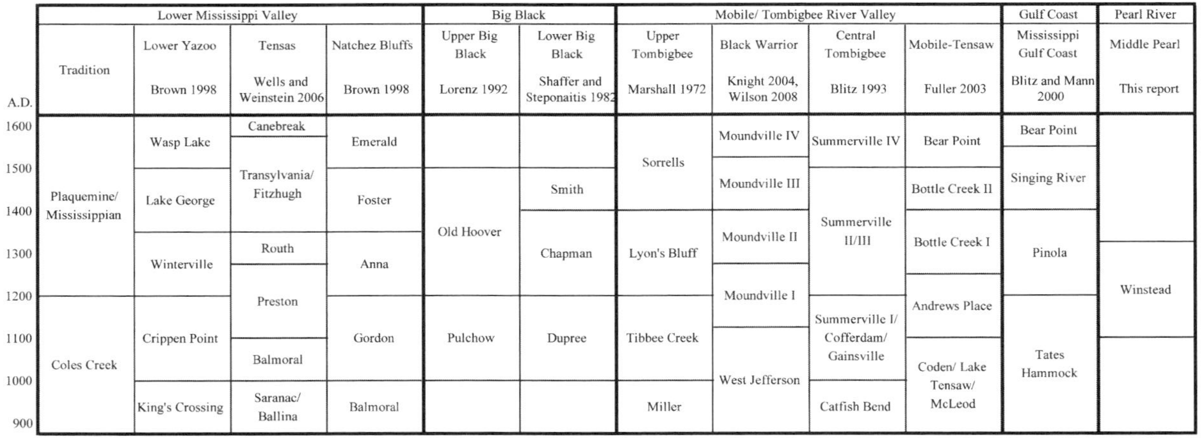

A.D.	Lower Mississippi Valley			Big Black		Mobile/ Tombigbee River Valley				Gulf Coast	Pearl River
Tradition	Lower Yazoo Brown 1998	Tensas Wells and Weinstein 2006	Natchez Bluffs Brown 1998	Upper Big Black Lorenz 1992	Lower Big Black Shaffer and Steponaitis 1982	Upper Tombigbee Marshall 1972	Black Warrior Knight 2004, Wilson 2008	Central Tombigbee Blitz 1993	Mobile-Tensaw Fuller 2003	Mississippi Gulf Coast Blitz and Mann 2000	Middle Pearl This report
1600	Wasp Lake	Canebreak	Emerald							Bear Point	
1500		Transylvania/ Fitzhugh	Foster		Smith	Sorrells	Moundville IV	Summerville IV	Bear Point	Singing River	
1400	Lake George			Old Hoover			Moundville III	Summerville II/III	Bottle Creek II		
1300	Winterville	Routh	Anna		Chapman	Lyon's Bluff	Moundville II		Bottle Creek I	Pinola	
1200		Preston					Moundville I		Andrews Place		Winstead
1100	Crippen Point	Balmoral	Gordon	Pulchow	Dupree	Tibbee Creek		Summerville I/ Cofferdam/ Gainsville		Tates Hammock	
1000							West Jefferson		Coden/ Lake Tensaw/ McLeod		
900	King's Crossing	Saranac/ Ballina	Balmoral			Miller		Catfish Bend			

Figure 1.2. Chronological chart showing the timing of different phases for the Middle Pearl and adjacent river valleys (Blitz 1993b; Blitz and Mann 2000; Brown 1998; Fuller 2003; Knight 2004; Lorenz 1992; Marshall 1977; Shaffer and Steponaitis 1982; Wilson 2008; Wells and Weinstein 2007).

and Scarry 1995), and the nature and diversity of leadership (Beck 2006; King 2006; Welch 2006).

There have also been numerous critiques of the application of the chiefdom model to the Mississippian, most notably Pauketat's (2007) book. Pauketat, as others have before him, objected to the social evolutionary connotations of *chiefdom* (Yoffee 1993) and the imprecision of the term (Feinman and Neitzel 1984; O'Shea and Barker 1996). Pauketat was also very concerned that the term *chiefdom,* especially in its minimalist connotations, fails to fit all Mississippian polities, particularly Cahokia (Pauketat 2007:159), and fails to provide a good explanatory framework for the Mississippianization of the late prehistoric southeast (Pauketat 2007:85). Despite these criticisms, Pauketat did not advocate completely abandoning the term *chiefdom,* merely "return chiefdom to a purely descriptive usage" (Pauketat 2007:13).

It is in this descriptive sense that *chiefdom* is used in this work. Like Muller (1997:41–42) I find *chiefdom* to be an adequate term to denote the majority of the late prehistoric polities of the Southeast. The term *chiefdom* is burdened with many antiquated connotations, but rather than necessitating discard of the term this merely means that it must be defined by each author for his or her own work (see Barker 2008 for a review of the history of the chiefdom concept). The same is true for many other more pedestrian terms archaeologists are accustomed to using that carry many differing and sometimes contradictory meanings like *temper, biface,* or *feature.* A frequent criticism of "chiefdom" or other social typologies is that even when such terms are rigorously defined there are always boundary cases over which one may argue the application of the term. It should come as no surprise that many of the most vocal critics of the social evolutionary typologies work on archaeological cultures most poorly served by those typologies, and in the Southeast these include Cahokia and Poverty Point. Unfortunately those who argue for the uselessness of *chiefdom* merely from its inapplication to a few cultures fall into the logical fallacy of the continuum. Terms like *bald* and *beard* still have utility even if most observers would disagree on whether specific individuals would qualify as being bald or as having a beard, and terms like *chiefdom* can still be valuable even if there are inevitable boundary cases that resist categorization.

Therefore, in this work *chiefdom* is used to connote societies with some degree of multigenerational centralized and hierarchical political authority and territorial integration but lacking rigid social classes or an elaborate bureaucracy. This usage differentiates chiefdoms from states and from other societies lacking centralized political authority. It also serves to differentiate the typical usage of *chiefdom* from short-lived expressions of political centralization that likely occurred in the past, which Milner and Schroeder

(1999) refer to as "presumptive chiefdoms." Such a definition is needed in this work because not all polities in the study area fit the chiefdom criteria.

Regional Perspectives on Mississippian Chiefdoms

Despite advances in our understanding of certain areas of Mississippian systems, little is known about Mississippian regional political systems because the requisite data are difficult to compile and analyze. Traditionally, the primary means of studying regional interactions is through analyses of trade and exchange. Archaeologists can trace the movements of raw materials and finished goods and surmise the types of interactions and exchanges that could make such networks possible. These kinds of studies have benefited tremendously from the chemical and physical analyses archaeologists can use to determine the source of raw materials (e.g., Emerson and Hughes 2000; Emerson et al. 2003; Gall and Steponaitis 2001; Steponaitis et al. 1996; Whitney et al. 2002; Wisseman et al. 2002).

Settlement patterns represent another critical avenue of investigation that can shed light on regional organization and competition during the Mississippi period. David Hally has done some of the most important research with regard to regional Mississippian systems. He examined the locations of mound sites in the southern Appalachian region and found that almost all contemporaneous mounds were located either less than 18 km or more than 32 km from each other (Hally 1993, 1999). These clusters of sites are interpreted as Mississippian polities, in which secondary centers are located within 18 km of the primary center and there is usually a buffer zone of at least 10–20 km between polities (Hally 2006). Spencer (1982:6–7, 1987:375) argued that a paramount chief's domain would likely be limited to a half day's travel from the political center, and he demonstrated how this has been documented for other chiefdoms around the world (Bauer and Covey 2002: 847–848; Cohen and Schlegel 1968:136; Helms 1979:51–53; Little 1967:240; Spencer 1990:6–8). This limit is largely due to the lack of internally specialized administrative units within chiefdoms (Wright 1977, 1984). Without internally specialized administrative organization, chiefs must avoid delegation of authority and must manage their domains from the center (Spencer 1987:375, 1990:7).

Hally's discovery is exciting for several reasons. First, it is an empirical confirmation of a theoretical expectation. As noted previously, scholars expected that hierarchical pre-state polities would encounter certain limits in their ability to control and consolidate an area. Furthermore, using the Hiker's formula developed by Gorenflo and Gale (1990) and the trail multiplier proposed by Tobler (1993), a distance of 18 km could be traversed in about four hours on foot by a reasonably healthy adult if there were a trail and the path were reasonably level (details of the formula are provided in Chapter 7). This means that Hally's distance corresponds well with Spencer's estimate of time. Second, the spatial patterning is unambiguous and would likely have been recognized by the Mississippian residents. Therefore, this represents one of the few times in which we can be fairly confident that the etic identification of space matches with the emic identification. Eighteenth-century maps produced by native informants for Europeans confirm that in later times, native settlements were conceived of as clusters of people with connections to other clusters (Waselkov 1989). These maps are probably best referred to as sociograms (Galloway 1998a), and they consistently employ the convention of representing socially cohesive groups of people as circles connected to each other with lines showing their cultural, political, or physical connections. These conventions were used for both maps depicting vast regions and maps showing the location of Chickasaw villages on a smaller scale (Waselkov 1998). Furthermore, prehistoric shell gorgets may have utilized similar symbolic conventions (Lafferty 1994). All of this indicates that the polity is a useful minimal unit of analysis for a discussion of regional interactions.

In the remainder of this research I will employ a strict definition of "polity" *sensu* Hally and Spencer, which defines a polity as a geographically discrete and bounded political unit typically covering an area within a half day's journey from the political center, typically 20 km in the Gulf Coastal Plain of the Southeast. The rest of this book is concerned with the types of social and political interactions that take place between polities. It is uncontroversial to say that there are differences in the quantitative sizes of Mississippian polities as measured by site size and the other proxy variables we have for population size. This work will argue that these quantitative differences translate into qualitative differences with respect to how polities operated internally and externally.

Paramount Chiefdoms in the Historic Period

There are several examples in the historic Southeast of one chiefly polity having some amount of control or influence over other polities. These are called paramount chiefdoms and known examples include Coosa, Cofitachequi, Ocute, and Tascalusa. Much of what is known about these chiefdoms comes from the written accounts of the Spanish expeditions of Hernando de Soto, who trekked throughout the interior Southeast between 1539 and 1542 (Clayton et al. 1993; Hudson 1997), and Juan Pardo in 1567 (Hudson 1990). Through the work of Charles Hudson, Marvin T. Smith, Chester DePratter, and others (Hudson 1994, 1997; Smith 2000), we have a reasonable estimate of the routes that the Spanish used and the archaeological sites that correspond to some of the locations described within the accounts.

The best known of these historic chiefdoms is Coosa (Hally 1994; Hally et al. 1990; Hudson et al. 1985; Smith 2000). According to Hally's reconstruction, the Coosa chiefdom incorporated more than seven polities and extended more than 400 km (Hally et al. 1990:132). The Little Egypt site has been identified as the likely home of the paramount chief. Unfortunately, the historical accounts do not provide very precise accounts of the exact political relationships between the polities. For example, the town of Chiaha was described as being "subject" to the Coosa chief (Smith 2000:35); however, very little is known about what such a status entailed. Smith (2000:94) and Hudson (1997:215–216) argue that the Coosa paramount was able to extract tribute from the subordinate polities, but the frequency, manner, and form of the tribute is entirely unclear. The fact that Soto was offered generous gifts of food during his expedition suggests that food may have been one form of tribute offered to elites. Furthermore, two decades after the Soto expedition, Tristan de Luna (Hudson et al. 1989) allied with the Coosa paramount to subjugate the Napochies, who were forced to contribute game, fruits, and nuts in tribute. Based on archaeological data for tribute during the protohistoric, Rees (1997) shows there is evidence that elites at Little Egypt (Hally 1980; Roth 1980) and Toqua (Bogan and Polhemus 1987; Polhemus 1987) were provisioned with food. This pattern of elite provisioning has been found at other sites, including Moundville and Bottle Creek (Jackson and Scott 1995, 2003; Scarry 2003a; Scarry and Steponaitis 1997; Welch and Scarry 1995), but there is little evidence to indicate how much, if any, of the provisions were being provided by extrapolity sources.

Unfortunately, the paramount chiefdom of Coosa is essentially invisible in the archaeological record (Hally et al. 1990:133). The only marker that seems to correspond with the boundaries of the paramount chiefdom is the distribution of Citico style rattlesnake gorgets. However, they are found interred with females and seem an unlikely symbol of the paramount chief or his political control (Hally et al. 1990:133). Because of the paucity of archaeological and historical data on the nature of the paramountcy, it is possible to construct a maximalist and a minimalist view of Coosa authority. As Smith (2000:93–94) states, it is possible that the Coosa paramount chiefdom was formed through conquest, and that the political center extracted regular tribute of goods, including foodstuffs. It is also possible that Coosa had little real power over the secondary polities, that the entity Soto recognized was merely a loose alliance, and that interpolity tribute was uncommon.

The lack of archaeological markers is interpreted by Hally et al. (1990:134) as evidence that the political relationship between paramount and subordinate polities was primarily symbolic in nature and that the paramountcy was likely ephemeral and short lived (Hally 1994). If the paramount chiefdom had been strongly centralized for an extended period of time, there would be clear evidence of a tributary relationship and an eventual change in settlement patterns. Current data indicate that all of the polities within the Coosa chiefdom are distributed as if there had not been a paramountcy, including the expected 10- to 20-km buffer zones. Furthermore, given the distance and effort required to transport bulk foodstuffs, most interpolity tribute is probably more likely categorized as wealth finance than staple finance (D'Altroy and Earle 1985). A paramount chief's requests for food from subordinate polities were probably restricted to personal visits, for use in feasts, or in order to compensate for emergencies such as crop failures or warfare.

Coosa is not the only historically identified paramount chiefdom in the Southeast. The Spanish also encountered Cofitachequi (Anderson 1994b; DePratter 1994; Waddell 2005) in South Carolina and Ocute in southern Georgia (Williams 1994). There are some disagreements about the extent of the Cofitachequi paramount chiefdom (cf. Anderson 1994b; DePratter 1994; Hudson et al. 1984), although it appears to have spanned approximately 200 km. Ocute (or Oconee) was much smaller and likely incorporated no more than a few polities. Hally (2006:31) provides an estimate that the paramount chiefdom extended for approximately 100 km and united a maximum of four polities. As with the Coosa paramountcy, the historical record provides very little information about the political relationships between the polities and few good archaeological markers to indicate a paramount chiefdom ever existed. Farther west in central Alabama, the Soto expedition encountered the territory of Tascalusa. Unfortunately, some of the major towns have not yet been identified archaeologically, making it difficult to estimate the size (Knight 2009). However, it is likely that Tascalusa was smaller than Coosa and more similar in size to Cofitachequi or Ocute. Finally, on their flight down the Mississippi River, the remnants of the Soto party were harassed for several days by warriors of the Quigualtam chiefdom and another unnamed chiefdom. Unfortunately, the nature of the data makes it impossible to interpret territory size.

Collectively, these accounts provide numerous historical examples that paramount chiefdoms were a regular feature of the protohistoric Southeast. Furthermore, since the social and political organization of the prehistoric Southeast was similar, we must assume that paramount chiefdoms existed throughout the Mississippian. However, the historic examples also indicate that even when historic data appear to provide solid evidence of extrapolity influence, it can be very difficult to identify directly with archaeological research. Fortunately, several researchers in the study area have found an indirect means of measuring interpolity competition through archaeological data.

Paramount Chiefdoms in the Prehistoric Gulf Coastal Plain

Several decades of research have made it clear that chiefs and elites depended on access to nonlocal esoteric goods in order to maintain their power. In some cases, such goods may have served as funds of power in a prestige goods economy (Brown et al. 1990; Earle 1987, 1997; Frankenstein and Rowlands 1978; Welch 1991). In this way, elites may have parlayed near monopolistic access to nonlocal goods into local wealth and prestige through gifts and exchange. Also, elites may have demonstrated their fitness for leadership by showing mastery over the exotic, the esoteric, and the otherworldly (Helms 1988). Items from far away were associated with power, and chiefs could demonstrate their association and control of such forces by simple physical possession of exotic goods. Marcoux (2007:239) has argued that at Moundville, nonlocal prestige goods were probably more important as display goods than as funds of power in a prestige goods economy because there is no evidence they were buried with nonelites or with elites outside the central Moundville precinct. Given the significance and archaeological visibility of nonlocal prestige goods, it seems useful to track changes in their abundance as a measure of changes in interpolity relationships. This is precisely what has been documented for the larger study region.

Case Studies

Two researchers have examined the changing levels of political centralization and esoteric goods at several sites in the region. In the first study, Steponaitis contrasted the development of the Moundville polity on the Black Warrior River and that of the Pocahontas polity on the Big Black River (Steponaitis 1991). Moundville has been extremely well studied (Jackson and Scott 2003; Knight 2004; Knight and Steponaitis, eds. 1998; Peebles 1979, 1987; Powell 1988, 1991; Scarry 1993; Steponaitis 1983; Welch 1991; Welch and Scarry 1995; Wilson 2008) and at 100 ha and with 29 mounds is one of the largest sites in the Southeast. Furthermore, it is at the center of a 40-km-long polity that included secondary mound centers during part of its history. In contrast, the Pocahontas site (Ford 1936; Rafferty et al. 2004; Rucker 1976; Shaffer and Steponaitis 1982, 1983) has a single platform mound and is surrounded by several Mississippi period conical burial mounds. The various burial mounds are interpreted as evidence of a segmentary social organization and horizontal social integration (Steponaitis 1991:221). In examining the abundance of nonlocal artifacts in the burial mounds, Steponaitis finds a large number associated with the Dupree phase (A.D. 1000–1200) but far fewer associated with the later Chapman (A.D. 1200–1350) and Smith (A.D. 1350–1500) phases. There is an approximately 80-percent decline from an average of 1.0 nonlocal item per burial to .2 per burial. Steponaitis (1991:222–227) links this decline to the rise of complex chiefdoms in the region, such as Lake George, Anna, and Moundville, at around A.D. 1200. Prior to this date most of the polities were of similar size and complexity. After this date, the elites in complex chiefdoms were capable of mobilizing more wealth, causing inflation in the value of prestige goods and precluding elites from smaller polities from fully participating in the exchange networks. Furthermore, it is also possible that Pocahontas came under direct control of the Lake George polity, located 50 km away. In either case, the evidence for interpolity competition is reflected in the changing abundance of sumptuary items.

In the second study, Blitz (1993a, 1993b) contrasted the development of the Lubbub Creek polity with that of Moundville by comparing the average number of nonlocal goods per burial. Lubbub Creek is a single-mound Mississippian site on the Tombigbee River located 53 km to the west of Moundville. At the Lubbub Creek mound site, there was a very slight increase in all types of nonlocal goods between Summerville I (A.D. 1000–1200) and Summerville II/III (A.D. 1200–1500), followed by a complete absence in Summerville IV (A.D. 1500–1600) (Blitz 1993a:166–175). The farmsteads surrounding the Lubbub Creek mound site had abundant marine shell and a little nonlocal stone in Summerville I deposits, a little marine shell and no nonlocal stone in Summerville II/III deposits, and no nonlocal burial goods in Summerville IV deposits. In contrast, at the same time as Summerville I, Moundville I (A.D. 1050–1250) phase burials had similar averages of copper and nonlocal stone and had fewer pieces of marine shell (Steponaitis 1991) than their Lubbub Creek neighbors. At the same time as Summerville II/III, Moundville started to consolidate politically (Knight and Steponaitis 1998), and there were sharp increases in all nonlocal goods. This was followed by small declines in marine shell and moderate declines in copper and nonlocal stone during the rest of Moundville II and III (A.D. 1250–1400 and A.D. 1400–1550) (Steponaitis 1991). By A.D. 1400–1500 both Moundville and Lubbub Creek were completely lacking nonlocal goods. As with Pocahontas, the data indicate that, before Moundville's political consolidation, Lubbub Creek had quantities of nonlocal goods similar to those of other mound centers in the region. After Moundville began to grow in size around A.D. 1200, there were sharp increases in the number of nonlocal goods at Moundville, whereas Lubbub Creek saw overall declines in marine shell and nonlocal stone but little change in copper. In total there was a change from

.32 nonlocal artifacts per burial to .18 nonlocal artifacts per burial between Summerville I and Summerville II/III, or a 56-percent decline. Although not as dramatic as those in the Pocahontas case, the Lubbub Creek data indicate that smaller polities in the shadow of larger polities generally had decreased access to nonlocal goods.

Collectively, these examples help describe the types of interregional interactions that were taking place in the Mississippian. Before A.D. 1200, the Coles Creek mounds of the Lower Valley included some examples of large multimound polities, but to the east, the chiefdoms all occupied small one- or two-mound sites of uniformly small size. The evidence indicates that sites like Pocahontas, Lubbub Creek, and Moundville all engaged in extralocal exchange at similar levels. At around A.D. 1200, sites like Lake George, Winterville, and Moundville all became significantly larger and developed into large, complex chiefdoms. Their access to extralocal goods increased while sites that did not grow substantially in size, such as Pocahontas and Lubbub Creek, had reduced access.

Forms of Interaction

There are several ways in which polities might have interacted with each other to create some of the patterning that is apparent archaeologically and historically. Clearly warfare has been frequently examined as one form of regional interaction (Hally 2006:32–33; Rees 1997:114–116; Steponaitis 1991: 207). Mississippian warfare (Dickson 1981; Dye 1990, 1994, 1995, 2009; Gibson 1974; Larson 1972; Steinen 1992) was largely characterized by raids and ambushes and was likely a constant presence in late prehistoric life (see also Anderson 1999:228). Steinen (1992) and Dye (1995) have linked warfare with competition among elites for prestige and power, although it may also have been oriented toward more decentralized and individualized goals such as revenge (Gibson 1974) or toward more economic goals such as seizing staple wealth, possibly due to naturally occurring crop shortages (Dye 2009:145–146). One goal of raid warfare might have been to destroy and desecrate temples and mortuary shrines that may have served to legitimize a chief's authority (Dye and King 2007).

Fortifications and settlement patterns are some of the most accessible indicators of the nature and intensity of warfare. In the Central Mississippi Valley, fortifications increased between the tenth and twelfth centuries, which may be evidence of increased conflict and greater mobilization and investment in response to warfare (Dye 1994, 1995:293). In contrast, the Black Warrior Valley saw a change from nucleated settlements to dispersed farmsteads over the same time interval, which may indicate that the political centralization of Moundville decreased the threat of warfare to its residents

(Steponaitis 1983:172, 1991:207). At Coosa, the core polities have little evidence of fortifications, while the edge polities have fortifications (Hally 1994; Smith 2000). This is interpreted as evidence that the core polities were not under threat since potential enemies would have to cross through areas occupied by allied communities, whereas the fringe polities were threatened. In a maximalist interpretation of Coosa power, it may also be possible that the fringe polities constructed the palisades in response to the growing coercive threat of Coosa itself.

Even when not directly implicated, warfare or the threat of coercive force was likely a prime factor in shaping interpolity relationships (Rees 1997). The rituals and feasting associated with warfare may have been responsible for many of the intrapolity exchanges of prestige goods, while ceremonies associated with alliance formation, negotiation, declaration of warfare, and negotiation of peace (Dye 1995:299, 2009) may have been important for many types of interpolity exchange. Many of these encounters would have involved elite-to-elite interactions and may have produced the types of prestige good exchange networks that are recognized archaeologically.

It is likely that there were other means of regional interaction that led to interpolity negotiation. In order for Steponaitis's (1991) model to be correct, there must have been a mechanism through which the elites of large chiefdoms could exercise their advantages in labor and goods in order to attract the attention of other powerful chiefdoms. Mound construction, feasting, and ritual performance are most often discussed as intrapolity symbols. They are viewed as tools by which elites could associate themselves with the most important physical and symbolic resources within a community and buttress their claims to authority. However, they may also have occasionally served as means of impressing interpolity guests. As Helms (1988, 1993) has indicated, individuals may have sought status by making journeys to distant places in order to associate themselves with extralocal power, and they may have sought to return with physical evidence of their journey. Especially large chiefdoms such as Moundville may have served as prized destinations for aspiring elites. Furthermore, the analysis of iconography from Moundville indicates an overwhelming focus on images of the Underworld and of death (Steponaitis and Knight 2004) and foreign elites may have sought out Moundville because of its perceived authority on these matters.

Method of Regional Analysis

The relationship between mound volume and duration of mound use has proven to be an important indicator regarding mound use during the Mississippi period (Blitz and Livingood 2004). Some archaeologists have interpreted the large size of some Mississippian mounds as evidence that they had been in use for a long time, while other archaeologists have thought that a large mound was a reflection of the ability of a chief or community to mobilize labor effectively. The question is whether the size of a mound can be interpreted as a proxy of a chiefdom's power and influence or whether it was just a mechanical result of the accretion of earth over time in the service of ritual. In order to address this question, a sample of data on the size, duration, and number of major mound construction stages was assembled for 35 mounds for which there were complete data. The primary finding was that mound construction at the largest sites is different from mound construction at smaller sites. When mounds from sites with nine or more mounds were excluded from the sample, there was a .64 correlation between mound volume and duration. This is interpreted as evidence that the rules governing the timing and frequency of mound construction permitted slightly more regular intervals at the smaller sites, but at the largest sites there was a breakdown in these patterns and no relationship at all between the size of a mound and the amount of time it was in use. The average interval between mound construction stages provides even more evidence that the largest and smallest Mississippian centers followed different rules with respect to mound construction (Livingood and Blitz 2004). Single-mound sites had longer average intervals between mound construction episodes than medium centers (2–8 mounds) or large centers (9+ mounds). Single-mound sites also had a stronger correlation between the number of construction episodes and the duration of mound use, indicating that the stages were probably constructed at more predictable intervals. These patterns are interpreted as indicating that, when contrasting single-mound sites to the largest centers, single-mound sites were much more likely to have augmented mounds in response to regular events, whereas the largest sites probably built mounds in response to unpredictable and dynamic political events. The medium-size sites fell between these two statistically and probably tended to use a mixture of strategies.

In summary, this research (Blitz and Livingood 2004; Livingood and Blitz 2004) found statistical evidence for modes within the data and that the largest sites used mound construction in a different manner from that used at small sites. Small sites likely conceived of mound construction and the attendant ritual in a different way. In other words, major Mississippian centers are not simply small sites writ large. Furthermore, it is likely that the social and political conditions that prompted the largest sites to modify their rules with respect to mound construction likely would have shifted their strategies with respect to other aspects of political life such as interpolity competition. Therefore, in a broad regional analysis there is reason to assume that large and small polities behave differently. They are not just different with respect to size and resources (e.g., Lorenz 1992), but they may also be pursuing different strategies commensurate with differences in the way they approach mound construction and other facets of Mississippian life.

In order to examine the pattern of interpolity relationships, three primary variables will be examined: (1) the distribution of prestige goods exchange, (2) the distribution of large and small polities, and (3) measures of political centralization and hierarchy. The goal is to determine how the Pevey site integrates with the distribution of large and small polities across the landscape and to see whether it is possible to identify the maximum distance at which large polities may have been able to interfere with or influence the fortunes of smaller polities.

As with many forms of archaeological data, these three variables must be interpreted carefully and situated in a cultural context. For example, the number of mounds at a site was a useful stratifying variable for the mound volume analysis, but it should not be assumed that it is an absolute indicator of polity strategy with respect to mound construction or interpolity interactions. This analysis is focused on the polities that had adopted a "large-polity" strategy; namely, those polities that appear to have asserted themselves in interpolity relationships, subordinated other polities, and were the least likely to have been subordinated themselves.

Identifying what sites adopted a "large-polity" strategy can be difficult. We cannot assume that all polities with nine or more mounds followed this strategy or followed it for the lifetime of the polity, or that no smaller polity was politically or diplomatically aggressive. Also, there may have been temporal and spatial variation in the cultural rules that affect the way we can interpret the central variables. Across the broader Southeast there were regional and temporal differences in mound construction practices. Payne (1994) found that there are regions of the Southeast that are more likely to have sites with nine or more mounds. For example, the study area for this project, stretching as it does from the Lower Mississippi Valley to the Black Warrior, is one such area that is well represented by sites with nine or more mounds. But to the east, in western Alabama and Georgia, there are no sites with more than eight mounds. This may be due to differences in chiefly authority or different cultural rules concerning mound construction. In addition, it is possible that site architecture in the study area might reflect various corporate group structures (Lindauer and Blitz 1997). For example, at Moundville paired sets of mounds may have been representative of segments of Moundville society (Knight 1998). If Mississippian communities elsewhere had different rules or had fewer numbers of segmentary divisions that were reflected in the architecture, this would lead to fewer numbers of mounds at the site. Furthermore, mound construction activity peaked in the lower South-

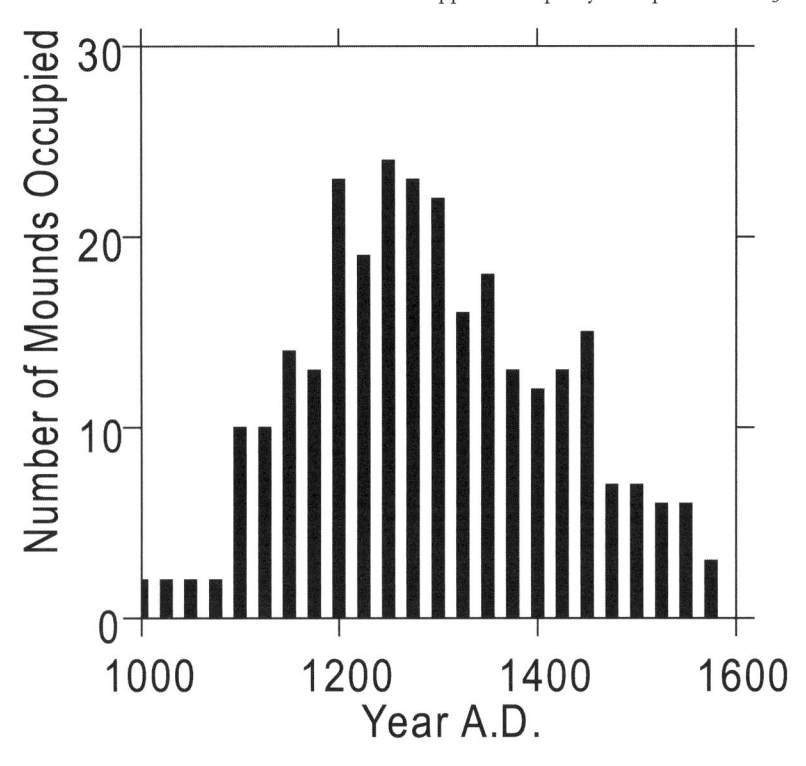

Figure 1.3. Number of Mississippian mounds in the Blitz and Livingood (2004) sample that were occupied during each year. The sample did not include Emergent Mississippian or Coles Creek period mounds. If a representative sample of those were included it would likely create an even more balanced normal curve. Assuming this small sample is representative, this graph is interpreted as indicating that the phenomenon of Mississippian mound use and construction peaked at ca. A.D. 1200–1300 in the Southeast.

east around A.D. 1200 and slowly declined (Figures 1.3 and 1.4). This could be interpreted as an overall decline in centralized authority or it could be a sign that the meaning of mounds and mound construction had changed over the centuries. Certainly, Coosa is evidence that a large paramount polity could emerge in the protohistoric Southeast without evidence of extensive mound construction (Little Egypt had only two or three mounds) or an extensive trade in prestige goods.

One solution to this problem is to select a study area that has less variation along these dimensions. The entire region stretching from the Lower Mississippi Valley to the Black Warrior River is populated with large mound sites and the time under consideration is relatively short. Unfortunately, the

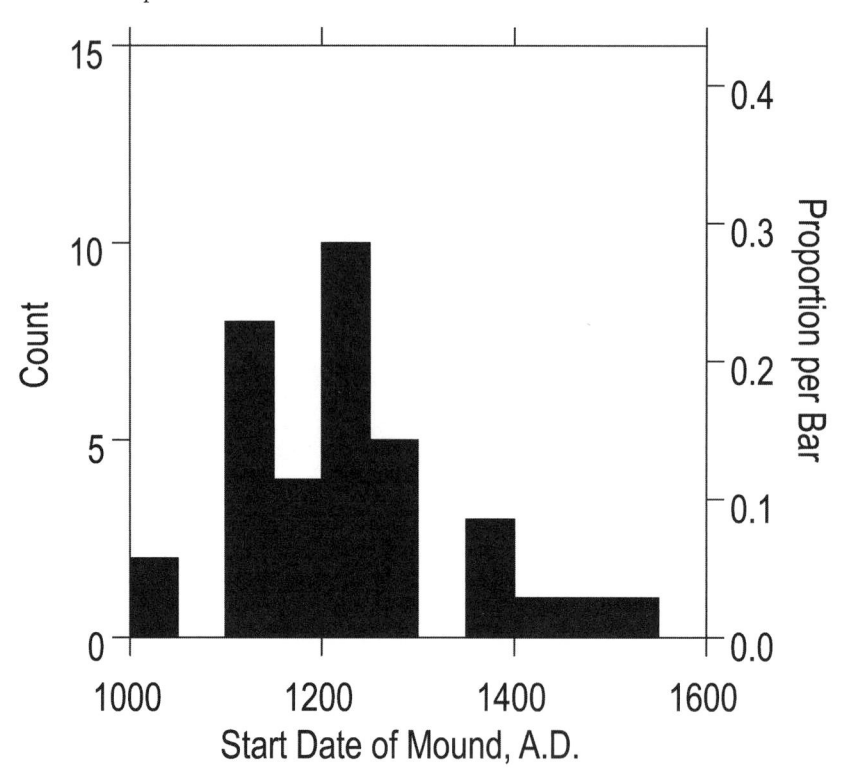

Figure 1.4. Histogram of the start date of mound construction in the Blitz and Livingood (2004) sample. In conjunction with the chronology shown in Figure 1.2, this helps reinforce the conclusion that most Mississippian mound construction peaked around A.D. 1200 and subsequently declined in frequency.

inclusion of the Plaquemine culture of the Lower Mississippi Valley complicates the analysis somewhat. The Plaquemine practiced a wide array of mortuary practices, including flesh burials in both extended and supine positions, secondary burials, and cremations (Jeter and Williams 1989:216–217; Kidder 2004:558; Neumann 1984:265). In some areas, such as the Natchez Bluffs, very few prehistoric burials have been documented, which presumably means they were practicing cremation or another form of secondary burial with low archaeological visibility (Steponaitis 1974). More generally, Plaquemine people were less likely to inter objects with the deceased than their Mississippian contemporaries. This makes direct comparison of archaeological evidence problematic, since the abundance of nonlocal items in burials has been such a useful metric for Mississippian sites in the study region.

Additionally, Plaquemine sites did not fully participate in the exchange of symbols typically associated with the Southeastern Ceremonial Complex (Kidder 2004:558; Phillips and Brown 1978; Williams and Brain 1983). However, Plaquemine polities were not completely parochial, and they were clearly interacting with their neighbors in numerous ways (Kidder 1998a, 2004). In particular, Bellaire style pipes (Brain and Phillips 1996:384–388) are distributed within the Lower Valley, at neighboring Caddoan sites, and at Moundville. Cahokian vessels are found at Lower Valley sites in the Yazoo (Williams and Brain 1983:409–412) and Tensas (Weinstein 2005; Wells and Weinstein 2007) basins. Probably most telling is that during the Coles Creek–Plaquemine transition, several Plaquemine polities began to grow in size at approximately the same time as their neighbors (Anderson 1996). As archaeologists begin to understand that the artifacts bearing "Southern Cult" motifs were symbolic of myths and legends that were a part of Mississippian life (Brown 2004; Diaz-Granados 2004; King 2007; Knight et al. 2001; Lankford 2004; Reilly and Garber 2007; Steponaitis and Knight 2004), the lack of such artifacts among the Plaquemine seems less mysterious. The Plaquemine culture likely shared different sets of beliefs about the world and exchanged different sets of stories about the supernatural. They may have been uninterested in participating in some of the rituals in which these objects were typically exchanged. Despite not participating in this sphere of Mississippian interaction, they still must have interacted politically on a regional scale, and this can be traced through some of the other variables available to us.

Measuring Political Centrality and Hierarchy

One of the flaws of a unilineal evolutionary approach to understanding social complexity is that it implies that rank or hierarchy is univariate. There have been numerous recommendations about how one can logically split the notions of complexity, such as McGuire's (1983) suggestion to divide it into heterogeneity and inequality, or Paynter's (1989) separation of social inequality and complexity. The argument taken in this work is that there are theoretically infinite numbers of variables that one could use to measure the outcomes and evidence associated with complexity, hierarchy, and rank and that these variables covary only slightly if at all. As archaeologists, we have access to only a handful of variables that let us assess the degree of hierarchy and centralization, and it makes sense to consider all of them and not to make the mistaken assumption that evidence of complexity in one measure (say site size) necessarily implies complexity in another (say the degree of elite provisioning). In this work, one of the steps is assessing relative complexity across a wide region using as many variables as we have available.

Summary

The purpose of this study is to find evidence for interpolity interactions in the study area between the Mississippi and Mobile/Tombigbee/Black Warrior river systems during the Middle Mississippi period. The goal is to see whether there was a geographic limit to the influence of the largest polities. This study relies on evidence from each polity along three dimensions: the distribution and abundance of prestige goods, the distribution of large and small polities as measured by number of mounds, and measures of political centralization and hierarchy. One of the key sites for this analysis is the Pevey site, and the next four chapters discuss the archaeological evidence from Pevey and the other Mississippian sites in Lawrence County. Special attention is paid to evidence for political centralization in comparison with other nearby sites. The final two chapters summarize the archaeological data from Pevey and analyze the regional data on interpolity interaction.

2
Archaeology of the Middle Pearl River

A number of previous investigators have worked in the area of the Pevey, Lowe-Steen, and Phillips Farm sites. Discussion of that work is preceded here with a description of the physiographic and environmental setting of the Middle Pearl River centered at Lawrence County, Mississippi. A detailed accounting of the three sites follows, including a description of previous research and an in-depth examination of the 1993, 1994, and 2000 excavations. Special attention is given to data that help situate these sites in a regional political context and contribute to an understanding of the degree of social and political hierarchy at these sites.

Physiographic and Environmental Description

The Pearl River is the first major river east of the Mississippi. From its source, it flows 146 miles southwesterly to near the city of Jackson and then 260 miles south to Lake Borgne and the Ringolets, which are arms of the Gulf of Mexico. The basin drains a total of 8,760 square miles (U.S. Army Corps of Engineers 1970). Geologically, the Pearl River is entirely within the Gulf Coastal Plain. All of Lawrence County falls in the Piney Woods physiographic province (Cross et al. 1974), which is characterized by uplands, rolling hills, and lowlands (Heartfield, Price, and Greene, Inc. 1982). Most of the Mississippian sites in the county are associated with the first floodplain terrace and Cahaba soils, which are found on level or nearly level surfaces, are well drained, and are regarded by modern agriculturalists as easy to till, unlikely to erode, and fertile throughout a wide range of moisture content (U.S. Department of Agriculture [USDA] 1978:9).

The Pearl River drainage has been relatively stable geologically and environmentally for at least the past 5,000 years (Burden et al. 1978). Forest types in Lawrence County primarily include loblolly pine–shortleaf pine but also include oak-gum-cypress, oak-pine, oak-hickory, and longleaf pine–slash pine (USDA 1978). Nuts may have been especially important food resources, and there are numerous nut-bearing trees in the Middle Pearl. Paleobotanical evidence from the Pevey site is discussed in Chapter 5.

The prehistoric inhabitants of Lawrence County probably exploited a wide variety of animal resources. There are 18 species of mollusks known from the Pearl River and its tributaries (U.S. Army Corps of Engineers 1975; Heartfield, Price, and Greene, Inc. 1982:2–26). There are also over 100 species of fish, 30 species of amphibians, 100 species of birds, and 50 species of mammals (Heartfield, Price, and Greene, Inc. 1982:2–28).

The Pevey Site (22Lw510)

Pevey is the largest archaeological site in Lawrence County and is the primary focus of this report. The site had at least nine mounds around a central plaza, which places it in the top 5 percent of Mississippian sites by number of mounds.

A Note on the Site Name

The site (22Lw510) was originally reported to archaeologists in 1961 and was recorded as the Mill Creek site because the mounds are located at the confluence of Mill Creek and the Pearl River. In his master's thesis, Baxter Mann (1988) used the name Pearl Mounds. Both names suffer from having a lack of specificity. There are thousands of Mill Creeks in the United States, including several dozen in the state of Mississippi alone; there are several Mill Creek archaeological sites in the Southeast; and there are several mounds known along the Pearl River. Thus, the site has been given its third name in 40 years of research and will be referred to herein as the Pevey site.

Previous Research: 1961–1988

The Pevey site (22Lw510) was first brought to the attention of professional archaeologists in 1961. J. E. Newman wrote a letter to Stewart Neitzel at the Mississippi Department of Archives and History, and the site was recorded as the Mill Creek site (Mann 1988:14). However, the communication contained little information about the site and the importance was not appreciated. In 1977, the site was again brought to the attention of the Mississippi Department of Archives and History by Mr. W. D. Clark of Columbia, Mississippi, and the Marion County Sheriff's Department. Mr. Clark was concerned about work that was being done at the site to clear it for agricultural purposes and felt that it was in danger of being destroyed (Mann 1988:14). The site was surveyed in order to gather the data necessary to nominate it to the National Register of Historic Places, and the importance of the site was communicated to the landowner. Clearing of the land was halted and the landowners have ceased all efforts that could endanger the core of the site. Currently, the six largest extant mounds (Mounds C, D, E, G, H, and I) are situated in woods and have not been disturbed by agricultural use of the surrounding land. The only major damage that has been recorded occurred sometime between 1977 and 1981 when a backhoe was used to loot Mound I (Mann 1988:15).

From 1977 through 1981 some analyses were performed on materials recovered from the initial surveys. The report by Samuel Brookes assigned all of the diagnostic lithics to the Middle and Late Archaic (Brookes ca. 1980s), and a report by John Stubbs analyzed the ceramics and noted an association with Coles Creek, Plaquemine, and Mississippian ceramic traditions (Stubbs ca. 1980).

The only other major work on the site occurred between the fall of 1981 and 1983. Baxter Mann and John Blitz conducted fieldwork at the site, and the results were reported in Mann's Master's thesis entitled "Archaeological Classification of Ceramics from the Pearl Mounds (22Lw510), Lawrence County, Mississippi" (Mann 1988). The site was mapped using a transit and stadia rod, and Mann and Blitz's map is the basis of the site map used in this report. They also made a surface collection of the central part of the site using 366 10-×-10-m collection grids. Finally, they excavated two 1-×-1-m test units (Mann 1988:49–50).

Mann's thesis noted that the vast majority of decorated ceramics found at the site can be comfortably identified using typologies established for the Lower Mississippi Valley (e.g., Brown 1998; Phillips 1970; Williams and Brain 1983), suggesting a cultural connection. Based on the identification of those ceramics to types and varieties used by Mississippi Valley archaeologists, he reported that the primary occupation of the site was coeval with the Anna phase (A.D. 1200–1350) of the Natchez Bluffs region. In addition to the Anna phase occupation, he identified a small Coles Creek (A.D. 600–1000) component and argued that the site was probably continuously occupied beginning in a phase equivalent to the Gordon phase (A.D. 1000–1200) in the Natchez Bluffs and that the site was likely abandoned during the Foster, Emerald, or Natchez phase (Mann 1988:86–88).

Mann also recognized that a far higher percentage of the undecorated ceramics from the Pevey site were shell tempered than has been documented in Anna phase Natchez Bluffs sites. He suggested three possible explanations. First, since most of the ceramics were recovered from the surface and lack stratigraphic context it is possible that the site dates to later periods such as the Foster, Emerald, or Natchez phases when shell tempering was much more frequent. Second, Mann suggested that residents of the Pevey site might have shared a cultural affinity with populations to the east and south where shell tempering during the A.D. 1200–1350 period was much more common. A final possibility is that the Pevey site served as a "point of interaction" (Mann 1988:88) between Lower Mississippi Valley people to the west and Middle Mississippian communities to the east. For example, the Pevey site could have been on a major overland trade route between the Natchez Bluffs and the Pascagoula drainage or Mobile Bay.

In 1982 the cultural resource management (CRM) firm Heartfield, Price, and Greene, Inc., produced a two-volume literature survey intended to describe the cultural resources of the Pearl River (Heartfield, Price, and Greene, Inc. 1982). The primary survey area, as commissioned by the U.S. Army Corps of Engineers, encompassed a 1-mile-wide corridor along the Pearl River from the Ross Barnett Reservoir to the mouth of the Pearl River. However, given the paucity of archaeological sites, the authors were able to expand their focus to include all known archaeological work in the entire Pearl River basin from the Ross Barnett Reservoir to the Gulf of Mexico. The results of the report were encapsulated by Bill Moore in a journal article (Moore 1987) and can be summarized by the opening passage, which states that "except for a few areas, this major drainage is virtually unknown archaeologically" (Moore 1987:191). Although there is some confusion about the Mississippian sites in Lawrence County, which reflected confusion in the state site file cards at the time, the study reports five known Mississippian mound sites in the study area. The sites are 22Ha515, 22Hi512, 22Lw510/22Lw511 (which is really 22Lw510), 22Lw514 (which is really 22Lw511), and 16Wa8.

Excavations: 1993 and 1994

During the summers of 1993 and 1994 the University of North Carolina at Chapel Hill conducted two field schools in Lawrence County. These field schools were directed by Tim Mooney, a doctoral student at North Carolina, and his advisor, Vincas Steponaitis. The work in Lawrence County was conducted in order to test one aspect of the Choctaw Genesis hypothesis (Galloway 1995), namely whether the site could be conclusively linked to the Sixtowns band of the historic Choctaw tribe. The investigator, Tim Mooney, was looking for two primary pieces of evidence. First, he sought to determine whether the Pevey site was abandoned in the sixteenth century, when Galloway's hypothesis suggested people were moving into the historic Choctaw homeland. Second, he was looking for material culture similarities between the terminal artifact types at the Pevey site and the earliest artifacts recovered from the Choctaw homeland. If both pieces of evidence could be found, this would help support Galloway's hypothesis.

These research questions shaped the excavation strategies. Because so little was known about the ceramic chronology of the region, the excavators selected areas for investigation based on their potential to yield large numbers of artifacts, especially ceramics. In 1993 a hand soil core auger was used to find locations at the site that had dense middens, and these were selected for excavation. In 1994 an effort was made to get excavation data from every mound at the site that had not been previously investigated. For the moderately sized mounds, units were placed in the flank, just at the edge of the summit. This placement maximized the chance of finding artifacts associated with a mound flank midden. By the end of the second season every mound had been investigated and the units were excavated to subsoil in all but the largest mound. The following section of this chapter describes the results of the 1993 and 1994 University of North Carolina excavations.

Site Description

There are currently nine mounds extant at Pevey (Figure 2.1). The mounds are arranged in two parallel rows extending down the gentle slope of an extension of the floodplain terrace. Mann (1988:7) recorded 10 mounds, but subsequent research has added and subtracted mounds from his original map. First, Mann designated a rise .5 m high located 100 m north of Mound J as Mound A. Testing in 1994 and 2000 showed there is no evidence for a mound at that location. However, the symmetry of the site, with two parallel rows of mounds, suggests that there may have been a mound at or near this location in the past. Second, Mann's map shows a Mound F in the floodplain approximately 50 m east of the floodplain terrace. This mound was 2 m high, but it was destroyed sometime between the summer of 1984 and the summer of 1993. If Mound F was a mound associated with the Mississippi period site, it was in an odd location and would have been subject to periodic flooding. Without any excavation data it is impossible to verify whether Mound F was a prehistoric feature. Finally, in 1994 Mound K was discovered and excavations confirmed it was a Mississippian mound missed by Mann's original map. In addition to the verifiable mounds, Mann (1988:6) also reported that a local informant recalled that there were at least four other mounds in the eastern half of the site that were destroyed prior to 1982. This is entirely possible, since over the past 50 years the land has been used for tree harvesting and agriculture, and the main dirt road running between the floodplain and floodplain terrace bisects the site. These forces have certainly caused some amount of damage to the mounds that are not currently in tree cover: Mounds B, I, J, and K (Figure 2.2). It is also possible that there are some small mounds extant to the south of Mill Creek. In 1984 there was little tree cover there and Mann (personal communication 2000) reported seeing some small "house mounds." Unfortunately, the land-

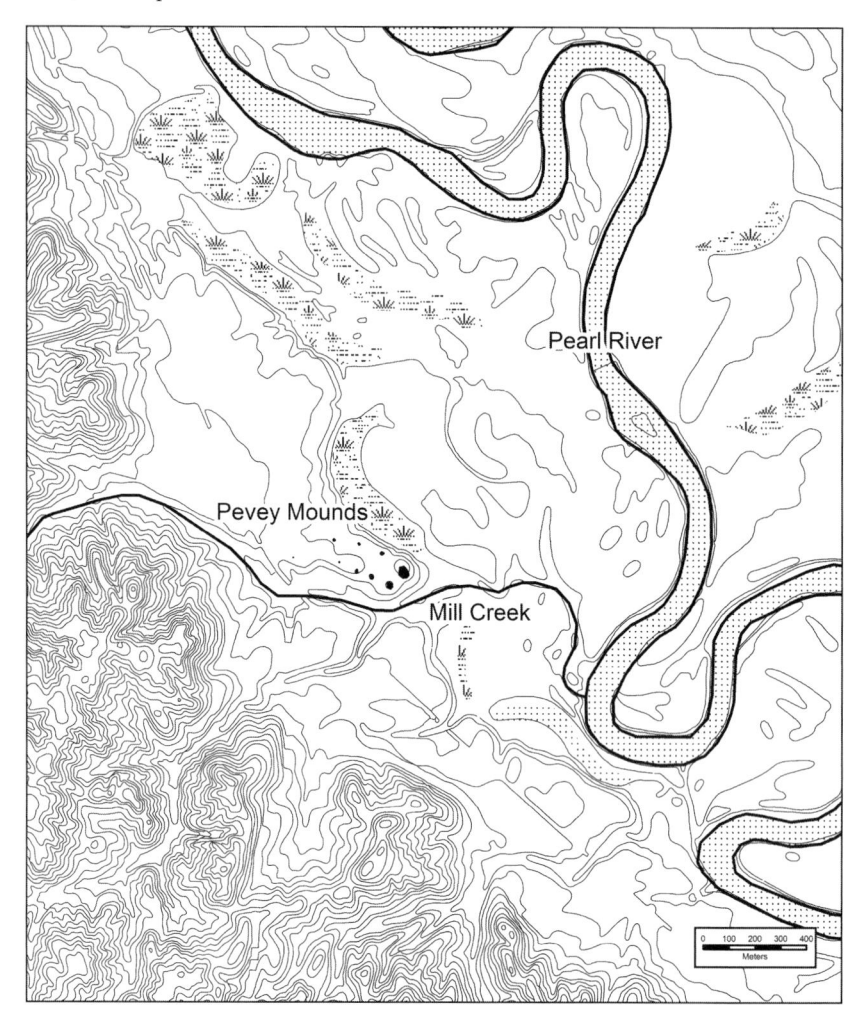

Figure 2.1. The topography of the Pevey site and surrounding area. Contours are in 10-foot increments. Mapping data from MARIS (Mississippi Automated Resource Information System). Swamp boundaries are based on U.S. Geological Survey topographic maps.

owners of the area south of Mill Creek have not been receptive to having archaeologists on their property. Therefore, there are only nine mounds at Pevey that can be clearly documented. In addition, based on the layout and symmetry of the site it seems likely that there was a mound to the north of Mound J that no longer exists, and local informants reported that there may have been a few more.

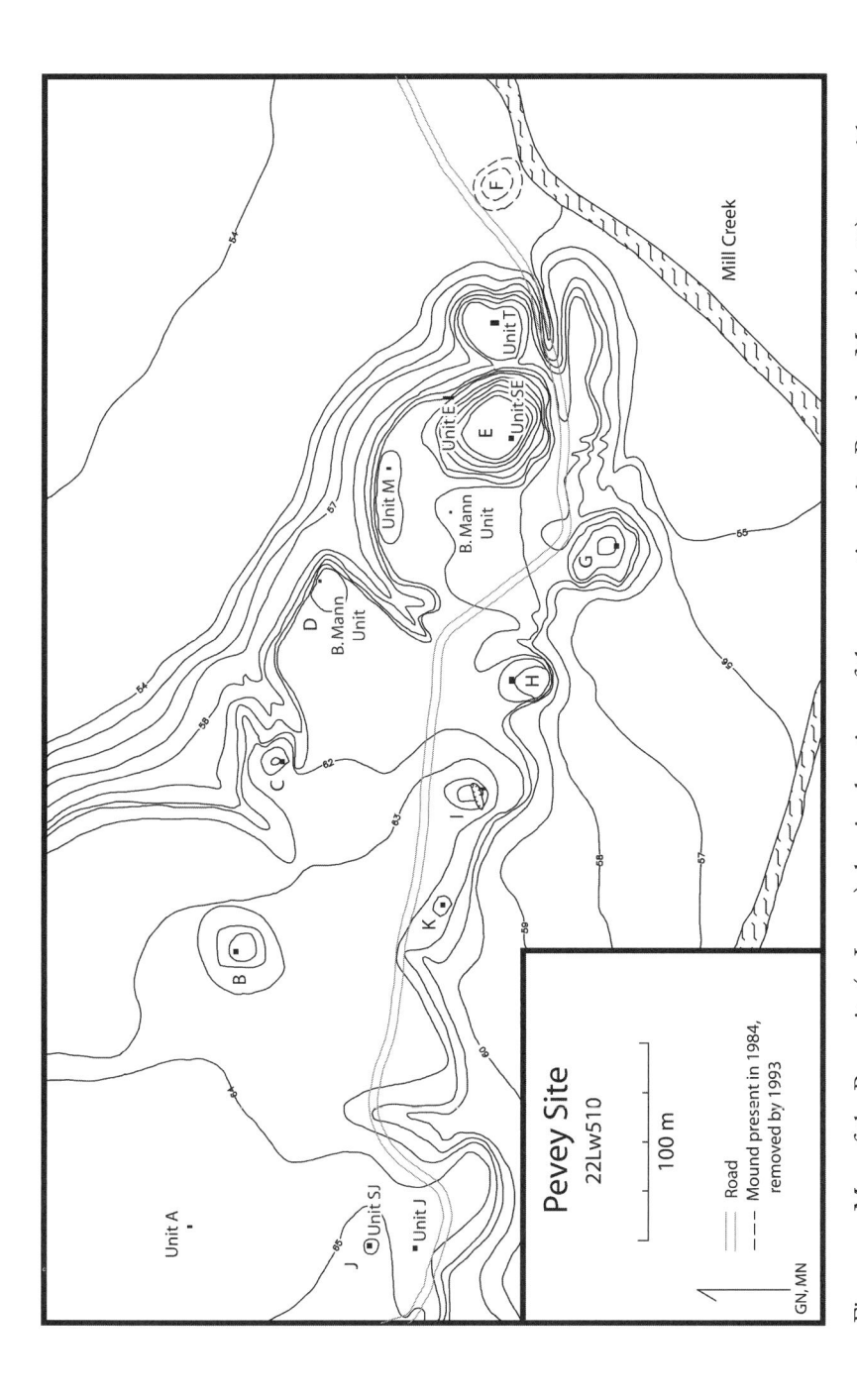

Figure 2.2. Map of the Pevey site (22Lw510) showing locations of the excavation units. Based on Mann's (1988) map with small modifications to show updated information on the mounds.

The Pevey site is located on the floodplain terrace of the west bank of the Pearl River (Figure 2.1). The site is bounded on the south by Mill Creek, which flows into the Pearl River. At present, that confluence is 1 km to the southeast of the site. The site is bounded on the east and on the north by a former channel of the Pearl River, currently a backwater swamp. The northern boundary of the site is very well defined by a sharp terrace edge that is 8–10 m high in places. The largest mound (Mound E) was built contiguous to the terrace edge, resulting in a 14-m height difference between the summit of the mound and the floodplain. The site itself sits at an elevation of 54 to 64 m above sea level.

The floodplain terrace extends for 800 m to the west of the site, where the topography changes dramatically to one of rolling hills that reach up to 140 m above sea level. The floodplain terrace to the northeast of Pevey is noteworthy in this section of the Pearl River drainage for being unusually large, flat, and very well bounded. The evenness of the terrace may be somewhat influenced by modern agricultural practices, but it is likely to have been reasonably flat in prehistoric times and it was certainly a well-defined natural space. It is demarcated by a 10-m-high terrace edge to the east and an abrupt boundary between floodplain terrace and uplands to the west. The entire terrace covers an area approximately 1,200 m from north to south and 800 m east to west. South of Pevey, across Mill Creek, the floodplain terrace is narrower but still rather well defined for a distance of 1.5 km.

The Pevey site is a remarkably large Mississippi period mound site. Using Claudine Payne's (1994) work we can compare the size of Pevey to that of other known sites. Payne gathered data on 536 Mississippian sites (not including Pevey). She evaluated the size of Mississippian mound sites using four key variables: number of mounds, mound precinct area, height of main mound, and volume index of main mound.

- With regard to number of mounds, Pevey's nine mounds place it in the top 5 percent of sites documented in Payne's tabulation. Only 24 of 467 sites for which she had data had nine or more mounds.
- Payne calculated mound precinct area for sites with four or more mounds by calculating the area of the rectangle that would enclose all of the mounds at the site. This method provides a mound precinct area of 11.5 ha for Pevey, which is greater than the median of 8.2 ha for Payne's sample. Payne presents the data in a histogram and from this one can read that Pevey's precinct size is exceeded by at most 28 Mississippian sites (Payne 1994:91).
- The main mound (E) at Pevey is 8 m in height, which is significantly larger than the 4.8-m mean for main mound height and is exceeded by

approximately 66 main mounds of the 353 that Payne recorded (Payne 1994:94).
- Payne calculates mound volume index as the product of the maximum length, width, and height of the mound in meters, which is then divided by 1,000. This index is the volume of the cubic solid that would completely contain the mound. Mound E at Pevey has a mound volume index of 36. This is exceeded by only 27 other Mississippian main mounds out of 271 that Payne recorded, which places Pevey in the tenth percentile.

It is possible to read too much into these statistics. First, although Payne's list of sites is the most complete one to date, it is still incomplete. Second, it is possible that regional cultural preferences may have played a role in shaping the parameters of site size. For example, Payne's (1994:88, 95) maps show that the sites with nine or more mounds, or with the largest mound precinct areas, occur disproportionately in the western half of the Mississippian world. Finally, as was discussed earlier, the size of mounds is influenced by numerous social and logistical factors and does not lend itself to simplistic interpretations. Presumably the number of mounds at a site and the size of a mound precinct area are just as complex to interpret. Therefore, these size statistics are presented merely to demonstrate in an approximate sense that the Pevey site is especially large compared with average Mississippian mound sites and is in the same order of magnitude of size as some of the better-known sites in the larger study area that were neighbors to Pevey, such as Bottle Creek, Anna, Lake George, and Moundville.

Thirteen separate blocks were excavated during the 1993 and 1994 seasons (Figure 2.2). In general, the excavation procedures called for excavating a 2-×-2-m excavation unit in each location of interest. The first half of the unit (1 × 2 m) was excavated in 20-cm arbitrary levels; the second half was excavated in natural levels corresponding to the stratigraphy noted in the first half. Flotation and water-screen samples were usually taken from every level and from every feature. All other soil was sifted through a ¼-inch screen to recover artifacts.

Within each excavation unit, related contexts were lumped together into analytical units. These are indicated on the sides of the profile drawings shown. Appendix 1 lists all of the excavated contexts and how these align with the analytical units. Typically, in blocks where natural levels were excavated, they were used as the basis for constructing the analytical units, and the arbitrary levels were matched up with those. The analytical units are utilized throughout the rest of this work as the basis for interpretations.

Discussion of the excavation units for Pevey will be done in a clockwise order around the mound precinct. Each of the excavation discussions below includes a mention of the important ceramics, and a complete inventory can be found in Appendix 1. Refer to Chapter 4 for a discussion of the methods used to derive the types and varieties and for a more detailed analysis of the ceramics and a comparison of the assemblages by unit. Also, refer to later chapters for inventories of the other artifact classes recovered from each unit. Chapter 6 contains a summary of the chronology and a discussion of the architectural evidence.

Excavation Unit A

Unit A was excavated in 1994 in order to test a small rise in the field that had been designated as Mound A by Mann. The excavation unit indicated there was no evidence of a mound at this location. A 1-×-2-m unit was excavated to 60 cm below the surface in 20-cm arbitrary levels. Only seven sherds were recovered from the unit, including a single piece of Coles Creek Incised, *var. unspecified*. There was no evidence of mound fill or of any manmade features in the stratigraphy.

In 2000 shovel testing was done on the floodplain terrace to the north of the mounds. One transect of shovel tests intersected the rise designated as "Mound A." The shovel testing revealed that in most of the field north of the mound precinct there is a layer containing moderate amounts of gravel 30–40 cm below the surface. However, under the "Mound A" rise, the gravel is denser and located just 20 cm below the surface, which might help to explain the slight mound-like rise in the field.

However, the fact that Unit A provided no evidence of a mound at the location mapped by Baxter Mann does not mean there was no "Mound A" in the vicinity when the site was occupied. The symmetry of the site strongly suggests a mound was here but has been destroyed by modern agricultural practices.

Excavation Unit B

Unit B was placed off center of Mound B, which is at present about 1 m tall (Figure 2.3). Mound B is currently located in a field without the benefit of any tree cover and has likely been reduced in size by plowing. The 2-×-2-m unit was excavated to subsoil 120 cm below the surface. The base of the unit had a single small post feature, and analytical unit 4 contained a significant quantity of daub (533 g). On the top surface of analytical unit 4 was a lens of daub, charcoal, and bone measuring approximately 50×25 cm. These data indicate that there was a structure at the site of Mound B before the mound was constructed. On top of this structure there were at least two major mound construction events, both employing grayish sandy loam.

22Lw510
Unit B W 1/2
East Profile

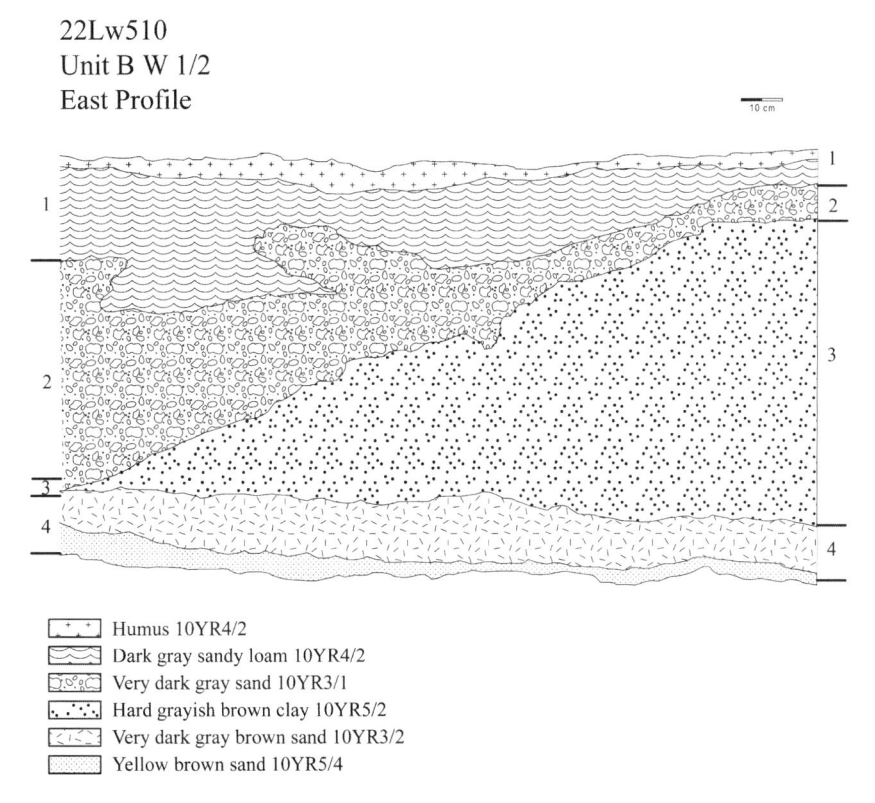

- Humus 10YR4/2
- Dark gray sandy loam 10YR4/2
- Very dark gray sand 10YR3/1
- Hard grayish brown clay 10YR5/2
- Very dark gray brown sand 10YR3/2
- Yellow brown sand 10YR5/4

Figure 2.3. Profile map of Unit B, west ½, east wall, 22Lw510.

The unit contained 136 sherds. The decorated varieties include Plaquemine Brushed, *var. Plaquemine* and two sherds of D'Olive Incised, *var. unspecified*. The sherds diagnostic to vessel form include two small bowls and three large jars. Plaquemine Brushed vessels were likely used for cooking or other utilitarian uses and the entire inventory is consistent with a modest domestic assemblage.

Excavation Unit C

The 2-×-2-m unit designated Unit C was excavated on the flank of Mound C to subsoil at a maximum depth of 250 cm (Figure 2.4). The mound contained evidence of at least three major building episodes. Beneath the mound was a single pit feature that was 24 cm deep and approximately 45 cm in diameter. The pit was filled with charcoal, bone, and some pieces of Mississippi Plain pottery. There were also four definite round postholes ranging in size from 12 to 21 cm in diameter and in depth from 21 to 30 cm. The post-

22Lw510
Unit C
West and North Wall Profile

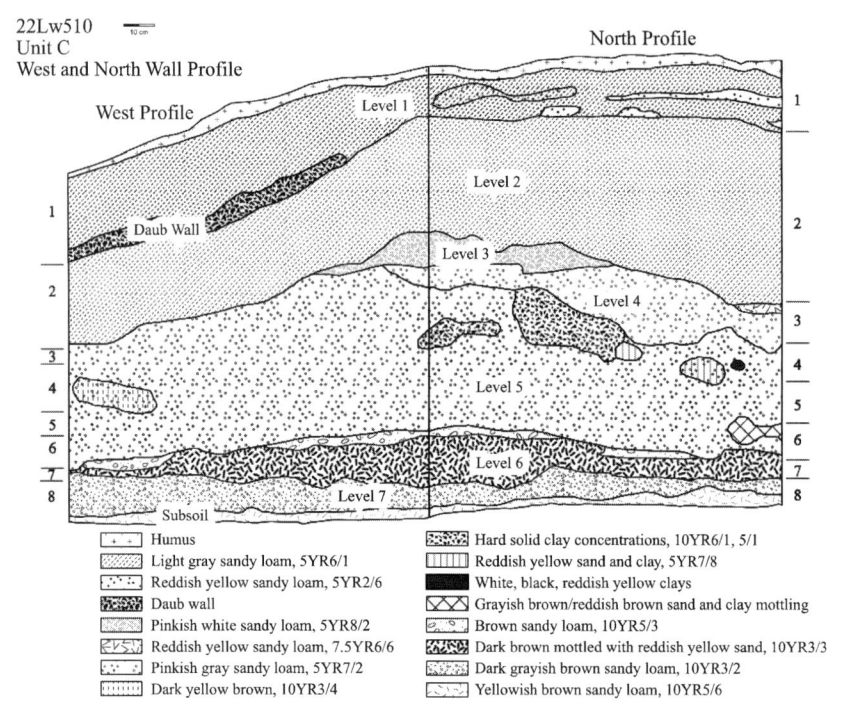

North Profile

West Profile

Level 1

Daub Wall

Level 2

Level 3

Level 4

Level 5

Level 6

Level 7

Subsoil

- Humus
- Light gray sandy loam, 5YR6/1
- Reddish yellow sandy loam, 5YR2/6
- Daub wall
- Pinkish white sandy loam, 5YR8/2
- Reddish yellow sandy loam, 7.5YR6/6
- Pinkish gray sandy loam, 5YR7/2
- Dark yellow brown, 10YR3/4
- Hard solid clay concentrations, 10YR6/1, 5/1
- Reddish yellow sand and clay, 5YR7/8
- White, black, reddish yellow clays
- Grayish brown/reddish brown sand and clay mottling
- Brown sandy loam, 10YR5/3
- Dark brown mottled with reddish yellow sand, 10YR3/3
- Dark grayish brown sandy loam, 10YR3/2
- Yellowish brown sandy loam, 10YR5/6

Figure 2.4. Unit C west and north wall stratigraphy, 22Lw510.

holes appear to trace the outline of a circular structure or the corner of a rectangular structure missing the corner post. The base of the mound also contained 545 g of daub, some ochre, shell, and animal bone. The ceramics include one sherd of Carter Engraved, *var. Carter*, a sherd of Coles Creek Incised, *var. Hardy*, and a sherd of Owens Punctated, *var. unspecified*, as well as some Addis and Mississippi Plain rim sherds. This level was covered by a thin layer of mottled brown fill.

The next living surface for which there is evidence was located on top of analytical unit 7. Here, excavators found a hearth feature in the northeast corner of the unit that was about 65 cm in diameter and two postholes about 23 cm in diameter that were filled with charcoal. The sherds associated with this surface include two Anna Incised, *var. Anna* sherds and a Carter Engraved, *var. Carter* rim from a restricted-mouth bowl. There was also a single crinoid bead.

Analytical units 3 to 6 are probably a series of episodes of mound fill, although there may have been a small living surface on the top of analytical unit 4. These fill episodes are mostly composed of a pinkish loam. Unit 2 appears to represent another major episode of mound fill, and the fill is a uniform light gray sandy loam. There was certainly a structure on the surface of analytical unit 2, and the wall of the structure collapsed into the western edge of Unit C and burned in situ. There also may have been some postholes associated with this structure in the eastern half of the unit. The ceramics associated with this occupation include two sherds of Parkin Punctated, *var. Hollandale,* two sherds of Carter Engraved, *var. Carter,* a sherd of D'Olive Incised, *var. unspecified,* a sherd of Mound Place Incised, and a sherd of Anna Incised, *var. Anna.*

In sum, the evidence from Mound C indicates that there were higher-status artifacts here than at Mound B. A crinoid bead and ochre were recovered as well as several plates and bowls associated with serving.

Excavation Unit SE

Unit SE was placed on the southern half of the summit of Mound E, the largest mound at Pevey (Figure 2.5). The SE designation signifies the "summit of Mound E," which is 6–8 m above the level of the plaza. This unit was critical to Mooney's research goal and was intended to gather evidence about the final occupation of Mound E in order to ascertain when the site was abandoned.

The unit was excavated to 130 cm below the surface. At the base of the unit (base of analytical unit 6) were a pair of parallel wall trenches and 20 post features indicating the presence of a structure that had likely been rebuilt at least once (Figure 2.6). A soil core auger test below this indicated that this structure was built on a layer of fill at least 1 m in depth.

This excavation unit was covered by approximately 40 cm of mottled orange, gray, and brown fill (analytical units 5 and 6). The second living surface at the top of analytical units 3 and 4 contained several post features. Likely there were two or possibly three separate living surfaces represented here separated by a centimeter of charcoal, clay, and soil each.

These surfaces were covered by 40 cm of dark fill (analytical unit 2) that was likely extracted from a nearby midden. The fill was capped by a living surface represented by a discontinuous lens of white sand 1–2 cm thick. On top of this was more midden-like fill to the surface of the unit. Analytical unit 1 contained a remarkable 13 kg of daub. This is evidence that there were one or more structures built on the terminal levels of Mound E.

Within this uppermost midden were a Maddox Engraved, *var. Silver City* sherd, six Anna Incised, *var. Anna* sherds, and three Plaquemine Brushed, *var. Plaquemine* sherds. Based on the *Silver City* sherd, it appears that the top of the mound may have been used later than much of the rest of the site, since *Silver City* is typically associated with the Foster or Emerald phases (A.D. 1350–1450) (Brown 1998; Williams and Brain 1983).

32   Chapter 2

22Lw510
Unit SE
North Profile

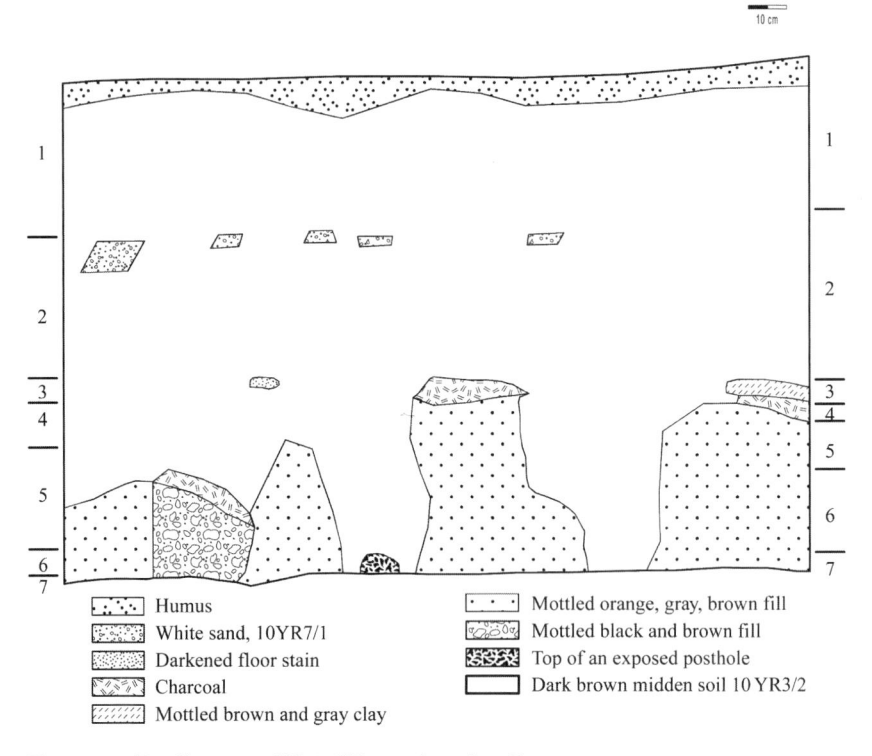

Figure 2.5. Profile map of Unit SE, north wall, 22Lw510.

The ceramic assemblage from the occupation levels of the unit includes Anna Incised, *var. Anna,* Anna Incised, *var. Australia,* Fatherland Incised, *var. unspecified,* Plaquemine Brushed, *var. Plaquemine,* Parkin Punctated, *var. Harris,* Moundville Incised, *var. unspecified,* Owens Punctated, *var. unspecified,* Evansville Punctated, *var. unspecified,* and Mound Place Incised.

Excavation Unit E

Unit E was placed at the northeastern base of Mound E, between the foot of the mound and the edge of the floodplain terrace. The excavation unit was ultimately extended to 4×1 m, with the southernmost 2×1 m designated as E, the 1×1 m to the north of that as E2, and the northernmost 1×1 m as E3. The unit was excavated as a 4-m-long, 116-cm-high step into the mound. The southern wall of the unit in Mound E was 116 cm tall and the northern wall

22Lw510
Unit SE
Unit Floor

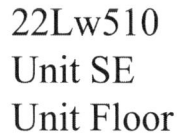

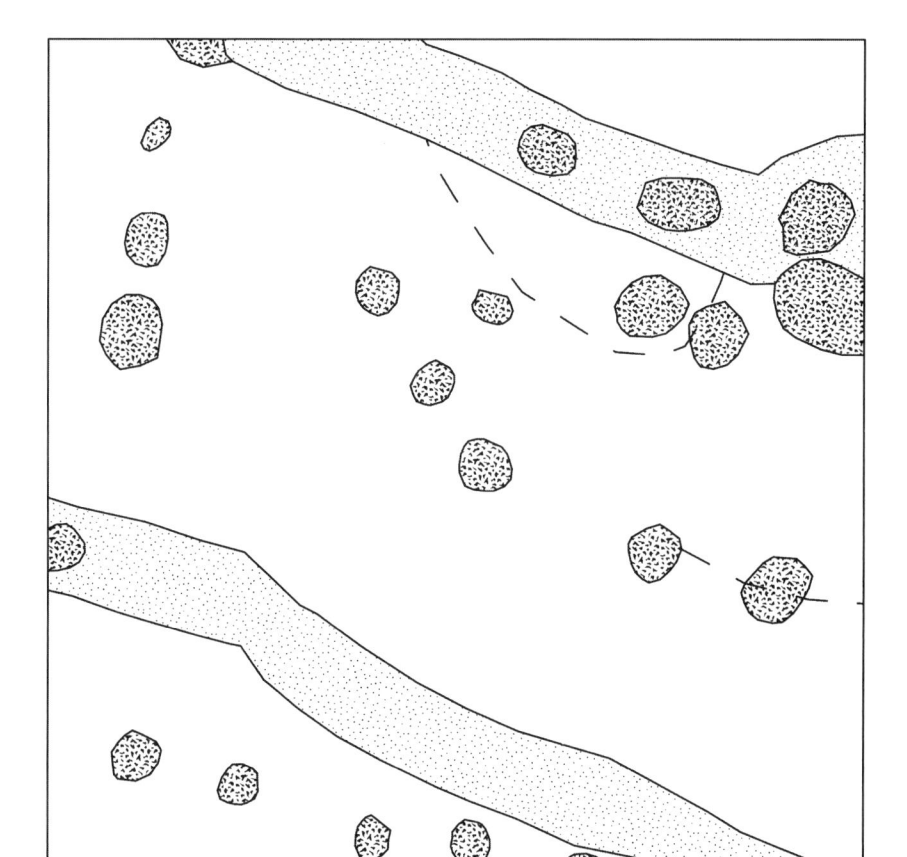

Figure 2.6. Map of Unit SE unit base floor, 22Lw510. This corresponds with the base of analytical unit 6. The postholes and wall trenches associated with this occupation level are shown.

of the unit was 1 cm deep and nearly level with the surrounding submound surface. The intent of the unit was to sample the mound flank midden that might have accumulated during the last stages of the Mound E occupation. No profile map was created in the field.

In sum, 1,081 sherds were excavated from Units E, E2, and E3, including 272 decorated sherds. The most common decorated sherds are Anna Incised, *var. Anna,* Plaquemine Brushed, *var. Plaquemine,* and Mound Place Incised. Other decorated types include Carter Engraved, *var. Carter,* Leland Incised, *var. Bethlehem,* Maddox Engraved, *var. Silver City,* L'Eau Noire Incised, *var. L'Eau Noire,* D'Olive Incised, *var. unspecified,* Barton Incised, *var. Midnight,* Grace Brushed, *var. Grace,* and Hollyknowe Pinched, *var. Patmos.* As with Unit SE, the presence of a Maddox Engraved, *var. Silver City* sherd suggests this was an area of the site that was used near the end of the site's occupation. In addition, the excavation unit contained much bone, charcoal, daub, and fire-cracked rock.

Excavation Unit M

There are two level areas surrounding Mound E that are circumscribed by the terrace edge. Either or both of these may have served as homes to elite residents or as sites of exclusive access if the space was utilized in a manner similar to that of other known Mississippian sites. Unit M is located on a small rise situated on the bluff edge between Mound E and the ravine separating Mounds D and E. Soil core probes indicated that this area had a dense midden, and this was later confirmed by excavation.

Because of time constraints imposed by the end of the field season, this unit was not excavated in a standard manner. The east half (1×2 m) of the unit was excavated to 120 cm below the surface (Figure 2.7). It is not clear from the notes whether the excavators thought they were at subsoil. Ten centimeters above the base of the unit, at the bottom of analytical unit 3, the excavators documented an occupation floor with evidence of posts and wall trenches from a rectangular structure (Figure 2.8). Above this floor was about 30 cm of fill, on top of which was a 20-cm-thick sheet of midden (analytical unit 2). On top of this midden was an undifferentiated grayish brown fill.

The west half of the unit was excavated to a depth of 20 cm, which just revealed the top of the midden. This midden was removed as Feature 1 and an additional .52 m^2 was excavated to the southwest corner of the unit in order to further trace the feature.

The unit contained 1,690 sherds, including 407 decorated sherds. Among the more remarkable finds was half of a L'Eau Noire Incised, *var. L'Eau Noire* vessel. This unit also contained two sherds with dates normally associated with the Foster phase (A.D. 1350–1500) in the Natchez region: one Maddox Engraved, *var. Silver City* and one Fatherland Incised, *var. Pine Ridge.* (It also contained two Owens Punctated, *var. unspecified* sherds that resemble *Menard.* These sherds could potentially date the unit even later than the Foster phase and this finding is discussed in detail in Chapter 4.) These

22Lw510
Unit M, E 1/2
West Wall Profile

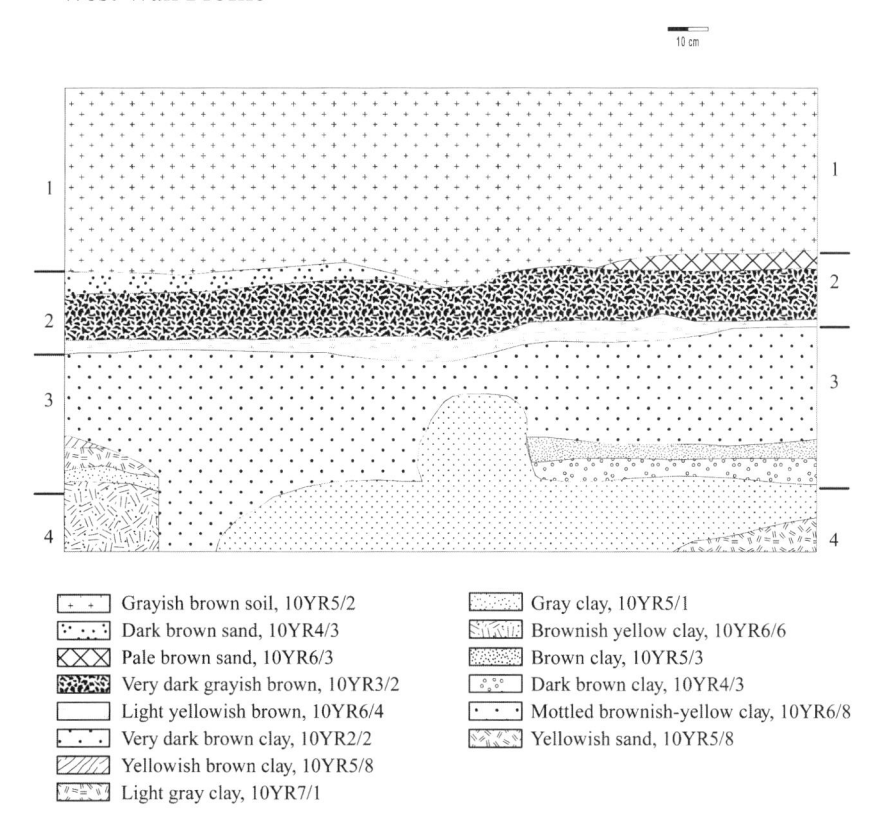

Pattern	Description	Pattern	Description
	Grayish brown soil, 10YR5/2		Gray clay, 10YR5/1
	Dark brown sand, 10YR4/3		Brownish yellow clay, 10YR6/6
	Pale brown sand, 10YR6/3		Brown clay, 10YR5/3
	Very dark grayish brown, 10YR3/2		Dark brown clay, 10YR4/3
	Light yellowish brown, 10YR6/4		Mottled brownish-yellow clay, 10YR6/8
	Very dark brown clay, 10YR2/2		Yellowish sand, 10YR5/8
	Yellowish brown clay, 10YR5/8		
	Light gray clay, 10YR7/1		

Figure 2.7. Profile map of Unit M, east ½, west wall, 22Lw510.

sherds were found in the upper levels of the unit. As with the evidence from Units E and SE, this suggests the area around Mound E might have been occupied later than most of the rest of the site. Finally, associated with the sheet midden in the east half of the unit was a piece of copper foil in the shape of a bilobed arrow.

Excavation Unit T

Off the eastern end of Mound E there is a bulge in the terrace wall edge. This space was bounded to the west by Mound E and to the north, south, and east by the terrace edge. At times when the floodplain was swampy or

22Lw510
Unit M E 1/2
Level 6 base

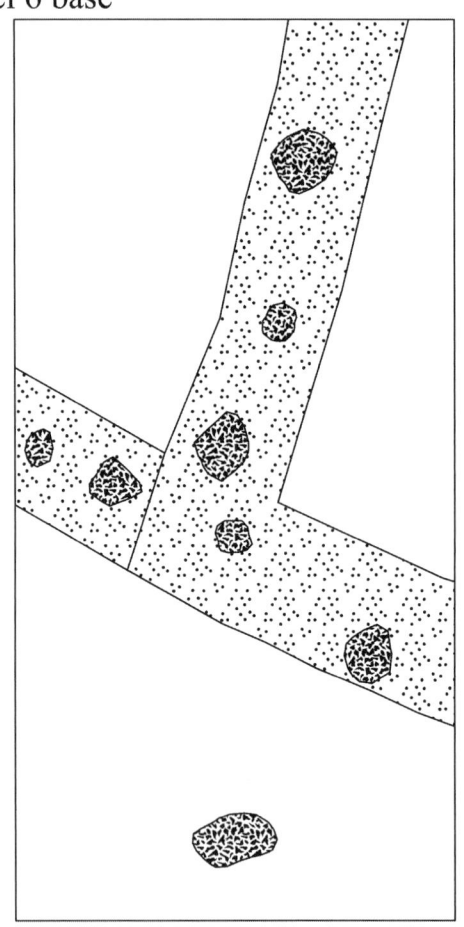

Figure 2.8. Map of Unit M, east ½, excavation level 6 floor plan, 22Lw510. This corresponds with the base of analytical unit 3. Wall trenches and post features associated with a structure at the base of the unit are shown.

22Lw510
Unit T
East Profile

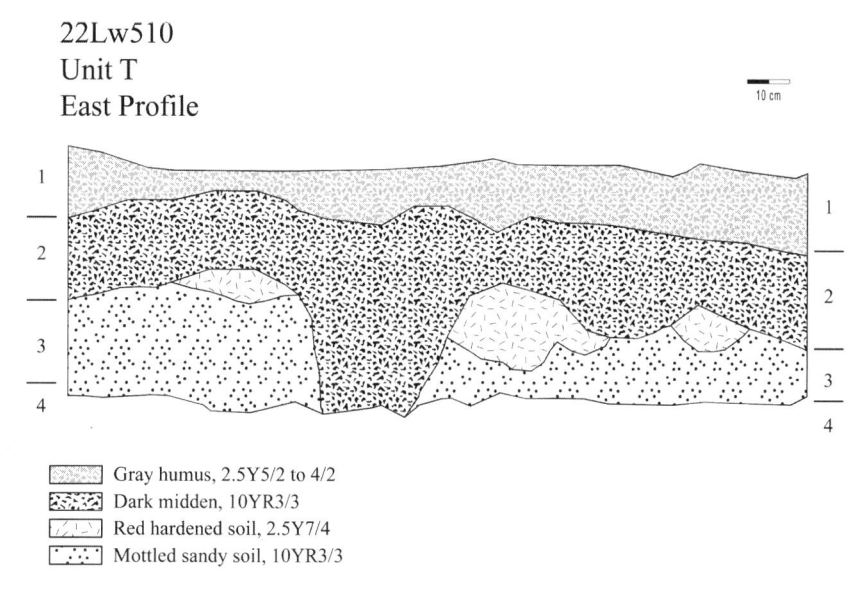

▒ Gray humus, 2.5Y5/2 to 4/2
▨ Dark midden, 10YR3/3
▧ Red hardened soil, 2.5Y7/4
▫ Mottled sandy soil, 10YR3/3

Figure 2.9. Profile map of Unit T, east wall, 22Lw510.

flooded, this would have been a very exclusive and highly restricted space. Two adjacent 2-×-2-m units were excavated there (Figure 2.9). These units were designated T (for "terrace") and, to the north, T2.

The units were excavated 30–35 cm deep to subsoil. The base of the units contained numerous post features. The yellowish soil surface contained areas of red that suggested the surface may have been burned (Figure 2.10). The units also contained an abundant amount of mussel shell at all levels, with especially high concentrations in T2 and the northern half of T. This living surface was covered by 20–30 cm of a mottled sandy soil (analytical level 3). There was likely a living surface here because the profiles indicate features were excavated down through this level. Analytical unit 2 was a ca. 30-cm-thick midden.

In total, 2,163 sherds were collected from these units. Decorated sherds include Anna Incised, *var. Anna,* Carter Engraved, *var. Carter,* and Plaquemine Brushed, *var. Plaquemine,* which are collectively the most common decorated types found in mound contexts. There were also Mazique Incised, *var. Manchac,* abundant amounts of Grace Brushed, *var. Grace,* and Hollyknowe Pinched, *var. Patmos,* Coles Creek Incised, *var. Hardy,* and L'Eau Noire Incised, *var. L'Eau Noire.*

Unit T is atypical of all the units on or adjacent to Mound E in that it has a very low percentage of decorated sherds (Table 2.1). For the whole site, 17 percent of all sherds were decorated. This proportion is slightly higher on the

38 Chapter 2

**22Lw510
Unit T
Unit Base Floor**

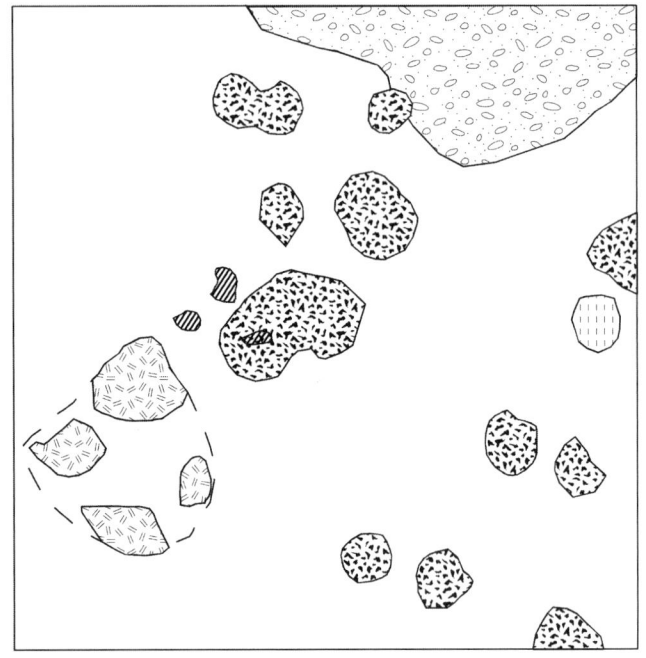

↑N

Symbol	Description
	Midden, post features
	Whitish clay with orange and black splotches
	Root or rodent disturbance
	Pieces of shell on the floor
	Red/orange burnt floor

Figure 2.10. Plan drawing of the base of Unit T, 22Lw510. The post features are shown.

summit of Mound E (19 percent) and extremely high at Unit M (24 percent) and Unit E (25 percent). It is also comparably high at the adjacent Mound G (23 percent). However, only 5 percent of 2,163 sherds recovered from Unit T are decorated. This is indicative of the high number of storage vessels from Unit T, which are generally larger and less likely to be decorated. Given its proximity to Mound E and the nature of the ceramic assemblage, it is possible the Unit T terrace may have hosted some feasting events.

Table 2.1. Percentage of decorated sherds in each excavation unit at Pevey

Unit	Total Sherds	No. of Decorated Sherds	% Decorated
A	7	1	14.3
B	139	17	12.2
C	425	50	11.8
E	669	153	22.9
E2	216	40	18.5
E3	196	79	40.3
G	717	164	22.9
H	287	56	19.5
H2	830	174	21.0
I	493	30	6.1
J	2	0	0.0
K	504	161	31.9
M	1,690	407	24.1
SE	417	81	19.4
SJ	16	4	25.0
T	1,233	73	5.9
T2	930	40	4.3

Excavation Unit G

Mound G is the second-largest mound at Pevey, and, based on the arrangement of mounds at the site, it was likely the second most exclusive mound after Mound E. The excavation unit was placed on the south edge of the Mound G summit (Figure 2.11). The unit reached a maximum depth of 2.4 m and was excavated to subsoil.

Below the mound, on top of the subsoil, there were two wall trenches with postholes inside the trench (Figure 2.12). Above this initial structure were 50 cm of midden with evidence of several structures. This midden contained an abundance of vessels associated with high-status serving, including five sherds of Anna Incised, *var. Anna* and eight sherds of D'Olive Incised, *var. unspecified.* These represent decorated shallow plates or bowls. There were also three sherds of a very finely made Carter Engraved, *var. Shell Bluff* carinated bowl. The surface of this vessel was finely burnished, the decorations were done with extreme care, and the walls of the vessel were 3.3 mm, about half the thickness of a typical Pevey vessel. Finally, there was a

40   Chapter 2

**22Lw510
Unit G
South Wall Profile**

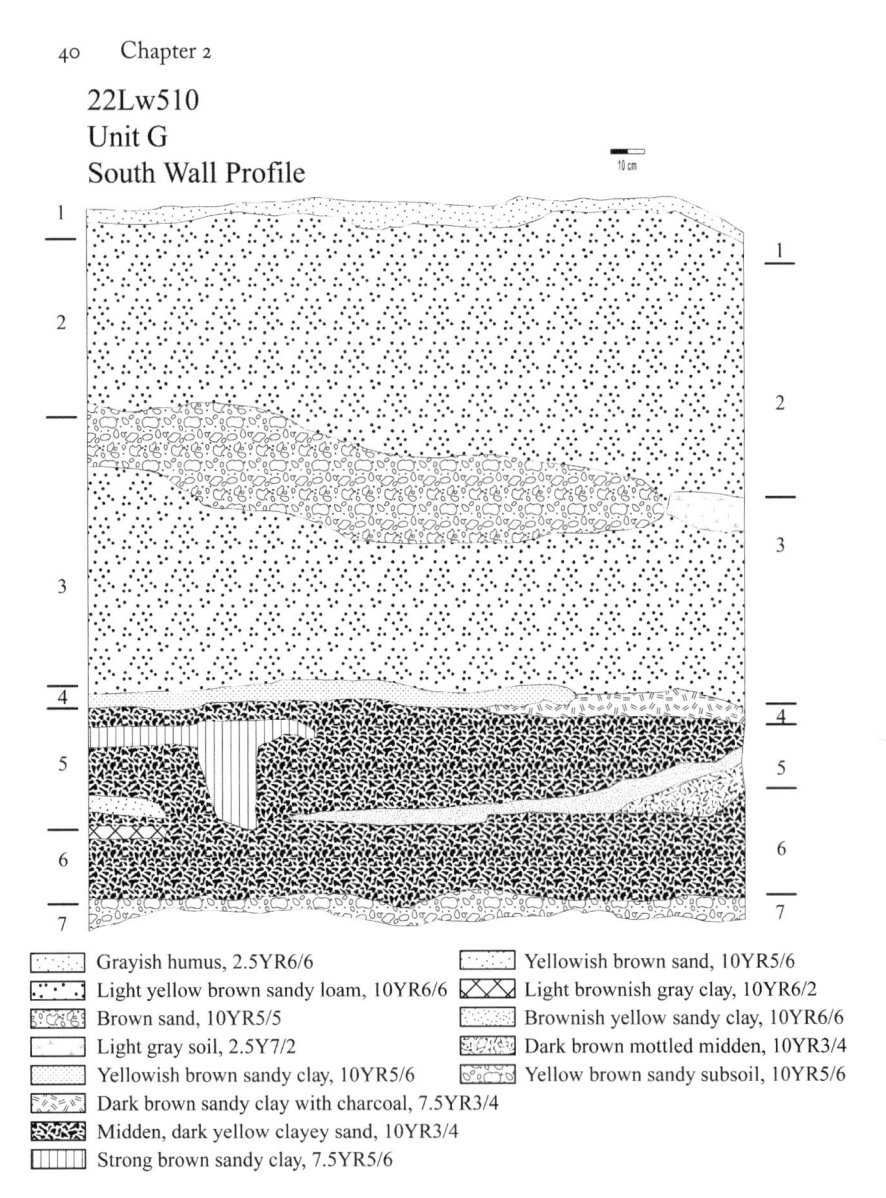

	Grayish humus, 2.5YR6/6		Yellowish brown sand, 10YR5/6
	Light yellow brown sandy loam, 10YR6/6		Light brownish gray clay, 10YR6/2
	Brown sand, 10YR5/5		Brownish yellow sandy clay, 10YR6/6
	Light gray soil, 2.5Y7/2		Dark brown mottled midden, 10YR3/4
	Yellowish brown sandy clay, 10YR5/6		Yellow brown sandy subsoil, 10YR5/6
	Dark brown sandy clay with charcoal, 7.5YR3/4		
	Midden, dark yellow clayey sand, 10YR3/4		
	Strong brown sandy clay, 7.5YR5/6		

Figure 2.11. Profile map of Unit G, south wall, 22Lw510.

crinoid bead and five sherds of Moundville Incised, three of which are from a Moundville Incised, *var. Moundville* jar that is either an import or an exact duplicate of the decorated jars common at Moundville.

The upper half of the midden layer contained more evidence of structures, including a hearth and a feature from which nine sherds of Anna Incised, *var. Anna* were recovered. Above these structures were 1.4 m of fill.

22Lw510
Unit G
Unit Base Floor

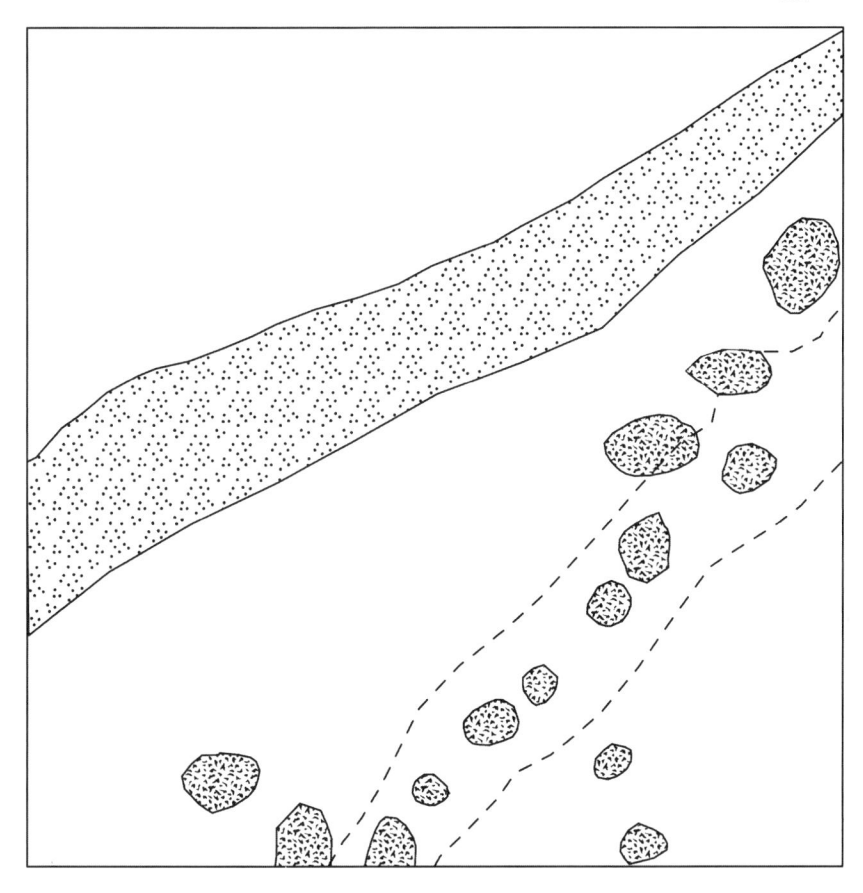

Figure 2.12. Plan drawing of the post features and wall trench at the base of Unit G, 22Lw510.

The fill contained lots of sherds including the expected Anna Incised, *var. Anna,* Carter Engraved, *var. Carter,* and Plaquemine Brushed, *var. Plaquemine,* as well as Barton Incised, *var. Barton,* Moundville Incised, *var. unspecified,* Grace Brushed, *var. Grace,* D'Olive Incised, *var. unspecified,* Mound Place Incised, and Fatherland Incised, *var. unspecified.*

Overall, the unit has one of the most exotic and high-status assemblages of any of the mounds. Moundville Incised, *var. Moundville* and Carter Engraved, *var. Shell Bluff* wares are possible long-distance exchange goods. Ad-

22Lw510
Unit H
East Wall Profile

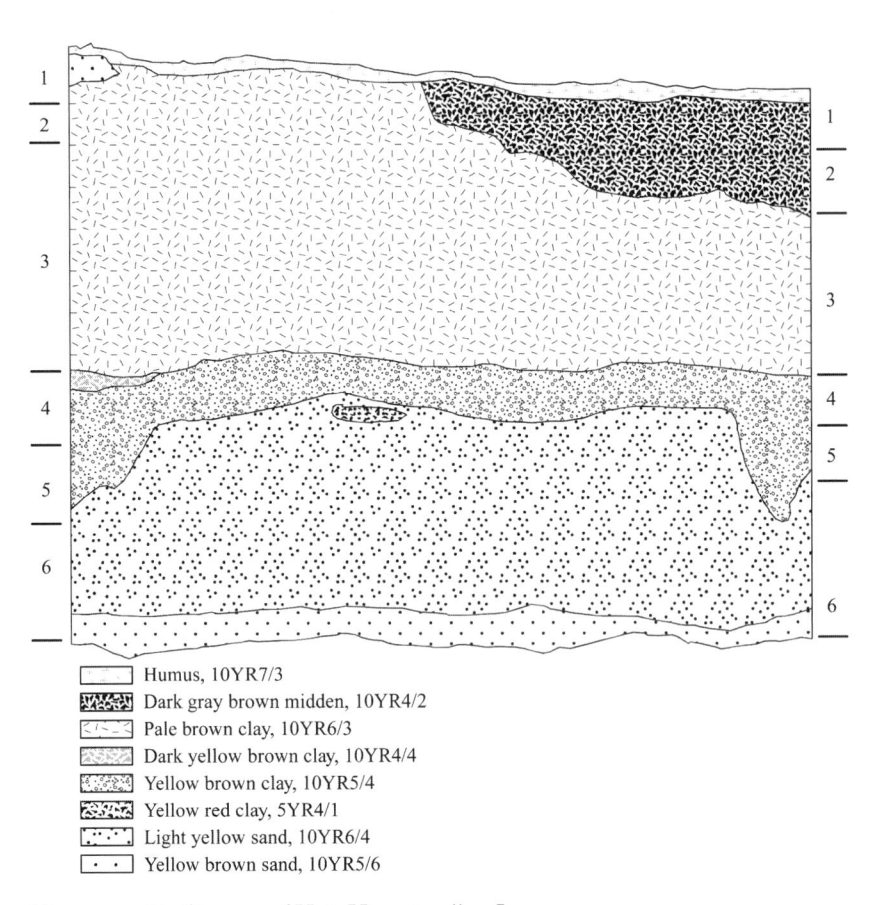

Humus, 10YR7/3
Dark gray brown midden, 10YR4/2
Pale brown clay, 10YR6/3
Dark yellow brown clay, 10YR4/4
Yellow brown clay, 10YR5/4
Yellow red clay, 5YR4/1
Light yellow sand, 10YR6/4
Yellow brown sand, 10YR5/6

Figure 2.13. Profile map of Unit H, east wall, 22Lw510.

ditionally, the collective assemblage reflects an orientation predominately toward serving and reflects a high degree of investment in vessel production. A total of 23 percent of all sherds recovered from the unit were decorated, compared with a 17-percent average for the whole site.

Excavation Unit H

Unit H was placed on the north edge of the Mound H summit. The unit was excavated a maximum depth of 175 cm to subsoil (Figure 2.13). At the base of the mound were a few assorted post features but no clear sign of a structure. The first major construction on the mound contributed about 50 cm of light yellow sandy fill (analytical unit 6). On top of this mound construction was a living surface with a possible wall trench containing two 8-cm-diameter post features. After this phase of the mound's use, the mound accumulated about 15 cm of yellow-brown clay midden (analytical units 4 and 5). The top of this surface contained some suggestion of a 100-cm-diameter hearth feature. The second major construction episode used a pale brown clay fill (analytical unit 3) to raise the mound surface to its present location. On top of this fill is evidence for a flank midden in the southern half of the unit (analytical unit 2).

The ceramics in this mound are the standard ones for mound contexts at Pevey: Anna Incised, *var. Anna,* Carter Engraved, *var. Carter,* Plaquemine Brushed, *var. Plaquemine,* and Mound Place Incised. In addition, there were a few sherds of Carter Engraved, *var. Sara* and Evansville Punctated, *var. Sharkey* found in the flank midden. There was also some Moundville Incised, *var. unspecified* found in the second major stage of mound fill.

Excavation Unit I

Unit I was excavated on the south flank of Mound I. It was excavated as a single 1-×-2-m unit in 20-cm arbitrary levels to a maximum depth of about 180 cm (Figure 2.14). The unit exposed a very orderly progression of alternating middens and mound fill. The base of the unit (top of analytical unit 3) contained two postholes and a hearth. One post feature was approximately 18 cm in diameter, and the other was obscured by the unit wall but possibly 10 cm in diameter. The hearth was located in the southeast corner of the unit and appeared to have a radius of 60–70 cm. The hearth contained lots of charcoal and fired clay.

This living surface was covered by a 10-cm-thick grayish brown midden and then a reddish brown mottled clay that represents evidence of the first construction stage. The flank then contains evidence of at least two other major construction stages. The middle, dark grayish brown, layer contained clusters of shell, sherds, and a piece of burned thatch. The unit also produced an abundant amount of shell.

The ceramics from Mound I are the standard ones from the site: Anna Incised, *var. Anna,* Carter Engraved, *var. Carter,* Plaquemine Brushed, *var. Plaquemine,* and Mound Place Incised. There were also some D'Olive Incised, *var. unspecified* and Harrison Bayou Incised, *var. Harrison Bayou* sherds.

Excavation Unit K

Unit K was placed in the suspected location of Mound K. This area is in the part of the site that has been partially cleared and was probably subject

Pevey Site
Unit I, East 1/2
East Profile

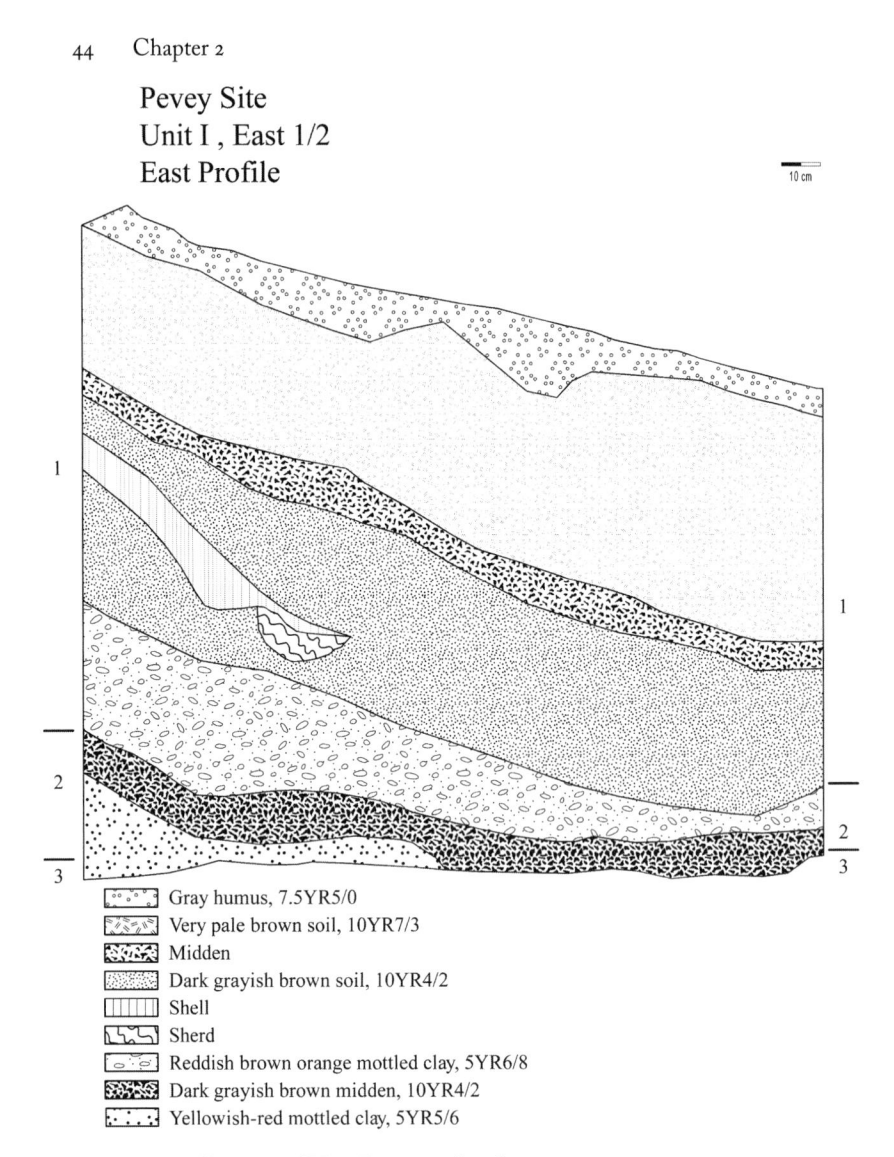

10 cm

- Gray humus, 7.5YR5/0
- Very pale brown soil, 10YR7/3
- Midden
- Dark grayish brown soil, 10YR4/2
- Shell
- Sherd
- Reddish brown orange mottled clay, 5YR6/8
- Dark grayish brown midden, 10YR4/2
- Yellowish-red mottled clay, 5YR5/6

Figure 2.14. Profile map of Unit I, east wall, 22Lw510.

to erosion and modern agriculture. This suspected mound was tested with a soil auger and found to have a midden, and Unit K was excavated here. The 2-×-2-m unit was excavated to a depth of 70 cm, which was far below the 40- to 45-cm-deep cultural deposits. The base of the unit had evidence of 5–10 possible post features. The five or six post features in the east half of the unit were not detected until the unit was well below the surface of the subsoil and were mapped as having 4- to 8-cm diameters. The four circular features mapped in the western half of the unit base range in size from 20 to 26 cm in diameter. There is also the suggestion that there may have been a wall trench in the unit. These structures were covered by a 40-cm-thick dark brown sandy midden.

The ceramics recovered include Anna Incised, *var. Anna,* Carter Engraved, *var. Carter,* Plaquemine Brushed, *var. Plaquemine,* and Mound Place Incised. There were 29 sherds of Anna Incised, representing a fairly high concentration. Although the evidence for the presence of a mound K is not definitive, a persuasive case can be made. First, the site symmetry suggests that such a mound should exist in the vicinity of Unit K. There is a slight suggestion of a mound rise on the surface, and under the surface a midden on top of a likely structure. Although there is no mound stratigraphy remaining, the quantity and type of sherds suggest this was a fairly important locale and most likely a mound.

Excavation Unit J

Unit J was a 2-×-2-m unit excavated to a depth of 40 cm. A total of two sherds were recovered and no culturally significant stratigraphy was noted. This unit was placed in the wrong location because of mapping problems and did not intersect with Mound J.

Excavation Unit SJ

Unit SJ was placed on Mound J. It was a 2-×-2-m unit excavated to an approximate depth of 60 cm. The excavators found a 10- to 30-cm-deep midden below the plow zone that was flecked with charcoal and contained daub. In the east half of the unit, on top of the midden, were four post features. There were only 16 sherds recovered from the unit, including one Anna Incised, *var. Anna* and one Carter Engraved, *var. unspecified.*

The Lowe-Steen Site (22Lw511)

The Lowe-Steen site is a two-mound Mississippian site located 18 km north of the Pevey site on the west bank of the Pearl River (Figure 2.15). The environmental setting of the Lowe-Steen site is considerably different from that of Pevey. Whereas Pevey is located on a terrace as high as 8–10 m above the floodplain, the Lowe-Steen site is located on a small peninsula of land situated less than 2 m above relict channel swamps flanking the site on three sides. This environment would have provided the residents of Lowe-Steen with easy access to bottomland and aquatic resources. Although we do not know which channel the Pearl River flowed through when the Lowe-Steen

46   Chapter 2

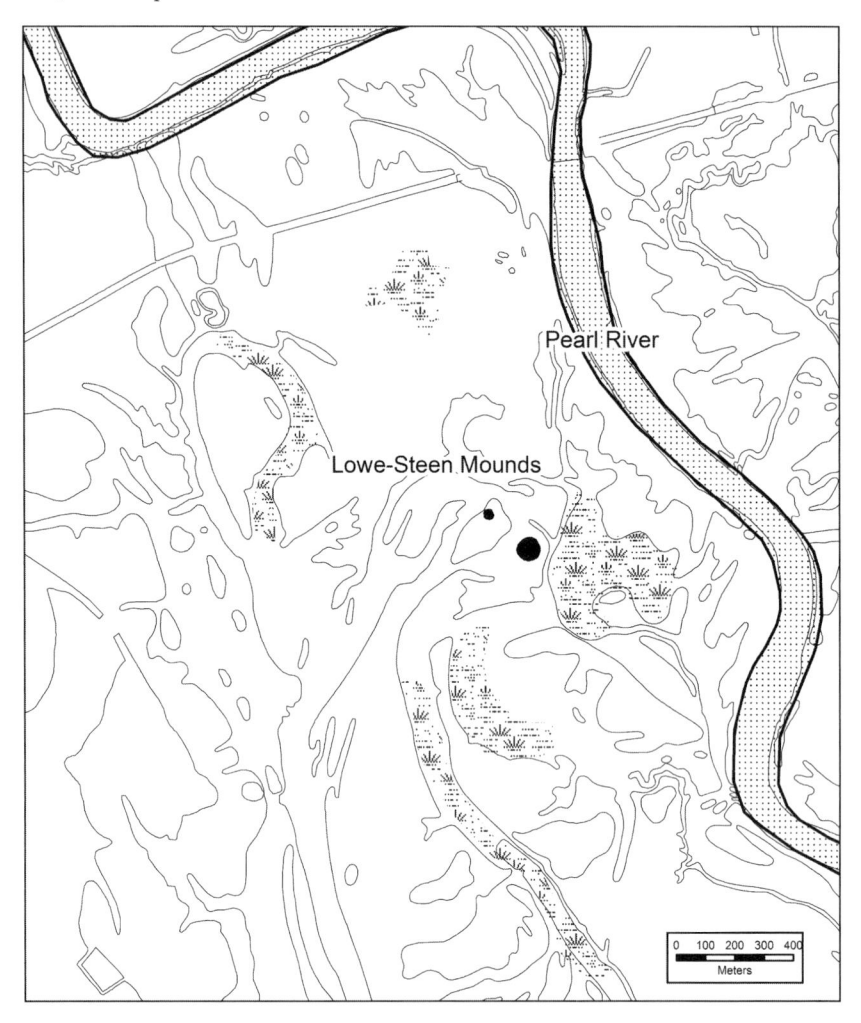

Figure 2.15. The environmental and topographic setting of the Lowe-Steen site. The contour lines are at 10-foot intervals and are based on data provided by MARIS. Swamp boundaries are based on the U.S. Geological Survey topographic map.

site was occupied, the present course of the Pearl River is 500 m from the site and the far edge of the floodplain indicates the river was never more than 1 km from the Lowe-Steen location.

The University of North Carolina Field School excavated at Lowe-Steen in 1993, and that work represents the only known archaeological excavations to have taken place at the site. The research goals were the same as for the

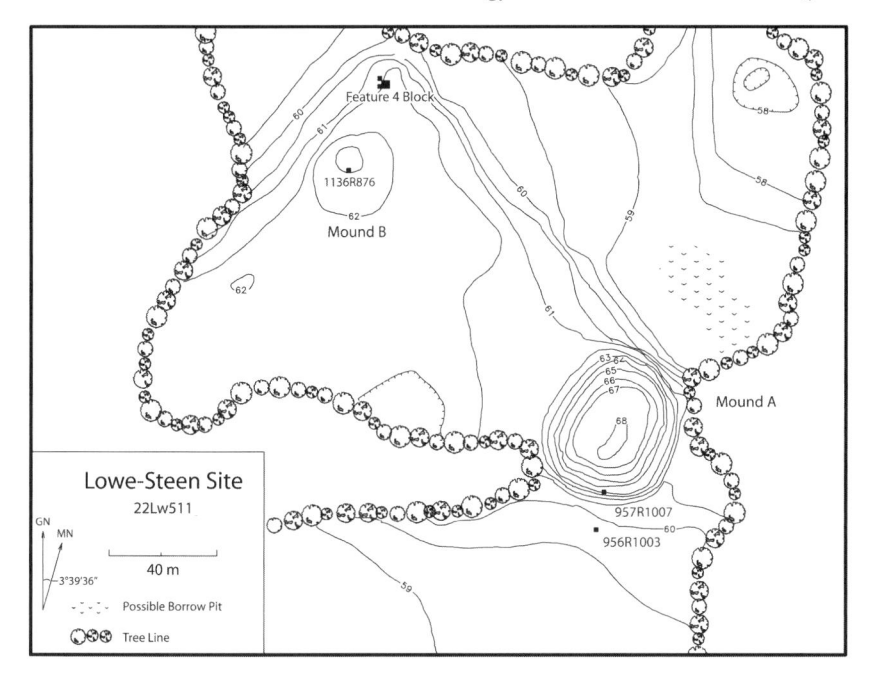

Figure 2.16. Topographic map of the Lowe-Steen site (22Lw511) showing the location of the excavation units.

Pevey site: to create a ceramic chronology and investigate the time period in which the site was abandoned. A total of four excavation units were opened: one unit each for Mounds A and B and two other units placed in locations that looked promising from surface collections and soil core auger tests (Figures 2.16 and 2.17).

Excavation Unit 956R1003

Unit 956R1003 was located 15 m south of Mound A and was discovered through surface collections and soil core auger testing to be a likely source of midden and artifacts. The unit was excavated to a depth of 96 cm as a 2-×-2-m block. The excavation revealed two separate living surfaces. Located on top of the subsoil was a layer of dark soil 10–15 cm thick that could have been a midden or a buried A horizon. On top of this was a discontinuous sand floor, topped by a 5- to 10-cm-thick charcoal-flecked midden, on top of which was another living surface. Associated with this surface was a hearth feature located in the southern half of the unit, oval in shape and measuring 65 cm wide and 60 cm long at the floor surface (analytical unit 4). Above this living surface was a 20-cm-deep midden located below the plow zone.

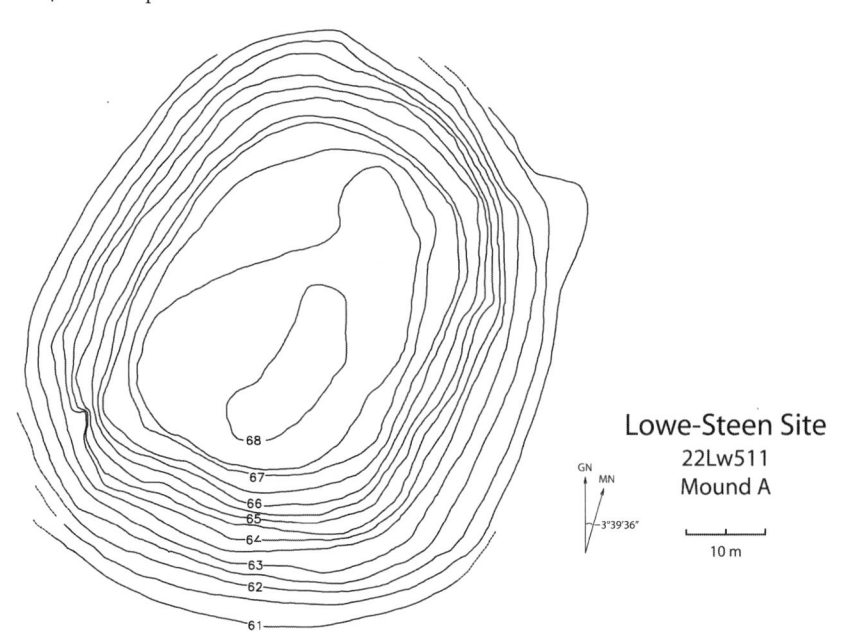

Figure 2.17. Topographic map of the primary Lowe-Steen mound, Mound A.

The top midden and plow zone contained Anna Incised, *var. Anna,* Plaquemine Brushed, *var. Plaquemine,* Mound Place Incised, Carter Engraved, *var. Carter,* Hollyknowe Pinched, *var. Patmos,* and D'Olive Incised, *var. unspecified* decorated sherds. Levels associated with the living floors and their middens yielded Barton Incised, *var. Barton,* Carter Engraved, *var. Carter,* and many examples of Plaquemine Brushed, *var. Plaquemine,* Carter Engraved, *var. unspecified,* and Mound Place Incised.

Excavation Unit 975R1007

Unit 975R1007, 2 × 2 m, was placed near the base of the south flank of Mound A. The west half of the unit was excavated in arbitrary 20-cm levels, and the east half of the unit was excavated in five separate natural levels. The unit was excavated to subsoil, which was 155 cm below the north edge of the unit and 90 cm below the south edge (Figure 2.18).

On the surface of the subsoil in the northern part of the unit there was a single post feature about 20 cm in diameter. These basal levels contained a large number of flakes and point fragments, suggesting there may have been a significant pre-Mississippian occupation and that not all of the features are necessarily Mississippian in age. There was 20 cm of brown soil

22Lw511
Unit 975R1007
East Profile

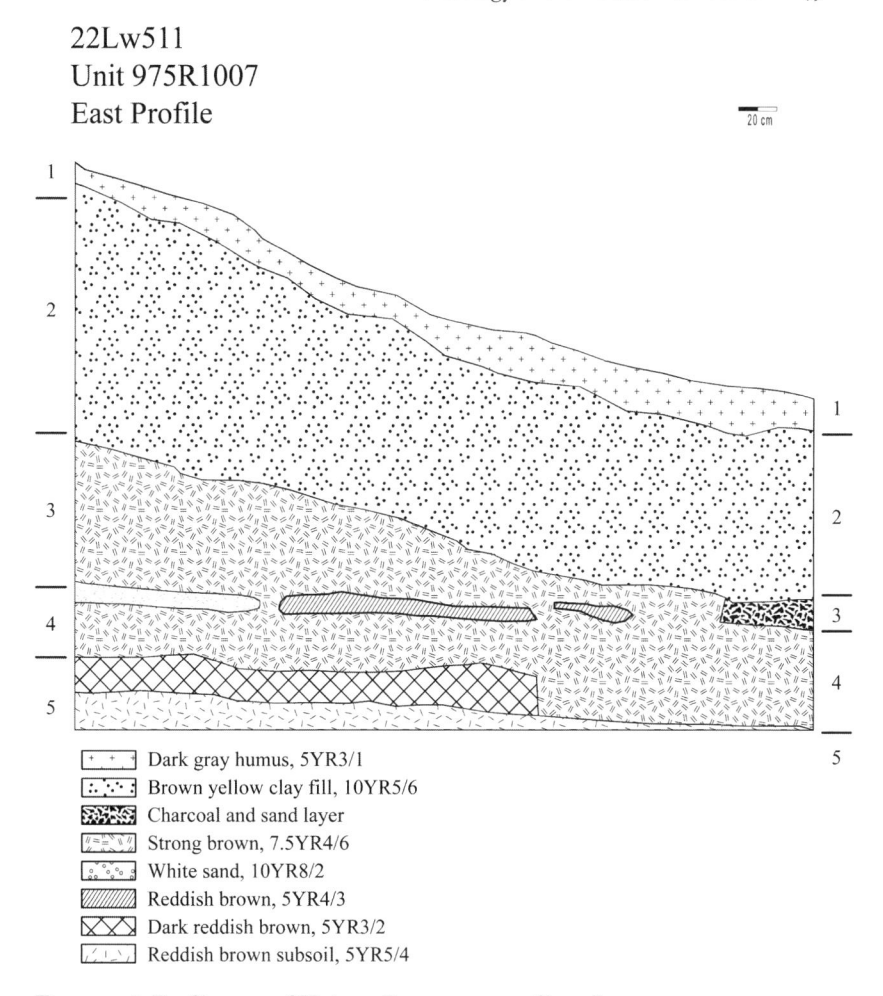

- Dark gray humus, 5YR3/1
- Brown yellow clay fill, 10YR5/6
- Charcoal and sand layer
- Strong brown, 7.5YR4/6
- White sand, 10YR8/2
- Reddish brown, 5YR4/3
- Dark reddish brown, 5YR3/2
- Reddish brown subsoil, 5YR5/4

Figure 2.18. Profile map of Unit 975R1007, east profile, 22Lw511.

above the subsoil (analytical unit 4) that contained charcoal and daub as well as sherds such as Plaquemine Brushed, *var. Plaquemine,* Anna Incised, *var. Anna,* Harrison Bayou Incised, *var. Harrison Bayou,* and Mound Place Incised. This soil may have been deposited as wash off the mound flank. Covering the wash was a sand layer living surface (base of analytical unit 3). At the time this surface was occupied, this unit would not have been covered by Mound A. There were two distinct levels of mound fill (analytical units 2 and 3) placed on this location.

Associated with the living surfaces were Harrison Bayou Incised, *var.*

Harrison Bayou, Anna Incised, *var. Anna,* Plaquemine Brushed, *var. Plaquemine,* Carter Engraved, *var. unspecified,* and Mound Place Incised.

Excavation Unit 1136R876

Unit 1136R876 was placed in Mound B. Before the unit was excavated it was not known whether the small rise was a mound, but the excavation proved conclusively that it is. The entire 2-×-2-m unit was excavated as a single block. The excavations started as 20-cm arbitrary levels, but after excavating through 15 cm of plow zone and 30 cm of fill the investigators encountered the top of the last visible living surface, and the excavators subdivided the excavations by level, zone, and feature. At the base of the cultural zone and top of the subsoil, the excavators mapped 29 post features. On top of the subsoil was a 20-cm-thick cultural zone (analytical unit 3) that was divisible into at least three living surfaces. It was filled with charcoal and daub, several of the surfaces were burned, and there was a hearth in the southern half of the unit. This cultural zone was capped by 30 cm of mottled light brown fill (analytical unit 2).

The unit yielded just 119 sherds, of which only six were decorated. A Plaquemine Brushed, *var. Plaquemine* sherd, a Mound Place Incised sherd, and an unclassified decorated on shell-tempered paste sherd were found in the hearth. Two D'Olive Incised, *var. unspecified* sherds and a Barton Incised, *var. Estill* sherd were located in other parts of the cultural zone.

Mound B is located in the middle of an active agricultural field and may have been damaged before investigation, so conclusions about this mound must be necessarily tentative. Excavations revealed that structures were built and rebuilt on top of Mound B numerous times. Little evidence of midden was gathered in this unit, however, indicating trash was deposited elsewhere, possibly adjacent to the mound.

Feature 4 Block

Soil auger testing indicated there was a substantial midden just below the plow zone. A total of six 2-×-2-m units (1178R892, 1182R892, 1178R894, 1180R894, 1180R896, 1185R892) were completely or partially excavated, tracing out the boundaries of a large black sheet midden that extended 5–40 cm deep below the base of the plow zone. The feature contained charcoal, ceramics, lithics, and some daub. There were no definitive architectural features and no map was produced of the entire block.

A total of 1,293 sherds were recovered from the units, including 128 decorated sherds. These included 64 Plaquemine Brushed, *var. Plaquemine* sherds, as well as Anna Incised, *var. Anna* and Grace Brushed, *var. Grace* sherds and a nearly complete Carter Engraved, *var. Carter* vessel.

Phillips Farm Site (22Lw593)

In 2000 I directed excavations at the Phillips Farm site. The goal of the season's fieldwork was to locate and document non-mound Mississippian sites in and around the Pevey and Lowe-Steen sites. At the conclusion of the 2000 season, the project focused on 22Lw593 for excavation because it was the most accessible of the known Mississippian sites and the best candidate for a Mississippian farmstead.

The site is located 3 km to the northeast of the Pevey site and 1.5 km east of the current channel of the Pearl River (Figure 2.19). It was originally recorded in 1992 by Tim Mooney, who was doing reconnaissance survey for the excavation projects that he would conduct the following season. The site is located near the edge of a 2-m-high terrace overlooking a relatively large cypress swamp located in a relict channel of the Pearl River. Numerous sites (Lw524, Lw525, Lw526, Lw527, Lw530, Lw531, Lw533) have already been documented along the edge of this relict channel, and this was a very heavily utilized area for millennia. These sites have mostly Late Archaic and Woodland components, but there are also a few Early Archaic and Middle Archaic components recorded. These sites are discussed more completely elsewhere (see Survey Block 6 in Livingood 2006:139–141).

Of particular interest during this work, however, was the note of a Mississippian component to 22Lw593. During a visit to the site in 2000, survey was conducted of a small part of the site that had been plowed but was not under cultivation. Collections revealed a definite Mississippian component with definable boundaries. An arbitrary grid was established at the site with the north–south axis parallel to the terrace edge, and shovel testing was conducted. These tests helped to determine where the excavation would begin.

A total of 14 contiguous 2-×-2-m units, as well as an additional 1-×-1-m unit, were excavated (Figure 2.20). The excavation procedures involved removing the 9- to 16-cm-thick plow zone and mapping the features on the surface of the subsoil. All soil was screened through ¼-inch hardware cloth for artifacts. Features were removed individually and some soil was retained for flotation analysis.

The most significant discovery was the outline of a large structure on the east half of the excavation block. Unfortunately, time did not permit a more complete excavation, and the precise boundaries of the structure cannot be determined. One possible scenario suggested by the postholes in the southern part of the unit is that there was a very large circular structure in this area, possibly 8 m in diameter. In support of this argument, most of the post features are of similar size, with a diameter of 8–10 cm and a depth of 20–28 cm below subsoil. Unfortunately, there are few enough posts that several ar-

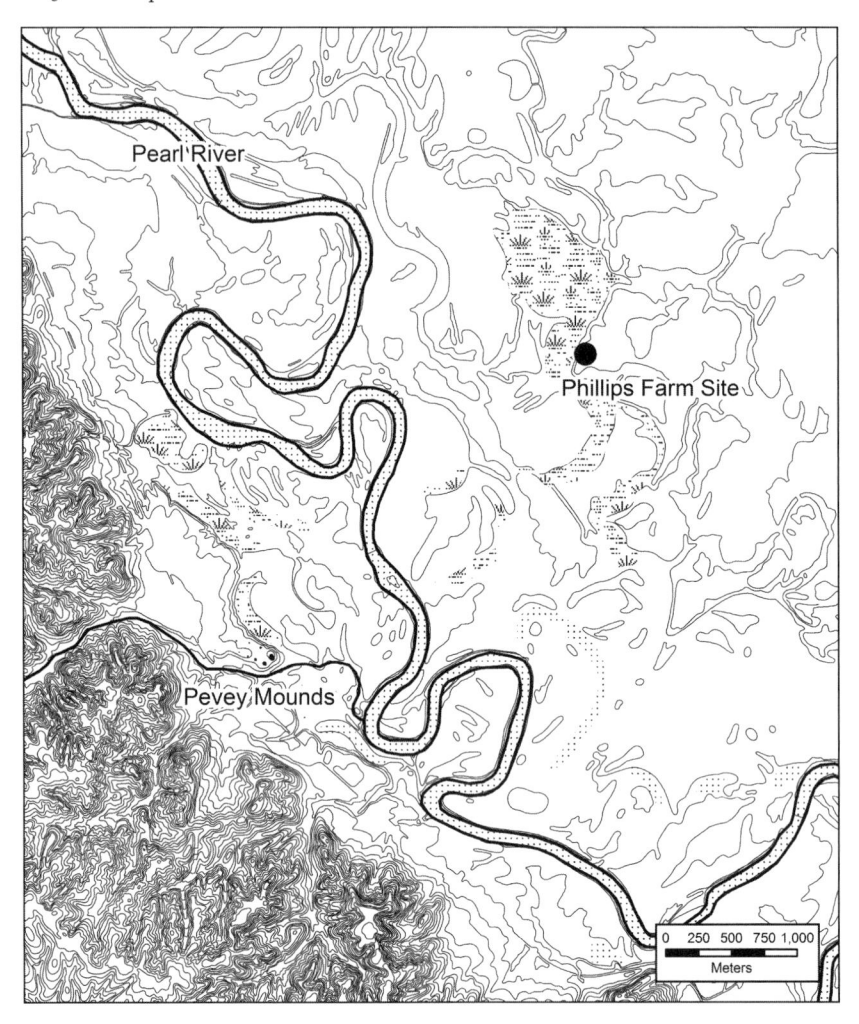

Figure 2.19. The environmental setting of the Phillips Farm site (22Lw593). The contour lines are based on MARIS data and are at 10-foot intervals. The map of the swamp is based on U.S. Geological Survey topographic maps and digital orthoquads provided by MARIS.

rangements are possible: (1) an 8-m-diameter circular structure, as suggested by the postholes in the southern part of the excavation, which does not match as well with the eastern postholes, however; (2) an ovoid structure, which fits nicely with the map of the known postholes but would be an unexpected architectural choice; or (3) three separate straight walls that could be part of two or three separate rectangular structures. This last proposal seems most

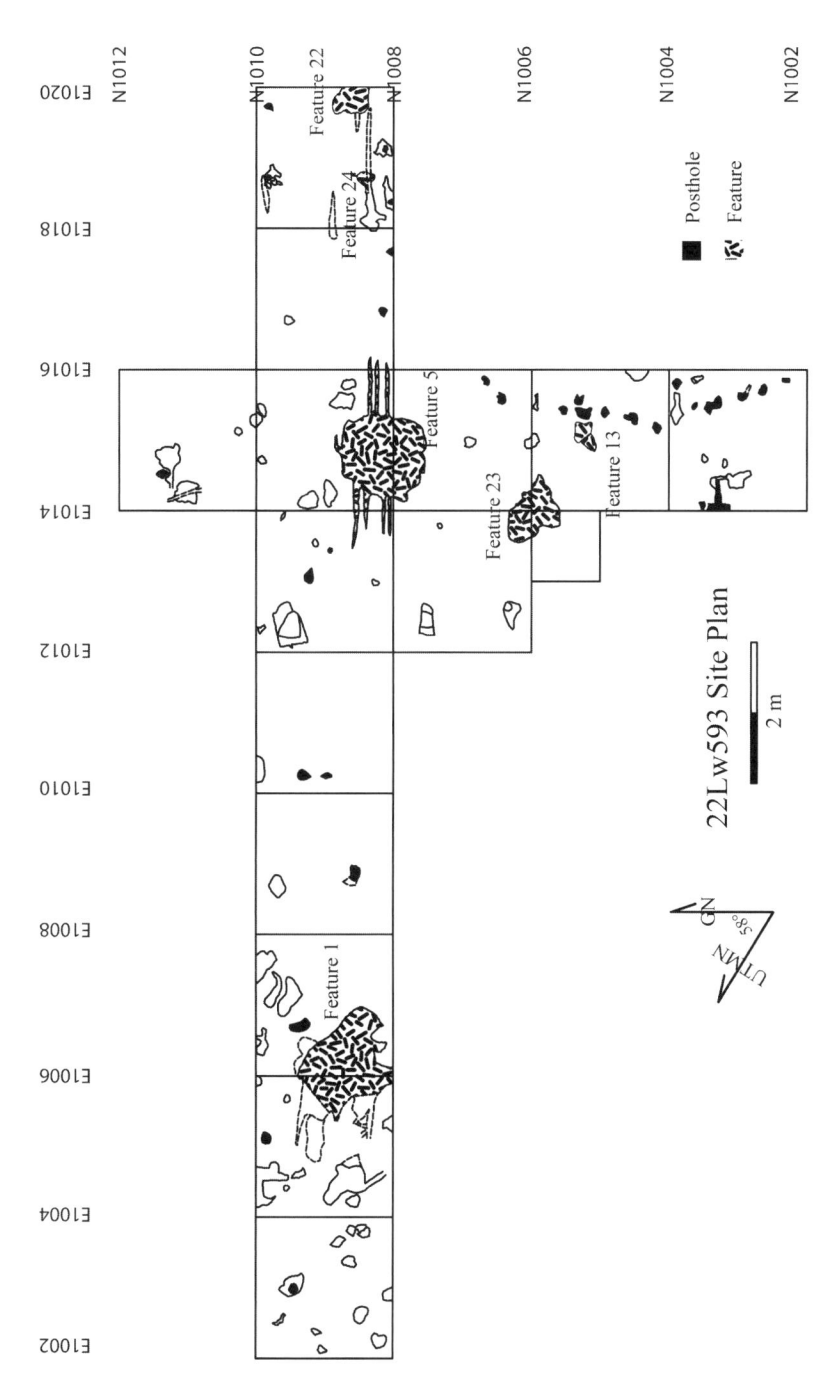

Figure 2.20. Map of the Phillips Farm (22Lw593) excavations.

likely because the proposed circular structure would be so unexpectedly large and because in Brown's (1985a) chronology of Natchez region architecture a rectangular structure would be consistent with the single radiocarbon date obtained from the site.

Several significant features were excavated at the site. Feature 1 was a broad, shallow pit with dark brown soil that contained some lithic debris. Feature 5 was an approximately circular feature 110 cm in diameter and 10 cm deep below the plow zone. It appears to have been a pit or shallow depression in which remains of a burned structure were deposited. The unit contained daub, charcoal, sherds, and flakes, and the soil was fire hardened. Feature 13 was a small 20-cm-deep pit that contained a large shell-tempered rim sherd. Feature 22 contained dark brown soil and some lumps of hardened clay. Features 23 and 24 both had darkened soil and a few artifacts.

Few diagnostic ceramics were recovered from the excavations. There were many decorated sherds that were too small to classify; the only one that was classified to type and variety was a single Plaquemine Brushed, *var. Plaquemine* sherd. One radiocarbon sample (cal A.D. 1475–1631) was analyzed from this site that suggests that this site postdates the Pevey and Lowe-Steen sites. A detailed chronological discussion can be found in the final chapter.

Summary

This chapter has reviewed archaeological evidence from the three Mississippian sites that have been excavated in Lawrence County. Excavations at the nine-mound Pevey site indicate that there is internal differentiation within the site. The areas around the large mound (Mound E), including the summit of Mound E (Unit SE), the flank of Mound E (Unit E), and the adjacent terraces (Units M and T), have assemblages that are likely associated with an elite household and feasting. The second-largest mound (Mound G) has the most likely candidates for high-status imported ceramics. In contrast, the mounds of the western half of the site are smaller and have less-remarkable, less-distinct, and more domestic-looking ceramic assemblages.

Excavations at the two-mound Lowe-Steen site investigated the flank of the large mound (Mound A), proved the existence of Mound B, exposed a large midden on the edge of the mound precinct, and investigated a midden and hearth to the south of Mound A. Excavations at Phillips Farm exposed evidence for one or more structures that may have been part of a Mississippi period farmstead.

3
Investigation of the Settlement Patterns of the Pevey Polity

During the 1999 and 2000 seasons I undertook a survey project in order to answer three questions: (1) did the Lawrence County Mississippians live in dispersed hamlets and farmsteads or in concentrated settlements, (2) were settlements concentrated around the two main mound sites or were they dispersed along the length of the Pearl River, and (3) how do the ceramic assemblages at non-mound Mississippian sites differ from those of the mound centers? Collectively, the answers to these questions could be compared with those for the other well-studied polities, such as Moundville, Lubbub Creek, and Old Hoover, in order to better understand the degree of political hierarchy.

To answer these questions, it was important to sample the full extent of the Pearl River drainage in Lawrence County. Also, since one of the five Mississippian sites known in Lawrence County prior to the survey project was in the uplands (22Lw549), it was considered important to sample across physiographic zones. Therefore, a stratified random research design was created (described in Livingood 2006) and within selected survey blocks my coworkers and I used a method adapted from Laurie Steponaitis's (1986:105–118) survey of the Lower Patuxent drainage, Maryland.

The challenge of Mississippian survey is that in order to locate small hamlets and farmsteads, it is necessary to use tightly spaced transects. For pedestrian survey we employed transects spaced 10 m apart in most cases and 5 m apart in a few instances. Transects were divided using both arbitrary and naturally gridded methods. All members of the survey crew were equipped with pin flags, collection bags, and permanent markers. Crew members would leave pin flags at the beginning and end of each transect section. The pin flag would be labeled with the name of the transect and section. One crew member would follow behind the others and would collect the pin flags and note the GPS location of each.

For some fields, crew members were instructed to use a 30-m chain in order to measure out gridded transect sections. In this case, all collection units were 30 × 3 m. However, it was quickly discovered that setting arbitrary 30-m transect sections was inefficient since many sections were devoid of artifacts. The project switched to a pedestrian survey method called naturally gridded transects. With this approach the crew was responsible for deciding where to end and begin each transect section. The crew used natural boundaries and changes in artifact density as clues. For example, in the large field of Survey Block 2, we found that most artifacts were located on small sandy ridges 10–20 m wide that meandered through the field. In places where those were found, the crew would collect the ridge as a single unified section. In other instances, drainage ditches or changes in soil color were used as boundaries to begin or end a transect section. When artifact cover was dense, crew members were instructed to keep section length to no more than approximately 30 m long. When there were no artifacts to be found, crew members could extend a section indefinitely, and some were hundreds of meters long.

Using GPS we were later able to calculate the artifact density. When crew members found particularly important artifacts, such as a projectile point or decorated ceramic, the crew was instructed to bag them separately as an artifact collection and to leave a pin flag. This permitted us to point plot important artifacts and helped refine the ability to map site components.

Unfortunately, the carefully constructed stratified random method for choosing survey locations did not survive exposure to the field. As with many places in the southeastern United States, Lawrence County landowners were increasingly abandoning the use of cultivated fields in favor of planting pine trees. The sale of fast-growing pine species, such as loblolly pine, was more profitable than other land uses. The result is that many fields in cultivation three to nine years before the survey began were planted in trees at the time of the survey. In the process of scouting locations for survey it became increasingly obvious very few survey strata still had cultivated fields of any appreciable size as of 2000. A few survey blocks were investigated as the research design called for, but eventually the stratified random sampling was discarded in favor of opportunistic survey. Further complicating matters was the lack of success finding Mississippi period sites. The few documented sites are described below.

Survey Results

A total of 10 survey blocks were examined. The details of the data collected are discussed in Livingood (2006). Only a few of the newly recorded sites were Mississippian in age: the ceramics recovered from them are listed in Table 3.1 and a map of all known Mississippian sites is shown in Figure

Table 3.1. Summary of all known Mississippi period sites in Lawrence County

Site Number	Name	Information
22Lw510	Pevey site	Large multiple-mound site.
22Lw511	Lowe-Steen site	Large two-mound site.
22Lw544		Larto Red-Filmed sherd, other sherds, Collins point. Possible farmstead.
22Lw549	Smith Estate No. 1	Shell-tempered sherds. Possible farmstead.
22Lw593	Phillips Farm site	Plaquemine Brushed, *var. Plaquemine,* numerous unclassified decorated and plain sherds. Possible farmstead, although not necessarily occupied at the same time as the Pevey and Lowe-Steen sites (see section on chronology in conclusion).
22Lw641	Coin Farm site	5 Addis Plain, *var. Addis* sherds. Likely farmstead.
22Lw644		1 Addis Plain, *var. Addis* and 1 Mississippi Plain. Farmstead.
22Lw657		1 Addis Plain, *var. Addis* and 2 Mississippi Plain. Farmstead located 1.1 km from Pevey mounds.
22Lw660		1 Carter Engraved, *var. unspecified,* 1 Mound Place Incised, *var. B,* 1 Plaquemine Brushed, *var. Plaquemine,* numerous plain sherds. Along with Lw661, a residential area associated with Pevey.
22Lw661		1 Plaquemine Brushed, *var. Plaquemine,* 1 unclassified decorated on Bell Plain, a few plain sherds. Along with Lw660, a residential area associated with Pevey.

3.1. Only the survey blocks with Mississippian components are discussed below.

Survey Block 1

Survey Block 1 was surveyed during the brief 1999 season, and it was not surveyed using the same procedures as we used the following year. This field was selected because it was located near the confluence of Bahala Creek and

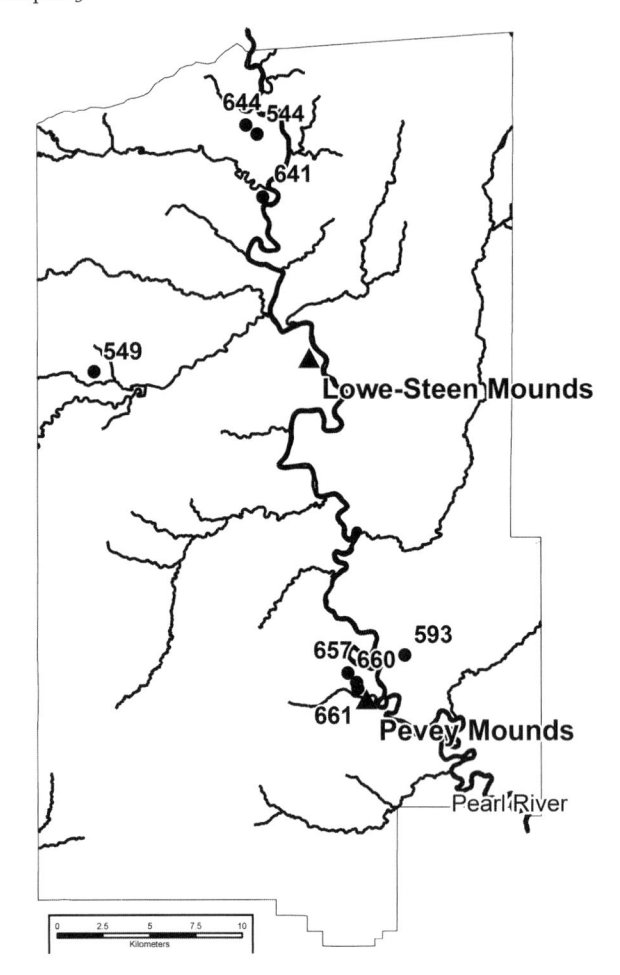

Figure 3.1. Map of all known Mississippi period sites in Lawrence County.

the Pearl River, and it is the only cultivated field in the survey area located at the confluence of a major stream and the Pearl River. The landowners had an extensive collection of points and some ceramics, much of which was collected on the property. The collection included a few examples of Anna Incised, *var. Anna* and some Addis-tempered sherds. The field was collected using a mixture of controlled and uncontrolled methods.

A single site was identified during the survey, although subsequent controlled surveys may be able to delineate other artifact concentrations in the area. The single site has a Mississippian and a Late Archaic component. This site contained five sherds of Addis Plain, *var. Addis* and has been designated the Coin Farm site (22Lw641). The Coin Farm site also contained a

McIntire point and 68 other lithic pieces. In addition, other parts of the field yielded one Addis Plain, *var. Greenville* and two Mississippi Plain sherds although not in densities sufficient to recognize them as a site. Other parts of the field also yielded some Middle Archaic, Late Archaic, and Woodland points, although with no discernable site patterns.

Based on the small number of Mississippian artifacts and their relatively close distribution, the Coin Farm site is likely a Mississippian hamlet. The site is located 400 m south of Bahala Creek and 150 m west of a backwater swamp that appears to be a relict channel of the Pearl River. It is also located near an intermittent stream, which the landowners report becomes a secondary channel of Bahala Creek during flood conditions.

Survey Block 2

Survey Block 2 is located in a large field in the northern part of Lawrence County, the largest cultivated field in the county at almost 250 ha or 100 acres. This field was the first surveyed using the gridded transect and naturally gridded transect methods. A total of 1,465 different collection units were used. Collection conditions were generally fairly good. Most of the areas were freshly plowed or had young cotton or peanut plants of less than 12 cm in height at the time of collection, while a few transects were collected in a young maize field when the plants were approximately 1 m high. During the field season, southern Mississippi was experiencing a drought, so wash conditions were generally poor for much of the season. Wash refers to the level of visibility of surface artifacts from soil. After a rain, surface artifacts are clean of dirt, and that condition is referred to as good wash. Despite the poor wash conditions, overall visibility in this field was good to excellent since the plowing had been relatively recent and the plants in the field were small and unobtrusive.

A total of 10 sites were recorded for this survey block. One of these sites, 22Lw644, has a Mississippian component as well as Late Archaic and possible Paleo-Indian components. One Mississippi Plain sherd and one Addis Plain, *var. Addis* sherd were found at the site within 40 m of each other. The site is located 4 km north of the Coin Farm site and 13 km north of the Lowe-Steen site. All together, 22Lw644 encompasses a large 25-ha area at the headwaters of an intermittent stream that currently drains into the Pearl River. It is also 220 m west of a relict channel of the Pearl River that is currently a backwater swamp and is 700 m southwest of the current channel of the Pearl.

Survey Blocks 8 and 9

During the 2000 season, a portion of a field north of the Pevey site was planted in watermelons. This portion was surface collected with naturally

60   Chapter 3

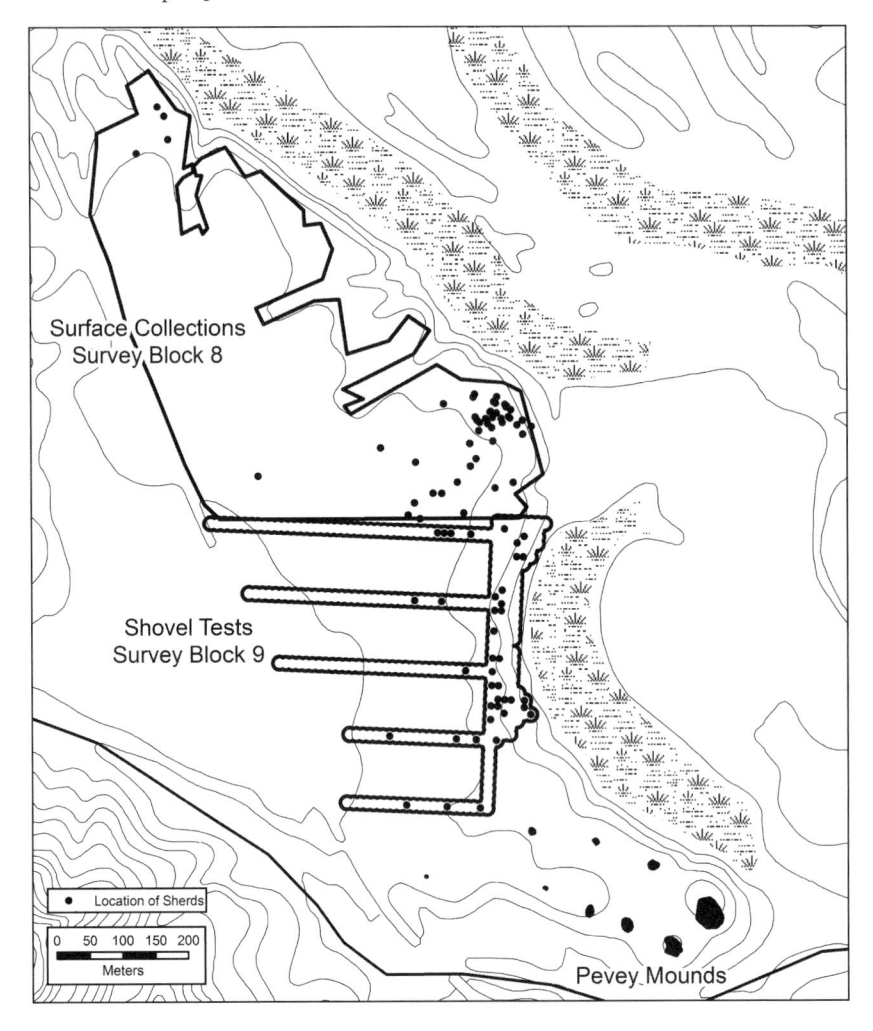

Figure 3.2. Map of the locations of ceramics found in Survey Blocks 8 and 9. Survey Block 8 was surface collected using 5-m transects and ceramics were piece plotted with GPS. Survey Block 9 was surveyed using a series of shovel tests. Both methods showed that ceramics are mostly concentrated near the bluff edge.

gridded transects at 5-m intervals and designated as Survey Block 8 (Figure 3.2). During the survey, it became obvious that most of the occupation was located within 50–100 m of the terrace edge. The area directly to the north of the Pevey mounds was still in pasture; a grid was established here coincident with the grid used to map the Pevey site, and 320 shovel tests were excavated at 10-m intervals as Survey Block 9. Shovel tests were attempted to a depth of 40 cm, but often gravel or other natural barriers made such depths impossible. All soils from the shovel tests were screened through ¼-inch hardware cloth for artifacts, and a record was made of the exposed stratigraphy. The goal was to shovel test the 40–60 m adjacent to the terrace edge. In addition, east–west transects were excavated across the field at 100-m intervals. These confirmed that most of the occupation of the site was restricted to the terrace edge, even as testing neared the mound precinct.

At the northern end of Survey Block 8, testing permitted us to examine all of the floodplain terrace surface between the terrace edge and the beginning of the upland boundary. These results suggest that, at the Pevey site, much of the Mississippi period occupation of the site may have occurred within 1 km to the north of the mound precinct immediately adjacent to the terrace edge. One concern is that the terrace edge might have eroded from its Mississippi period location. The landowners report extensive erosion along the terrace edge. It is possible we are missing some of the Mississippian occupation and that the artifacts have been deposited on the floodplain below.

The three main locations in these survey blocks for Mississippian settlement appeared to be at Lw657, Lw660, and Lw661. These areas were all issued state site numbers for the purpose of permanently recording the locations, but Lw660 and Lw661 are probably more accurately called precincts of the Pevey site. Lw660 and Lw661 likely represent a concentration of multiple households within 150–700 m of the mound precinct. Lw657 is most likely a smaller concentration of households, perhaps a farmstead, located 500 m north of the northern edge of Lw660 and 1,100 m north of the mound precinct. All three of these settlements are located along the terrace edge, which would have been home to the Pearl River or a relict channel during their occupation. Three sherds (one Addis Plain, *var. Addis* and two Mississippi Plain) were recovered from Lw657. Fifty-eight sherds were recovered from Lw660, including one Carter Engraved, *var. unspecified,* one Mound Place Incised, *var. B,* and one Plaquemine Brushed, *var. Plaquemine.* Eleven sherds were recovered from Lw661, including one Plaquemine Brushed, *var. Plaquemine.* All of the sherds from this site are mapped in Figure 3.2. We also found a large number of lithics along the terrace edge. Diagnostic lithics recovered are representative of the Middle Archaic, Late Archaic, Woodland, and Late Woodland/Mississippi periods.

Survey Block 10

Survey Block 10 involved shovel tests conducted at and near the Phillips Farm site (22Lw593). These tests were done over the area later selected for excavation and along the edge of the terrace. Twenty-one Mississippian sherds were recovered including 17 Addis Plain, *var. Addis,* 2 Mississippi Plain, and 1 unclassified decorated on Baytown Plain. These shovel tests helped determine the area to excavate; the primary results for this site were discussed in Chapter 2.

Settlement Patterns

Before the survey project, there were only five known Mississippian sites in Lawrence County (Table 3.1). These included the Pevey site, the Lowe-Steen site, the Phillips Farm site, Smith Estate No. 1 (22Lw549), and 22Lw544. Smith Estate No. 1 (22Lw549) had been recorded in 1983 during a pipeline survey. It is located in the uplands in the eastern part of Lawrence County near Bear Creek. This site is recorded in the state site files as having some shell-tempered sherds. Lw544 had been recorded in the northern part of the county near Survey Block 2. It is noted as having a Collins point, a Larto Red-Filmed sherd, some other sherds, and debitage. Based on the size of the sites and the paucity of artifacts, these locations likely represent Mississippian farmsteads.

During the 1999 and 2000 survey seasons, five more sites with Mississippian components were located. The Coin Farm site (22Lw641) had several Addis Plain, *var. Addis* sherds. Just to the north, 22Lw644 was recorded as having some Addis Plain, *var. Addis* and Mississippi Plain sherds. Finally, Lw657, Lw660, and Lw661 were documented with numerous Mississippi period ceramics in the area north of the Pevey mounds.

Survey coverage remains relatively incomplete for the county, so conclusions on the Mississippi period settlement of Lawrence County must necessarily be tentative. One of the original goals was to discover the type of settlement pattern. Across the Southeast, Mississippian people utilized a wide variety of settlement strategies that were likely chosen to suit the local environment and social conditions. Following Hammerstedt (2001:1–2), there are three major classifications of Mississippian settlement types: (1) mound/village centers with dispersed farmsteads loosely clustered around them, (2) an even dispersal of sites across the landscape, and (3) nucleated towns/centers with no outlying farmsteads. Examples of mound/village centers with farmsteads clustered around them include the Kincaid polity (Muller 1978, 1986, 1993), the Lubbub Creek polity (Blitz 1993a), and Moundville (Hammerstedt 2001; Welch 1998). Examples of an even dispersal of sites include Late Lamar occupations of the upper Oconee (Kowalewski and Hatch 1991) and the Apalachee settlements of the Florida panhandle (Payne and Scarry 1998). Examples of the strategy of nucleated settlement with no outlying sites include the Dallas phase (Polhemus 1987) and the Parkin phase (Morse 1990).

Since Lw544, Lw549, Lw593, Lw641, and Lw644 represent small, dispersed

Table 3.2. Percentage of decorated and undecorated sherds by site

Site	Undecorated (%)	Decorated (%)
22Lw510 (Pevey)	82.35	17.65
22Lw511 (Lowe-Steen)	88.77	11.23
22Lw593 (Phillips Farm)	92.86	7.14
22Lw641	100.00	0.00
22Lw644	100.00	0.00
22Lw657	100.00	0.00
22Lw660	93.10	6.90
22Lw661	81.82	18.18
Total	83.89	16.11

Mississippi period sites, we can definitely rule out the third pattern as a suitable model. Survey coverage is too incomplete to know how evenly dispersed sites are over the landscape, but based on the proximity of Lw657, Lw660, and Lw661 to the Pevey site, it seems most likely that the Lawrence County Mississippians conformed to the first pattern and located farmsteads according to environmental and political factors. One of these political factors appears to be proximity to a central civic center (Steponaitis 1978). The residents also clearly preferred to settle on the terrace edge adjacent to the floodplain and near backwater swamps. This pattern is typical across much of the Mississippian world and it provided easy access to farmland on the terrace, fish and waterfowl in the backwater swamps, and nuts and terrestrial game in the uplands (Smith 1985).

Unfortunately, little can be said about what types of decorated ceramic varieties were present at the non-mound sites and how they contrast with those at the mound sites since so few decorated sherds were found during the survey that could be identified to type and variety. Even the excavated Phillips Farm site had relatively few identifiable decorated sherds.

It is still possible to analyze the frequency of decoration (Table 3.2). The Pevey site and nearby 22Lw661 have the largest proportion of decorated sherds at 18 percent. The Lowe-Steen site is slightly lower at 11 percent. The other sites have no more than 7 percent. This clearly indicates the specialized nature of the assemblage at the Pevey site. It also indicates that Lw661, which is located only 150 m from Mound B and the edge of the mound precinct, may have been the site of specialized activities and may best be considered a component of the Pevey site. The Lowe-Steen site has a lower percentage of decorated sherds, but this may be a result of sampling bias.

64   Chapter 3

Table 3.3. Percentage of decorated and undecorated sherds by site type

Site Type	Undecorated (%)	Decorated (%)
Mound (22Lw510, 22Lw511)	83.67	16.33
Non-mound, no association with mound center (22Lw593, 22Lw641, 22Lw644)	93.10	6.90
Non-mound, proximate to Pevey (22Lw657, 22Lw660, 22Lw661)	91.67	8.33
@	83.89	16.11

Table 3.4. Percentage of decorated and undecorated sherds by mound or non-mound sites

Site Type	Undecorated (%)	Decorated (%)
Mound (22Lw510, 22Lw511)	83.67	16.33
Non-mound (all others)	92.73	7.27
Total	83.89	16.11

The majority of the sherds from the Lowe-Steen site come from Feature 4, which is an off-mound midden. In contrast, the majority of the excavations at Pevey are in mounds.

The results appear to show that there are noticeable differences between mound and non-mound assemblages with respect to the frequency of decorated sherds. Table 3.3 shows that, collectively, mound sites have a 16-percent frequency of decorated sherds, the non-mound sites in proximity to Pevey have an 8-percent frequency, and the other non-mound sites have 7 percent. When considered together, the non-mound sites have a 7-percent frequency of decorated ceramics (Table 3.4). These data show that there was an increased effort expended to manufacture the mound site ceramics.

Another attribute we can contrast is the choice of temper. From Table 3.5 it appears that coarse shell–tempered sherds are slightly more prevalent at the major mound sites (70 percent Mississippi Plain at Pevey and 76 percent at Lowe-Steen) than at the non-mound sites (48 percent at Phillips Farm and 31–67 percent at the others). However, this may be related to chronological differences between Phillips Farm and the mound sites and the differential preservation of sherds in the plow zone. The shell in shell-tempered sherds can be easily leached by groundwater, which makes the sherds fragile.

Table 3.5. Count of sherds by site and temper

Site	Collection Type	Addis Plain, var. Addis	Baytown Plain	Bell Plain	Addis Plain, var. Greenville	Mississippi Plain	Sand Tempered	Total
22Lw510 (Pevey)	Excavation	1,906	46	197	491	6,107	10	8,757
22Lw511 (Lowe–Steen)	Excavation	486	5	21	31	1,728		2,271
22Lw593 (Phillips Farm)	Excavation	92		2	6	95	1	196
22Lw641	Surface collection	5						5
22Lw644	Surface collection	1				1		2
22Lw657	Surface collection	1				2		3
22Lw660	Surface collection	35	1		4	18		58
22Lw661	Surface collection	4	1	1		5		11
Total		2,530	53	221	532	7,956	11	11,303

Subsequent plowing can destroy these sherds so they are not identifiable in surface collections. This has been noted across the Mississippian Southeast (Hammerstedt 2001; Holstein and Little 1986; Milner 1998) and may be contributing to a greater recovery of Addis sherds from surface collections and shallow excavations such as the Phillips Farm site.

Summary

Because of the lack of cultivated fields, the survey project was only moderately successful in identifying Mississippian sites in Lawrence County. Five Mississippian sites were newly identified, bringing the total of known Mississippian sites to 10. However, three of those sites (Lw510, Lw660, and Lw661) represent Pevey and an associated residential area. Therefore, the known Mississippian sites of Lawrence County are best enumerated as two mound sites and six likely farmsteads. The farmsteads are mostly clustered around the major mound sites, but this may be a by-product of survey coverage. Non-mound ceramic assemblages have less than a 7-percent frequency of decorated sherds compared with a 16-percent frequency at mound sites. Also, non-mound sites have fewer coarse shell–tempered sherds than the mound sites, but this is likely influenced by differential preservation in the plow zone.

4
Temper and Culture

Ceramic Analysis

The primary tools for addressing the research questions in this project are ceramics. They provide a means to situate Middle Pearl River polities in a regional history and provide insights into issues of trade, exchange, migration, and cultural and political interaction. In the Lower Mississippi Valley and surrounding regions, the primary tool for analyzing ceramics is the type-variety system. The nomenclature of the Lower Valley type-variety system originated with James A. Ford's early work on sites in the region and the ceramic types are documented in numerous reports by Ford and colleagues (Cotter 1951, 1952; Ford 1935a, 1935b, 1936, 1951; Quimby 1951, 1957). These types crystallized in Phillips, Ford, and Griffin's (1951) survey report of the Lower Mississippi Valley and assumed their modern nomenclature in Phillips's (1970) survey of the Yazoo.

One of the challenges of extending a type-variety system to a neighboring valley is reconciling the categories to a new set of material culture. Some of the types fit and others must be modified. Mann (1988) had already recognized that most of the decorated types found at the Pevey site were closely associated with decorated types found in the Lower Mississippi Valley, particularly the Natchez Bluffs region. Additional research (Livingood 1999) recognized that there were some discontinuities, particularly with regard to paste characterization. These discontinuities require special attention because, as Mann (1988) recognized, the Pearl River assemblage contains provocative mixtures of shell and grog tempering. The utilization of two major tempering modes will be examined in this chapter because the dichotomy between grog and shell has played a major role in defining cultural boundaries in some models of Lower Valley prehistory.

Grog vs. Shell and Plaquemine vs. Mississippian

In order to understand the importance some archaeologists have placed on shell tempering in the Lower Valley, it is helpful to understand how the Plaquemine period and culture came to be defined. Plaquemine is currently associated with the Lower Mississippi Valley from the Gulf Coast to just south of the Arkansas River. The region is shaped as an inverted triangle encompassing the southern Yazoo Basin, Natchez Bluffs, Lower Ouachita River, and Red River valley. The term *Plaquemine* first appeared in two figures in Ford and Willey's 1941 synthesis of eastern U.S. prehistory (Ford and Willey 1941:Figures 2 and 6). The concept had been developed by James Ford and George Quimby based on their work on the Louisiana State Archaeological Survey between 1938 and 1941. Ford's original chronology of ceramic-producing cultures of the Lower Valley utilized three stages: Marksville, Coles Creek, and Natchez (Ford 1935a, 1936, 1938; Quimby 1942:256, 1951). From this chronology, Coles Creek was eventually split into three eras: Troyville, Coles Creek proper, and Plaquemine. Ford conceived of Plaquemine as a spatially intermediate pottery complex between the Caddo to the west and the other Mississippian groups to the north and east. In this manner, "Plaquemine thus came into being as a somewhat vague designation for post–Coles Creek, pre-Natchez, non-Caddo, and non-Mississippian pottery assemblages in the Lower Valley" (Rees and Livingood 2007:4–5). It had the distinction of being "defined more in terms of what it lacks than what it possesses" (Jennings 1952:267; see also Jeter and Williams 1989; Kidder 1998b; Rees and Livingood 2007).

From these inauspicious beginnings, Quimby offered forth several defining characteristics of Plaquemine, many of which are still in use today. These include the presence of plates with interior incising and jars with brushed decoration, the use of truncated pyramidal mounds around a plaza, and post construction (Quimby 1951:128). Later archaeologists refined Quimby's definition to further permit researchers to distinguish between Plaquemine and its spatial and temporal neighbors (Ford 1951; Phillips 1970; Phillips et al. 1951; Quimby 1942, 1951, 1957).

Our modern definition of Plaquemine comes primarily from the work of Philip Phillips (1970). He labeled Plaquemine as a culture and recognized it, as others had before him, as separate and distinct from Mississippian culture. He further subdivided the archaeological material into spatially and temporally discrete archaeological phases (Phillips 1970:950–952). Jeter and Williams (1989:212) recognized that part of this exercise involved assigning each particular phase to either Plaquemine or Mississippian culture. The primary tool for constructing the phases became ceramics. To this end, Phillips developed and refined the type-variety system of ceramic classification into its current form. One of the features of the type-variety system is that it is inherently hierarchical. Some traits are chosen as higher-order traits and are used to distinguish types. Other trait differences are subsumed under these as more minor differences and are used to distinguish varieties. The top-level traits to distinguish types in the Lower Valley system are a combination of paste (i.e., shell tempering, grog tempering, sand tempering, etc.) and major decorative intent (i.e., rectilinear incising, curvilinear incising, brushing, punctating, etc.). These traits were selected because they could be identified macroscopically and because they were relevant to the cultural classifications in which Phillips and his colleagues were interested. One of the consequences of these decisions is that the definition of Plaquemine we inherit from Phillips is almost entirely based on ceramics. Furthermore, the presence or absence of shell tempering became the axiomatic means of differentiating Plaquemine and Mississippian cultures (Kidder 1998b:131; Rees and Livingood 2007; Williams and Brain 1983:337, 340).

Williams and Brain (1983:338) argued that Plaquemine could best be defined as a hybridization of Coles Creek and Mississippian cultures. Based on data from the Lower Yazoo, they argued that Coles Creek residents on the frontier began to slowly adopt Mississippian practices such as shell tempering, the Mississippian jar, and wall-trench house construction. This diffusion of ideas was followed by migrations of small numbers of Mississippian people and direct person-to-person contact between major Mississippian and Plaquemine sites. In this model, the divisions between shell-temper-using and grog-temper-using people are not merely cultural but rather viewed as an emic rivalry.

This approach of assigning phases to either Plaquemine or Mississippian has created some challenges in some instances. For example, there is disagreement about whether to classify the Bayou Petre phase in the Mississippi Delta (Brown 1985a:283; Phillips 1970:951–953; Weinstein 1987:98) or the Preston phase (Hally 1972:605–607) in the Tensas Basin as Plaquemine or Mississippian. This has led some scholars to argue that the interpretation of Plaquemine as "Mississippianized Coles Creek" does not generalize well outside of the Lower Yazoo (Kidder 1998b:131). Furthermore, archaeologists may be placing too much importance on the presence or absence of shell tempering and such a dichotomy may be glossing over some obvious similarities (Hally 1972; Kidder 1998b:132).

There seems to be a growing consensus that, at least for some regions, the presence or absence of shell tempering may be overemphasized (Kidder 2007; Rees and Livingood, eds. 2007) and that the Plaquemine/Mississippian dichotomy is not as clearly defined as the Phillips, Williams, and Brain models postulate. However, the primary tools of the Plaquemine archaeologist are ceramics and archaeological phases, and these were created with the assumption that the shell/grog divide was paramount in labeling and investigating the Plaquemine/Mississippian dichotomy. Therefore, archaeologists working with mixed-temper assemblages are forced to engage these concepts, at least nominally.

One of the further challenges is that the primary defining paste of the early Plaquemine in the Pearl River, Natchez Bluffs, and surrounding regions is called "Addis," which is a label for a diverse category of paste types with grog as an inclusion. Addis Plain was originally documented by Quimby (1942:265–266, 1951:107–109) as a "clay-tempered type" and a major diagnostic of Plaquemine culture. Phillips (1970:48–49) designated Addis as a variety of the type Baytown Plain and defined it as the "clay-tempered plainware of the Mississippi period from the Medora and Plaquemine phases in the Delta and Lower Red River regions to the Mayersville phase in [the Lower Yazoo]." Interestingly, Phillips (1970:60–61) also acknowledged the similarity between his Baytown Plain, *var. Addis* and his Bell Plain, *vars. Holly Bluff* and *St. Catherine*, which contain finely pulverized shell sometimes in quantities so small that their inclusion seems to be "accidental." Williams and Brain (1983:92) retained *Addis* as a variety of Baytown Plain but used Bell Plain, *var. Greenville* to describe Addis with the addition of shell temper to the paste. They also retained Bell Plain, *var. Holly Bluff* to describe heterogeneous Addis-like sherds in which shell tempering is slightly more prevalent than in Bell Plain, *var. Greenville*. Steponaitis (1974:116) proposed elevating Addis to the level of type and defined it as having a heterogeneous organic grog-tempered paste but allowed for the presence of shell in some types. Steponaitis then relocated the *Greenville* and *St. Catherine* varieties from their position under Bell Plain to be varieties under Addis Plain. This is the system currently in use in the Lower Mississippi Valley (Brain 1989; Brain et al. 1994; Brown 1985a, 1998).

There are two fundamental explanations for the tortured history of these types. First, shell tempering was defined a priori as a first-order attribute since it was thought to be diagnostic of the Plaquemine/Mississippian cultural divide. This explains why Phillips would place the *Addis* variety under Baytown Plain and the closely related *Holly Bluff* and *St. Catherine* varieties under Bell Plain. However, for archaeologists working in phases where these closely related types are common, this system of nomenclature can be unwieldy. Another explanation for the difficulties archaeologists have had in defining and arranging these taxa is that in the phases in which potters were freely choosing between shell and grog temper, a larger number of permutations is possible; designing a system to accurately describe these permutations is problematic. Support for this argument can be found in merely counting the number of plainware varieties in use in the Lower Mississippi Valley. Despite large quantities of coarse shell–tempered ceramics, only three varieties of Mississippi Plain are in common use in the Plaquemine world: *Coker, Mainfort,* and *Yazoo.* However, there are eight varieties commonly used to categorize fabrics with fine-sized grog tempering and grog and shell tempering in the Plaquemine period: the Addis Plain varieties *Addis, Greenville, Junkin, Ratcliffe,* and *St. Catherine* and the Bell Plain varieties *Bell, Holly Bluff,* and *New Madrid.*

Michael Galaty (2008) has used a ceramic ecology approach to argue that, on a regional scale, differences in tempering choices in Mississippi might be related to differences in the types of clays and tempering agents available to potters. For example, he argues persuasively that pre–Mississippi period potters in west Mississippi may have lacked access to sand suitable for tempering and relied instead on grog, whereas potters in east Mississippi may have preferred the easily available sand. Although he does not specifically address the regional differences in the use of grog and shell, his work raises the possibility that macroregional differences in temper might be related to ecology, not culture.

It is because of the complicated relationships between paste categories and uncertainty about how well the current typological definitions apply outside of the region for which they were designed that this analysis uses a conservative approach to the study of fabric types.

Methodology

Approximately 25,000 pieces of ceramics were recovered by the projects discussed in this volume (the 1993 and 1994 University of North Carolina Field School excavations and my 1999 and 2000 survey and excavations). The first step in the analysis was to screen all ceramics through a ½-inch geological sieve. All ceramics that passed through the screen were labeled sherdlets. They were counted and weighed by provenience, and they were not used in any other analyses. There were over 11,000 sherds remaining.

The sherds were first sorted into the simplified temper categories (Mississippi Plain, Bell Plain, Addis, Addis Plain, *var. Greenville,* Baytown, sand tempered) and according to whether they were diagnostic for vessel form and/or decoration. All nondiagnostic sherds were counted and weighed within their temper category and set aside. All diagnostic sherds were sorted into the type appropriate for their decoration or plainware variety. Also, when appropriate, several attributes related to vessel form, including rim diameter, rim type, vessel shape, and rim treatment, were recorded. Furthermore, in an effort to test the applicability of fabric type categories to this assemblage a

Table 4.1. Counts of sherds analyzed, by site

	Sherd Count		
Site	Total	Decorated	Diagnostic for Vessel Form
22Lw510 (Pevey)	8,757	1,546	881
22Lw511 (Lowe-Steen)	2,271	255	254
22Lw593 (Phillips Farm)	196	14	8
22Lw641	5		
22Lw644	2		
22Lw647	3		
22Lw660	58	4	3
22Lw661	11	2	1
General surface collections	43	4	8
Total	11,346	1,825	1,155

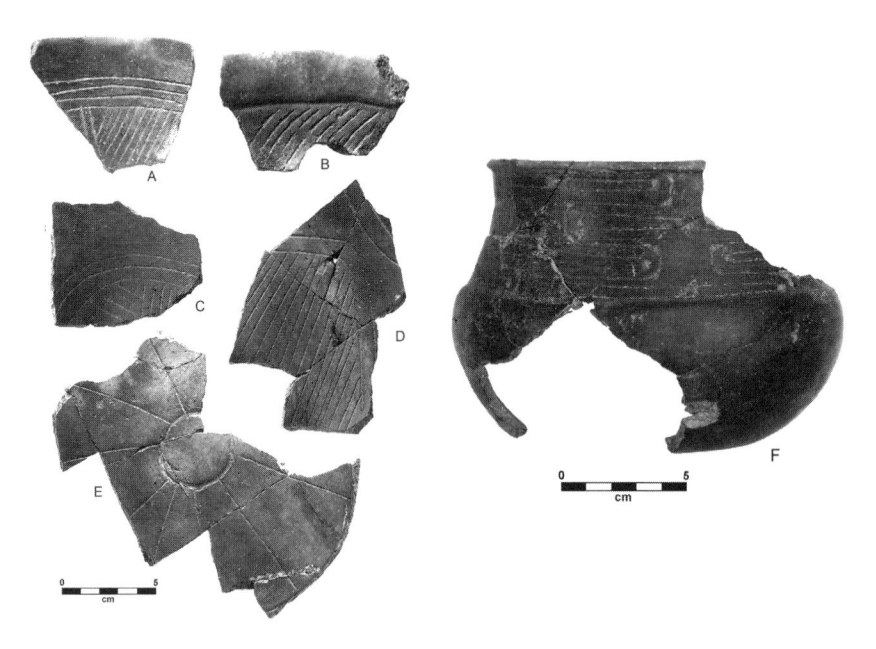

Figure 4.1. Anna Incised, *var. Anna* sherds from the Pevey site. A, 165/22Lw510; B, 156/22Lw510; C, 289/22Lw510; D, 272/22Lw510; E, 310/22Lw510; F, L'Eau Noire Incised, *var. L'Eau Noire* vessel, 153/22Lw510.

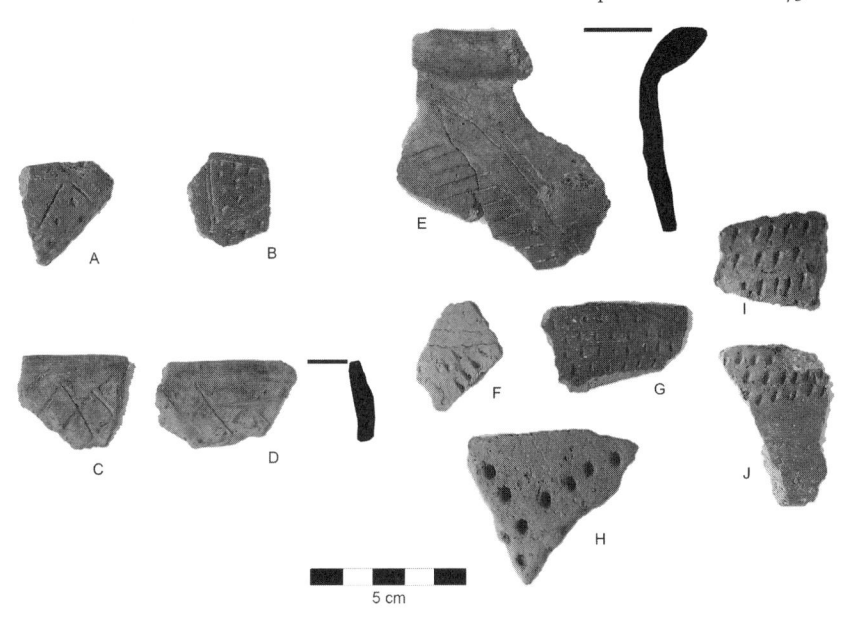

Figure 4.2. Decorated sherds from the Pevey site. A, Avoyelles Punctated, *var. Dupree*, 125/22Lw510; B, Avoyelles Punctated, *var. Dupree*, 154/22Lw510; C and D, Barton Incised, *var. Barton*, 241/22Lw510; E, Moundville Incised, *var. Moundville*, 250/22Lw510; F, Owens Punctated, *var. unspecified*, 154/22Lw510; G, Owens Punctated, *var. unspecified*, 149/22Lw510; H, Parkin Punctated, *var. Transylvania*, 148/22Lw510; I, Parkin Punctated, *var. Harris*, 155/22Lw510; J, Parkin Punctated, *var. Harris*, 385/22Lw510.

microscopic study was made of a small sample of diagnostic ceramics. The methods are described below, and the results were used to create new temper modes or categories. These modes were then used in a reanalysis of the decorated sherds.

Ceramic Overview

There were 11,346 sherds studied for this project: 1,825 of these had some form of decoration, and 1,155 were diagnostic for vessel form (Table 4.1, Figures 4.1–4.4). Decorated sherds were sorted into types and varieties based on the descriptions in Brown (1998), Fuller (1998), Fuller and Stowe (1982), Phillips (1970), Steponaitis (1974, 1983), and Williams and Brain (1983) as summarized in Livingood (2006).

Most of the types found in the Middle Pearl match up well with the decorative descriptions previously published from neighboring valleys, with the notable exception of Mound Place Incised. In the Lower Valley termi-

Figure 4.3. Decorated sherds from the Pevey and Lowe-Steen sites. A, Carter Engraved, *var. Sara,* 272/22Lw510; B and C, Carter Engraved, *var. Sara,* 270/22Lw510; D, Carter Engraved, *var. unspecified,* 241/22Lw510; E and F, Carter Engraved, *var. Shell Bluff,* 250/22Lw510; G and H, Carter Engraved, *var. Carter,* 1/22Lw511; I, Carter Engraved, *var. Carter,* 331/22Lw510; J, Carter Engraved, *var. Carter,* 215/22Lw510.

nology, varieties are distinguished based on the presence or absence of adornos and the size of shell tempering (Brown 1998). A larger number of Mound Place varieties are documented for the Pensacola and Moundville area (Fuller 1998; Fuller and Stowe 1982:66–68; Steponaitis 1983:335–336). Given the large number of Mound Place Incised sherds from the Pearl River; the fact that the decorative intent on the Pearl River spans Bell Plain, Mississippi Plain, and Greenville fabrics, which does not match the previous definitions; the fact that it is not always clear from the sherd fragment whether an adorno is present on the vessel; and the lack of congruence with the Pensacola variety decorations, I opted not to use these types. Instead, I established provisional types to separate wide from narrow and neat from sloppy execution. In this case, *var. A* refers to wide and neat lines, *var. B* to wide and sloppy lines, and *var. D* to narrow and sloppy lines. *Var. C* was reserved for narrow and neat lines but no examples were found.

The initial analysis and classification of ceramics indicated that Middle Pearl potters were making interesting and complex choices with regard to

Temper and Culture 75

Figure 4.4. Decorated sherds from the Pevey and Lowe-Steen sites. A, Mound Place Incised, *var. unspecified*, 153/22Lw510; B, Mound Place Incised, *var. unspecified*, 350/22Lw510; C, Mound Place Incised, *var. A*, 310/22Lw510; D, Mound Place Incised, *var. unspecified*, 289/22Lw510; E, Mound Place Incised, *var. D*, 149/22Lw510; F, Mound Place Incised, *var. A*, 310/22Lw510; G, D'Olive Incised, *var. unspecified*, 243/22Lw510; H, Evansville Punctated, *var. Sharkey*, 310/22Lw510; I, Evansville Punctated, *var. unspecified*, 362/22Lw510; J, Evansville Punctated, *var. unspecified*, 356/22Lw510; K, Fatherland Incised, *var. Pine Ridge*, 155/22Lw510; L, Grace Brushed, *var. Grace*, 166/22Lw510; M, Hollyknowe Pinched, *var. Patmos*, 3/22Lw511; N, Hollyknowe Pinched, *var. Patmos*, 4/22Lw511.

temper. The most common fabric found at the Pevey and Lowe-Steen sites was coarse shell tempering (72 percent of all sherds). However, Pearl River potters assigned special importance to Addis paste sherds because they executed most of their decorative motifs on these wares: 52 percent of all decorated sherds have Addis Plain, *var. Addis* paste, 17 percent of decorated sherds have a *Greenville* paste, and only 27 percent have a Mississippi Plain paste. Despite the preference for Addis pastes, several decorative techniques span multiple temper types. If we consider all of the interior-decorated plates and bowls (Anna Incised and D'Olive Incised) together, 60 percent are executed on Addis paste, 25 percent on *Greenville* paste, and 14 percent on Mississippi Plain paste. Based on these initial observations, it is clear that Middle Pearl potters were comfortable using a wide variety of temper combinations. Additionally, it is not obvious whether the plainware varieties developed primarily for the Lower Yazoo and Natchez regions are the most appropriate varieties to use to classify the ceramics from the Middle Pearl River.

Digital Microscopic Analysis of Temper

Macroscopic analysis of the Pevey and Lowe-Steen ceramics casts doubt on whether the fabric types used in the Natchez Bluffs region were the best means of categorizing these sherds. At the type level, these categories include Mississippi Plain for coarse shell–tempered sherds, Bell Plain for fine shell–tempered sherds, and Addis Plain for heterogeneous organic grog-tempered sherds. The type Addis Plain also includes a variety, *Greenville*, that permits some shell tempering. Since the Pearl River assemblage contains significant numbers of grog-, shell-, and grog-and-shell–tempered sherds it was not clear where the most useful analytical boundaries should be established. In order to be worthwhile, fabric categories should identify modes in the technical choices the potters made, which can assist in delineating differences in time, space, or function.

We know that many ethnographically studied potters (Arnold 1985; Krause 1985) follow a paste recipe in preparing clay for use. Potters often clean their clays to remove extraneous particles and then add carefully prepared tempering agents. Some potters mix temper with the prepared clays until the paste reaches a desired texture. For example, the Ibibio of Nigeria add grog or sand to the clay until it reaches the correct consistency called *aduang nbibiot* (Nicklin 1981:173; Rice 1987). Other potters follow a recipe that specifies the ratio of clay and temper (Rice 1987:121). For example, some Kavango potters in southern Africa mix two parts grog to three parts clay (Blandino 1997:26), while the Shipibo-Conibo of eastern Peru have a ratio of clay to temper of two to three (DeBoer and Lathrap 1979).

It is possible to test the Middle Pearl ceramics to check for modes in the distribution of temper size and abundance. If there are modes they can be used to reconstruct the paste recipes used by the potters. Armed with knowledge of the paste recipes, we can evaluate the utility of the commonly used plainware varieties for classifying the ceramic assemblage. Furthermore, it seems likely that, of all of the decisions a potter makes, the decision of temper is often one of the most resistant to change over time. Vessel form and decoration can change over decades in pre-state societies, but temper choices typically persist for centuries. In most pre-state societies, pottery production is a household activity (Arnold 1985:100–101; Sinopoli 1991:98–102; van der Leeuw 1977), and it is presumed that knowledge about pottery production is handed down through generations within the household. Whereas more visible aspects of pottery production such as vessel form and decoration might be subject to changing personal or group concepts of pottery construction, less visible and more technological decisions about temper are frequently more resistant to change (Carr 1995a, 1995b). Because of this, with sufficient information about paste recipes it might be possible to tease apart different communities of production, especially when multiple tempering agents encode greater information.

Since the terms used in ceramic studies such as *paste* and *temper* are often defined differently by different authors, it is important to be clear about how they are used in this project. For example, archaeologists disagree on whether temper refers to material that must be intentionally added by the potter (Rye 1976:109) or whether it also encompasses naturally occurring additives (Rice 1987:407; Skibo et al. 1989:123). They also disagree on whether it can be best characterized as nonplastic inclusions (Bronitsky and Hamer 1986:89), nonclay additives (Skibo et al. 1989), or any additives including other clays (Rye 1976:109). The definition each author chooses usually follows their research interest and background. For example, petrographers (i.e., Stoltman 1991:109–110) and ceramic scientists dislike intentionality as an element of the definition because it can be hard to detect and is irrelevant to the physical characteristics of the finished pot. In this work I will follow the definition common to Lower Mississippi Valley archaeologists in which "temper" refers to aplastics intentionally added to a clay to improve its physical properties and "inclusion" refers to all aplastics in a clay, whether they were added deliberately or were naturally occurring. "Paste" is defined as the clay plus all inclusions. Therefore, a "paste recipe" refers to all of the rules a potter follows to create the paste used to form a vessel, including where the clay should be gathered, how it should be processed, what temper should be added and in what quantities, and how the clay should be handled and treated before and during vessel creation.

The Sample and Methods

Twenty-nine sherds from the Pevey (22Lw510) and Lowe-Steen (22Lw511) sites were used for this analysis (Table 4.2). All of the sherds are diagnostic of vessel shape, decoration, or both. The sherds were deliberately chosen to represent the different temper combinations under investigation and to be representative of different vessel forms and functions. Of the 29 sherds, 24 were excavated from Unit M at the Pevey site. Of the sherds not from Unit M, two come from Unit H and one from Unit I, while the final two come from Feature 4 at Lowe-Steen.

The only technique appropriate to gather data on temper abundance and size from this sample is ceramic petrography, which is the practice of examining ceramics microscopically to study clay characteristics and inclusions.

Table 4.2. Results of the digital petrographic analysis of temper

Sample	Site	Type	Temper Type	Sample Area (mm²)	Non-Temper-Voids (%)	Grog (%)	Shell (%)	ELBPA
PRP1	22Lw510	Grace Brushed, *var. Grace*	Mississippi Plain	271.04	8.70	5.97	15.97	0.60
PRP2	22Lw510	Plaquemine Brushed, *var. Plaquemine*	Addis	135.85	13.96	14.44	.00	.00
PRP3	22Lw510	Anna Incised, *var. Anna*	Greenville	196.91	2.93	1.70	.87	.53
PRP4	22Lw510	Anna Incised, *var. Anna*	Greenville	216.60	6.94	1.92	.70	.35
PRP5	22Lw510	Anna Incised, *var. Anna*	Greenville	168.41	5.78	11.03	1.03	.33
PRP6	22Lw510	Anna Incised, *var. Anna*	Greenville	140.77	8.39	11.39	.34	.36
PRP7	22Lw510	Anna Incised, *var. Anna*	Greenville	173.31	8.30	4.40	5.10	.97
PRP8	22Lw510	Anna Incised, *var. Anna*	Greenville	142.41	5.69	1.62	1.88	.85
PRP9	22Lw510	Bell Plain	Bell Plain	130.85	3.56	3.45	1.56	2.32
PRP10	22Lw510	Mound Place Incised	Addis	145.69	9.98	5.99	1.42	6.53
PRP11	22Lw510	Addis Plain, *var. Addis*	Addis	119.43	4.49	20.76	.86	1.14
PRP12	22Lw510	D'Olive Incised, *var. unspecified*	Mississippi Plain	89.65	17.01	4.14	19.17	.21
PRP13	22Lw510	D'Olive Incised, *var. unspecified*	Mississippi Plain	79.02	6.65	3.05	7.03	.69
PRP15	22Lw510	Mazique Incised, *var. unspecified*	Addis	206.13	10.69	10.20	.00	.44
PRP16	22Lw510	Mississippi Plain	Mississippi Plain	156.18	4.07	1.91	13.63	1.67
PRP17	22Lw510	Mississippi Plain	Mississippi Plain	140.29	12.51	1.21	10.51	1.98

PRP18	22Lw510	Mississippi Plain	Mississippi Plain	190.52	2.59	1.77	15.90	3.46
PRP19	22Lw510	Mississippi Plain	Mississippi Plain	211.75	6.20	3.30	21.80	2.08
PRP20	22Lw510	Mississippi Plain	Mississippi Plain	158.81	3.92	.00	18.02	4.66
PRP21	22Lw510	Plaquemine Brushed, *var.* Plaquemine	Addis	192.42	3.99	16.16	.00	.05
PRP22	22Lw510	Plaquemine Brushed, *var.* Plaquemine	Addis	137.61	20.50	8.40	1.10	1.50
PRP23	22Lw510	Grace Brushed, *var.* Grace	Mississippi Plain	96.35	2.60	2.00	45.19	.00
PRP24	22Lw510	Grace Brushed, *var.* Grace	Mississippi Plain	111.24	11.21	.36	3.49	2.09
PRP25	22Lw510	Plaquemine Brushed, *var.* Plaquemine	Greenville	178.96	3.58	5.29	.58	.73
PRP26	22Lw510	D'Olive Incised, *var.* unspecified	Mississippi Plain	114.52	11.30	3.61	5.51	.60
PRP27	22Lw510	Carter Engraved, *var.* Carter	Greenville	98.79	6.50	4.20	7.70	5.21
PRP28	22Lw510	Grace Brushed, *var.* Grace	Bell Plain	125.186	6.14	.87	6.72	1.55
PRP29	22Lw511	Plaquemine Brushed, *var.* Plaquemine	Addis	121.168	4.15	14.24	.00	.89
PRP30	22Lw511	L'Eau Noire Incised, *var.* L'Eau Noire	Bell Plain	154.854	2.61	4.83	.49	.29

Note: There is no sample PRP14, as it had been used in a previous neutron activation study but was unsuitable for thin sectioning. ELBPA = Estimate of large birefringent particle abundance.

High-tech chemically based approaches such as X-ray diffraction or neutron activation can provide only a partial picture because they are unable to chemically distinguish grog from the clay matrix. Ceramic petrography has been a part of American archaeology since the days of Anna Shepard (1976), but most modern analysis owes much to Jim Stoltman, who systematized the use of point-counting techniques borrowed from geological petrography in order to bring a higher level of rigor and accuracy to the field (Stoltman 1989, 1991, 2001). Today, most ceramic petrographers use a point-counting technique to quantify inclusions, which involves overlaying the sample with a grid of points in order to obtain representative counts of constituent particles. This technique is excellent at measuring the abundance of constituent particles, and it remains the gold standard for measuring inclusion density (Livingood and Cordell 2009).

This analysis employed computer-assisted petrographic analysis (CAPA) (Livingood 2006; Livingood and Cordell 2009; Velde and Druc 1998). CAPA starts with a digital image of a ceramic thin section and uses digital image analysis software to help produce a map of the section that identifies the constituent particles. For some particle types, the software can do most of the work. It can be scripted to automatically identify a class of particles with a high degree of accuracy and precision. In other cases, a human operator is required to map the particle types, but the software can help by producing false-color images that make identifying the particles much easier.

CAPA has a few benefits over traditional microscope-based petrographic analysis (Livingood and Cordell 2009). First, it is less expensive under some circumstances, since an inexpensive consumer-quality flatbed scanner can produce images of sufficient resolution to identify temper particles. Second, CAPA produces a complete map of the thin section, which provides greater information than that provided by point counting. Since every particle is individually identified and measured, every possible metric related to particle count, size, shape, orientation, and location can be generated. Third, under some circumstances, this procedure can be faster than manual point-counting techniques. This is especially true if the samples are relatively homogenous and the features of interest are distinct. Fourth, the digital nature of the analysis makes it much easier to revise and correct analyses and to share results.

Each thin section was scanned at 3,200×1,600 dpi using an Epson Perfection 1640 scanner with a transparency adapter and polarizing film. Two scans were produced from each thin section (Figure 4.5): the first scan was produced with plane-polarized light and the second with cross-polarized light. Next, the images were aligned as layers within Adobe Photoshop. Software from Reindeer Graphics called Image Analysis Toolkit (Russ 1999) was used

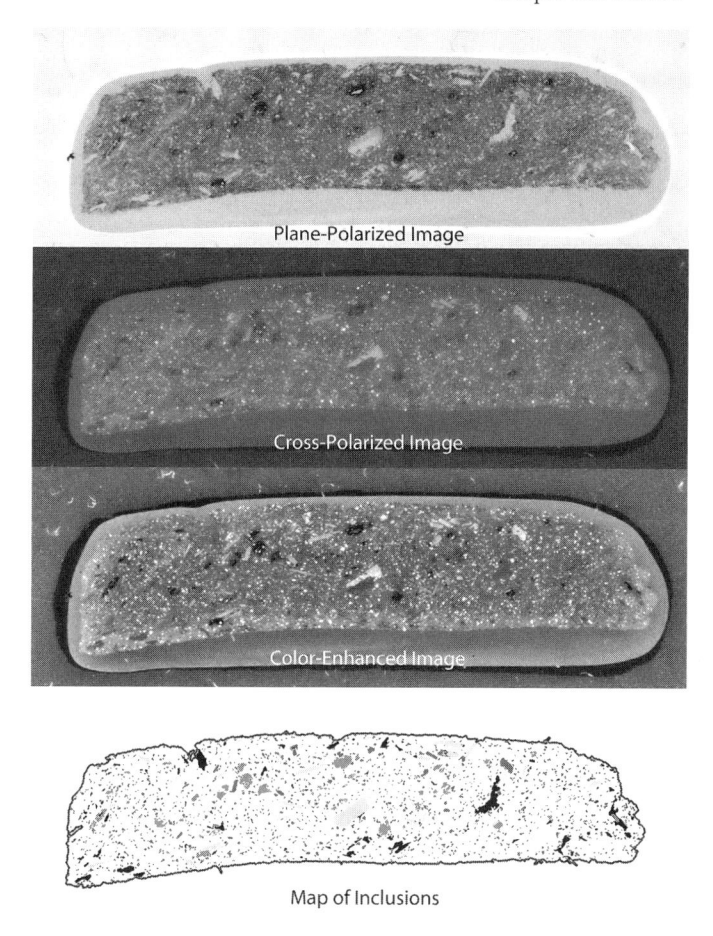

Figure 4.5. The plane-polarized, cross-polarized, and color-enhanced images and the inclusion map of a thin section (sample PRP27). The first two of these are the inputs and the second two are the outputs in the digital image analysis.

to create derivative images from these two layers by manipulating the information in their color channels (Figure 4.5). If the image can be manipulated in such a way that the desired features are distinguished by color, intensity, or texture, it is possible to automate the process of identifying the pixels corresponding to the features. Under cross-polarized light certain crystals appear to have unusual or bright colors because they split the light into two rays with different refraction indices. This property is referred to as birefringence, and these particles are very easy to identify with the software. In general, the identification of birefringent particles and voids was almost entirely automated, the automatic identification of shell was fairly accurate but required some editing, and the identification of grog was primarily done by hand. The end result of each identification is a series of Boolean images for every type of feature of interest (Figure 4.5). Every pixel in a Boolean image is either black, indicating it is a part of the feature, or white, indicating it is not. A function in the Image Analysis Toolkit software produces measurements of the features in the Boolean images for analysis in a spreadsheet or statistical analysis software package.

At a scanning resolution of 1,600 dpi there are approximately 63 pixels per mm in the finished scan. Based on the Wentworth scale (Rice 1987:38), silt particles would appear to be .2 to 3.9 pixels wide, very fine sand would appear to be 3.9 to 7.9 pixels wide, fine sand 7.9 to 15.7 pixels wide, and medium sand 15.7 to 31.5 pixels wide. Obviously, larger particles are easier to identify and map precisely. However, there are no easy rules to determine the minimum size at which a feature must be scanned in order to accurately distinguish it. That size depends on the degree of visual contrast between the particle and the surrounding matrix. However, tests definitively proved that 3,200×1,600 dpi is not sufficient to accurately identify particles the size of very fine and fine sand (Livingood and Cordell 2009). Because measuring particles of that size is not crucial to the research goals of this project, all measurements of birefringent particles with an area less than .2 mm^2 were discarded from consideration in this study. Therefore, all measurements of birefringent particles in this study pertain only to larger particles. The results were presented in Livingood (2006).

The majority of birefringent particles in these samples are sand, which appears to be a natural inclusion. Traditional petrographic analysis by Ann Cordell (2004) also found a small number of naturally occurring constituents such as muscovite mica in some of the samples that also have high birefringent values. However, because they are rare and because they are irrelevant to the study goals, no effort was made to differentiate between particles with high birefringent values. Furthermore, in order to accurately measure all of the birefringent particles in the sample, it is typically necessary to take two cross-polarized scans, with the sample rotated 90 degrees between scans, and together these will identify all of the birefringent particles. Since the orientation of birefringent particles is assumed to be random, however, it is possible to estimate their total abundance by doubling the area measured from a single cross-polarized scan. This produces a reasonably accurate estimate adequate to the research goals of this project. Therefore the values reported in Table 4.2 to measure the abundance of birefringent particles in the sample are most accurately called an estimate of large birefringent particle abundance (ELBPA), and they have been calculated by doubling the sum of the area of all birefringent particles at least .2 mm² in area identified in the analysis of a single cross-polarized image. This estimating avoids making any claims about the abundance of birefringent particles of a smaller size. It can be effectively interpreted as a proxy for the abundance of medium to large sand particles or, more precisely, an estimate of the sum of the surface area of all sand with particle size greater than .2 mm².

Shell particles and voids were easily identified using automated techniques of image analysis. Voids that had a length four times greater than breadth and minimal curvature were assumed to be from leached shell and are included with the shell totals.

In a separate study, four samples were measured using both techniques (Livingood and Cordell 2009). I examined the samples using CAPA while Ann Cordell, a professional ceramic petrographer at the University of Florida, used traditional microscope-based petrographic point counting. Once the problems of identifying smaller birefringent particles using the scanning resolution of 3,200×1,600 dpi were controlled for, CAPA was deemed sufficiently accurate to proceed with additional petrographic analyses. In the test, there was one sample for which the grog measurements were significantly different. The problem was that some hematite, ferric concretions, lumps or stains were incorrectly identified as grog. Although the problem was fixed, it underscored the difficulty of distinguishing grog from other natural stains even when using traditional microscope-based analysis (Di Caprio and Vaughn 1993). Great care has been taken in this analysis to try to ensure that only recycled pieces of pottery intentionally added as temper have been classified as grog. However, these classifications can sometimes be difficult and it should be expected that the range of error is greater for this temper identification than for shell, voids, or ELBPA.

Following the standards of petrographic point counting (Stoltman 1989, 1991), Table 4.2 reports the size of each thin section and the percentage of nontemper voids inside each sample. The percent abundance of each temper type is the ratio of temper area to matrix area, not including voids. Voids in the sample from leached shell are counted as shell temper.

Analysis

Before presenting any results, it is important to present a few caveats. First, there is the standard warning that this is a small sample and any patterns discovered must be considered merely suggestive. Second, there is no expectation that any conclusions drawn from these Pearl River ceramics will generalize to the rest of the Plaquemine area or anywhere else. In fact, there are

84   Chapter 4

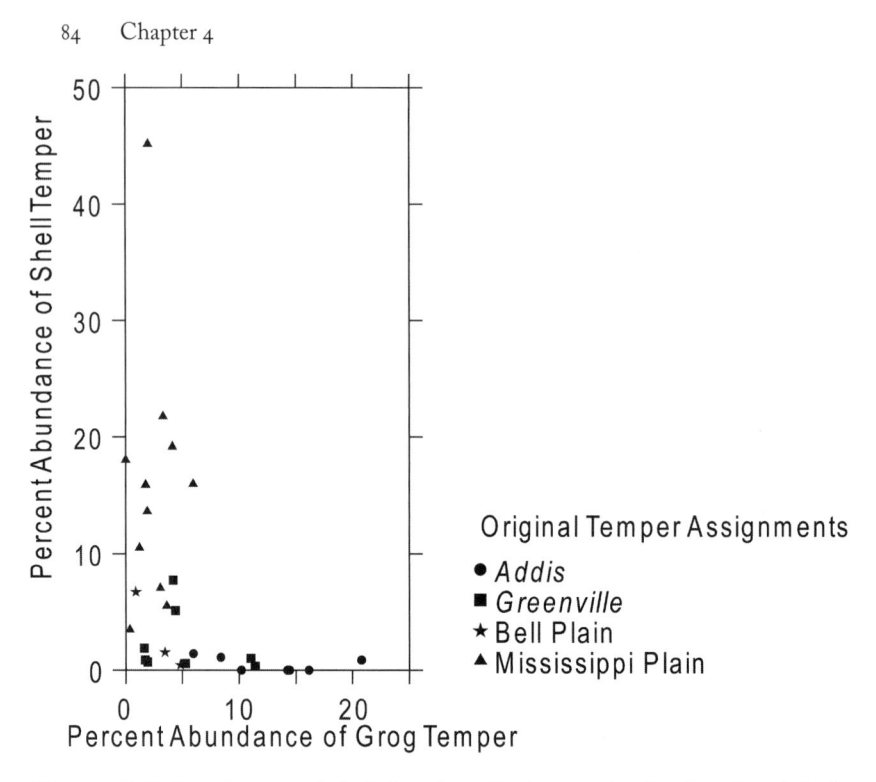

Figure 4.6. Biplot of grog and shell abundance in the sample, showing the original temper assignments.

strong reasons to suspect that the Pearl River assemblage might be a unique reflection of the social, historical, and ecological needs of the Middle Pearl community.

Figure 4.6 shows the biplot of the percentage of shell and grog with each sample coded by the original plainware variety classification. At first glance, a few important observations can be made. First, there is a single outlier that is a heavily shell-tempered sherd. Second, the graph has a general L shape. Eight of the samples have a relatively high abundance of shell (>10 percent) and low abundance of grog (<6 percent). Another eight of the samples have a relatively high abundance of grog (>8 percent) and a low abundance of shell (<1.2 percent). The remaining 13 samples have relatively small amounts of both grog (<8 percent) and shell (<10 percent). Another observation is that there is limited fit between the macroscopically observed temper and the microscopically measured categories. While the most heavily shell-tempered sherds were all correctly identified as Mississippi Plain and the most heavily grog-tempered sherds were classified as Addis Plain, *var. Addis*, there is a lack of fit in the intermediate classifications. Some sherds classified as Mississippi Plain appear to be nearly indistinguishable, using abundance measurements, from some Bell Plain and Addis Plain, *var. Greenville* sherds. Also, some sherds classified as Addis Plain, *var. Greenville* are quantitatively similar to sherds classified as Addis Plain, *var. Addis.* Clearly the human eye is only moderately successful at assessing temper abundance at these scales when the edges of the categories are so close. This is not an unexpected finding. In a summary of petrographic studies of Mississippi ceramics, Galaty (2008) found that almost every study noted a lack of correspondence between microscopic descriptions of fabric and ceramic types that were designed to describe macroscopic attributes such as decoration and form.

Other than the abundantly grog-tempered and abundantly shell-tempered specimens, it is not immediately clear whether there are any modes present in the data. It is entirely possible that if we increased the sample size we would see a continuous distribution of values, and that the reason there are problems in applying the type-variety system to classifying fabric is that we are trying to apply discrete categories to what is in fact a continuum. It is also possible that an increase in sample size would help to bring into focus modes present in the data. Since the Middle Pearl River potters took such care with so many observable aspects of pottery manufacture such as finely grinding temper particles, generally practicing careful incising and engraving techniques, and frequently polishing the finished vessels, it is probably safe to assume that they were careful in their clay preparation and followed some form of paste recipe. If that is the case, here are the modes suggested by the data (Figure 4.7, Table 4.3).

The cluster boundaries described below were constructed by considering the results of various cluster analyses, visual inspection of the graphs, a consideration of homogeneity of vessel form and type within clusters, and the analytical utility of proposed cluster definitions. Temper size was also used to construct these clusters, but abundance was found to be a much more useful metric. Generally, sherds with smaller temper sizes also had smaller abundances, while sherds with larger temper particles had higher abundances. Also, birefringent particles, which mostly represent quartz sand, are absent from the cluster descriptions because there is little correlation between ELBPA and any of the other major variables and all of the observed birefringent particles seemed to be rounded grains (Rice 1987:410), suggesting that the sand is a naturally occurring aplastic inclusion.

Cluster 1

If we exclude the clear outlier (sample PRP23 with 45 percent shell tempering; Table 4.2), the first set of clusters contains sherds with a large quantity of shell and little or no grog. All of the sherds in clusters 1A, 1B, and 1C have

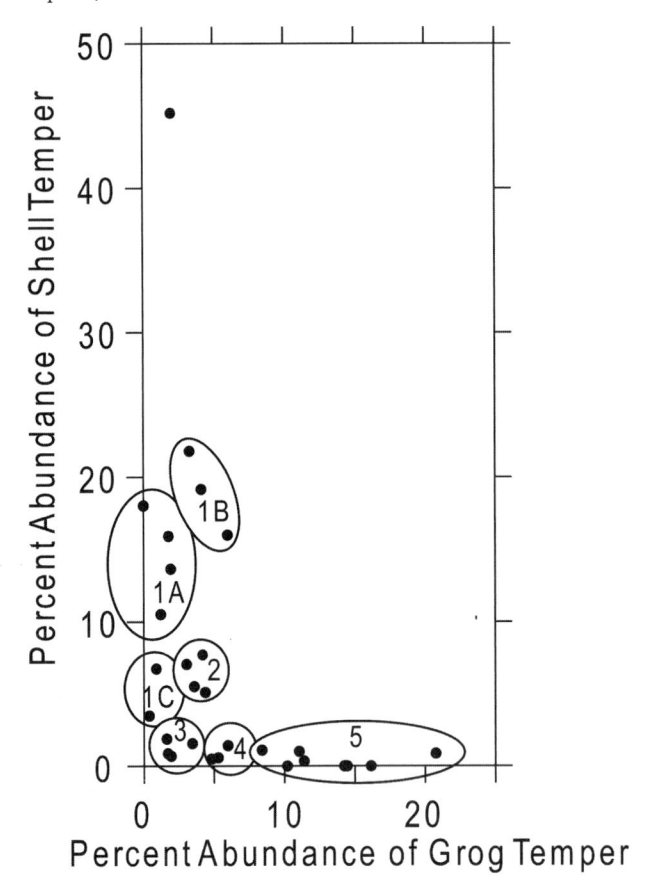

Figure 4.7. Biplot of the sherds in the sample showing cluster boundaries.

ratios of shell to grog between 5:1 and 10:1 and could be combined on this basis alone. However, since they also have significantly different amounts of shell and grog and tend to cluster according to vessel type, they are being subdivided as indicated.

Cluster 1A. The sherds in this cluster have shell abundance between 10 percent and 18 percent and grog abundance less than 2 percent. This cluster contains four sherds of Mississippi Plain.

Cluster 1B. This cluster is defined as having a high abundance of shell (15–22 percent) and moderate amounts of grog (3–6 percent). The sherds in this sample include one piece of Mississippi Plain, a Grace Brushed, *var. Grace* sherd, and a D'Olive Incised, *var. unspecified* vessel. When considering the total amount of temper added to the vessel (grog plus shell), this cluster contains the greatest amount of total temper of any of the clusters.

Table 4.3. Summary of clusters identified through digital petrographic analysis

Cluster	Summary Description	Plainware Varieties	Decorated Varieties
1A	Heavy shell temper. All utilitarian vessels.	4 Mississippi Plain	None
1B	Heavy shell temper plus moderate amounts of grog. Mixed serving and utilitarian vessels.	3 Mississippi Plain	1 Grace Brushed, *var. Grace*, 1 D'Olive Incised, *var. unspecified*
1C	Moderate shell and no grog. All utilitarian vessels.	1 Mississippi Plain, 1 Bell Plain	2 Grace Brushed, *var. Grace*
2	Nearly equal ratio of grog to shell in moderate amounts. All serving vessels.	2 Addis Plain, *var. Greenville*, 2 Mississippi Plain	2 D'Olive Incised, *var. unspecified*, 1 Anna Incised, *var. Anna*, 1 Carter Engraved, *var. Carter*
3	Very little temper. All serving vessels.	3 Addis Plain, *var. Greenville*	3 Anna Incised, *var. Anna*
4	Moderate grog temper with little shell temper. Mostly serving vessels.	2 Bell Plain, 1 Addis Plain, *var. Addis*, 1 Addis Plain, *var. Greenville*.	1 L'Eau Noire Incised, *var. L'Eau Noire*, 1 Plaquemine Brushed, *var. Plaquemine*, 1 Mound Place Incised, *var. unspecified*
5	Heavy grog tempering. Mixed serving and utilitarian vessels.	6 Addis Plain, *var. Addis*, 2 Addis Plain, *var. Greenville*	4 Plaquemine Brushed, *var. Plaquemine*, 2 Anna Incised, *var. Anna*, 1 Mazique Incised, *var. unspecified*

Cluster 1C. The two sherds in this sample are both Grace Brushed, *var. Grace* sherds and have between 3 and 7 percent shell and almost no grog.

Cluster 2

This cluster is defined as having a shell-to-grog ratio between 1:1 and 2:1. This cluster has grog between 3 and 5 percent and shell between 5 and 8 percent. All of the sherds in this sample are highly decorated serving vessels, including one sherd of Anna Incised, *var. Anna,* two sherds of D'Olive Incised, *var. unspecified,* and one sherd of Carter Engraved, *var. Carter.*

Cluster 3

This cluster contains three sherds that might have been called "untempered" in the nomenclature of Ford or Quimby. All three sherds in this cluster contain less than 2 percent shell and grog, and all three sherds come from Anna Incised, *var. Anna* vessels.

Cluster 4

This cluster contains four sherds with moderate amounts of grog tempering (3–6 percent) and little shell tempering (<2 percent). The vessels in this cluster include an example each of Bell Plain, Mound Place Incised, *var. unspecified,* Plaquemine Brushed, *var. Plaquemine,* and L'Eau Noire Incised, *var. L'Eau Noire.*

Cluster 5

This cluster contains all of the highly grog-tempered sherds. With a larger sample size it might be possible to subdivide this cluster, but for now it is being left undifferentiated. The sherds in this cluster have between 8 and 21 percent grog and less than 1 percent shell. This cluster includes four examples of Plaquemine Brushed, *var. Plaquemine,* two examples of Anna Incised, *var. Anna,* one sherd of Addis Plain, *var. Addis,* and one sherd of Mazique Incised, *var. unspecified.*

If we assume that these clusters are at least partially correct, what is their significance? First, temper modes correspond fairly well to variations in vessel function, which suggests that there may have been widely shared notions that different ratios of grog, shell, and clay were appropriate for different applications. Almost all the serving vessels (plates and shallow bowls, and decorated varieties such as Anna Incised, Carter Engraved, L'Eau Noire Incised, Mound Place Incised, D'Olive Incised) are found in clusters 2, 3, and 4, and the clays in clusters 1A and 1C were used exclusively for storage and cooking vessels. The clays in clusters 1B, 4, and 5 were used for mixed purposes. Note that there is not a good correspondence between decorative type and cluster. For example, there were six Anna Incised, *var. Anna* sherds in the sample that were constructed using temper combinations from three clusters. Likewise, the five sherds of Plaquemine Brushed, *var. Plaquemine* span two clusters, the three sherds of Grace Brushed, *var. Grace* span two clusters, and the three sherds of D'Olive Incised, *var. unspecified* span two clusters.

Second, this study found a fairly strong association between high total temper abundance (grog plus shell) and cooking/storage tasks, while the majority of presumed serving wares have low total temper abundance. This may be explained functionally: coarsely tempered vessels may perform better in tasks involving heat, such as cooking (Bronitsky and Hamer 1986; Steponaitis 1983:37–45). It may also be explained aesthetically: Pearl River potters seemed to prefer a more uniform, polished, "temperless" look for serving vessels.

Finally, the data indicate that there were a greater number of temper combinations being used than are described by the original fabric types borrowed from the Lower Mississippi Valley. Furthermore, the clusters do not map very well to the existing plainware varieties, as shown in Table 4.3. This might indicate that there were different tempering practices being used in the Middle Pearl because of cultural or ecological differences, or it might indicate the expected lack of correspondence between macroscopic and microscopic categories. In trying to apply these established types, it is interesting to observe that very few samples are completely lacking in grog or shell and there appears to be no real analytical difference between samples that contain trace amounts and those for which a temper is absent. Therefore, the distinction between Addis Plain, *var. Addis* and Addis Plain, *var. Greenville* does not seem very important for this assemblage. However, the ratio between grog and shell and the relative abundance of both do seem to be important. Sherds with lots of shell or lots of grog get assigned to clusters 1 or 5, respectively. The remaining sherds get classified according to whether they are almost "temperless" (cluster 3) or contain slightly more shell than grog (cluster 1C), slightly more grog than shell (cluster 4), or about equal amounts of both (cluster 2).

These results provide empirical evidence that the frustrated efforts to classify the Pearl River ceramics using the four paste categories of Addis Plain, *var. Addis,* Addis Plain, *var. Greenville,* Mississippi Plain, and Bell Plain were like trying to fit a square peg into a round hole. In reality, the categories needed should rely more on observing the ratio between grog and shell temper.

Macroscopic Application

The next step of the analysis was to reanalyze a portion of the assemblage macroscopically using the microscopically identified temper modes. All of the decorated sherds as well as some of the nondecorated rim sherds set aside for reference were reanalyzed (n = 1,172) and assigned a temper mode based on the clusters identified during the microscopic analysis. During the analysis, it became apparent that clusters 1A and 1B were largely indistinguishable macroscopically. They were therefore collapsed into a generic clus-

Table 4.4. Assignment of sherds to temper modes, by original assignment of temper type

	Percentage of Sherds					
	Cluster 1	Cluster 1C	Cluster 2	Cluster 3	Cluster 4	Cluster 5
Addis Plain, *var. Addis*	.3	.1	6.8	8.8	51.3	32.7
Bell Plain	15.8	42.1	15.8	.0	26.3	.0
Addis Plain, *var. Greenville*	1.3	7.5	24.3	8.4	52.2	6.2
Mississippi Plain	55.6	14.3	20.6	.9	8.5	.0

ter 1. Cluster 1C was retained, however, since it was identifiable macroscopically.

Table 4.4 shows the percentage of each original temper identification reassigned to each temper mode. The results indicate the same rough correspondence demonstrated in the smaller sample above. Sherds originally classified as Addis Plain, *var. Addis* were largely assigned to clusters 4 and 5. Mississippi Plain sherds were largely assigned to clusters 1, 1C, and 2. *Greenville* sherds were largely classified in clusters 2 and 4. Again, there is only partial overlap between the preestablished temper types and the temper modes.

Of foremost interest in this reanalysis are the types that are arbitrarily separated by fabric type. For example, in this sample brushed sherds on an *Addis* paste are classified as Plaquemine Brushed while brushed sherds on a shell-tempered paste are classified as Grace Brushed. Shallow plates and bowls with interior incising on *Addis* paste are classified as Anna Incised while those on shell-tempered paste are classified as D'Olive Incised. Figure 4.8 shows histograms of the temper modes if these types are considered together. What is clear is that for both of these modes, classic Addis grog tempering as represented by clusters 3, 4, and 5 predominates. However, some examples are also made on coarse shell–tempered or mixed grog-and-shell–tempered pastes.

Figure 4.9 shows histograms of temper modes for all vessel forms (to be discussed in the next section). This graph should be approached cautiously since only decorated sherds were completely analyzed for temper mode and most undecorated rim sherds were not analyzed. Since there are far more Addis-tempered rim sherds categorized by temper mode, there may be a bias toward Addis-tempered sherds in this figure.

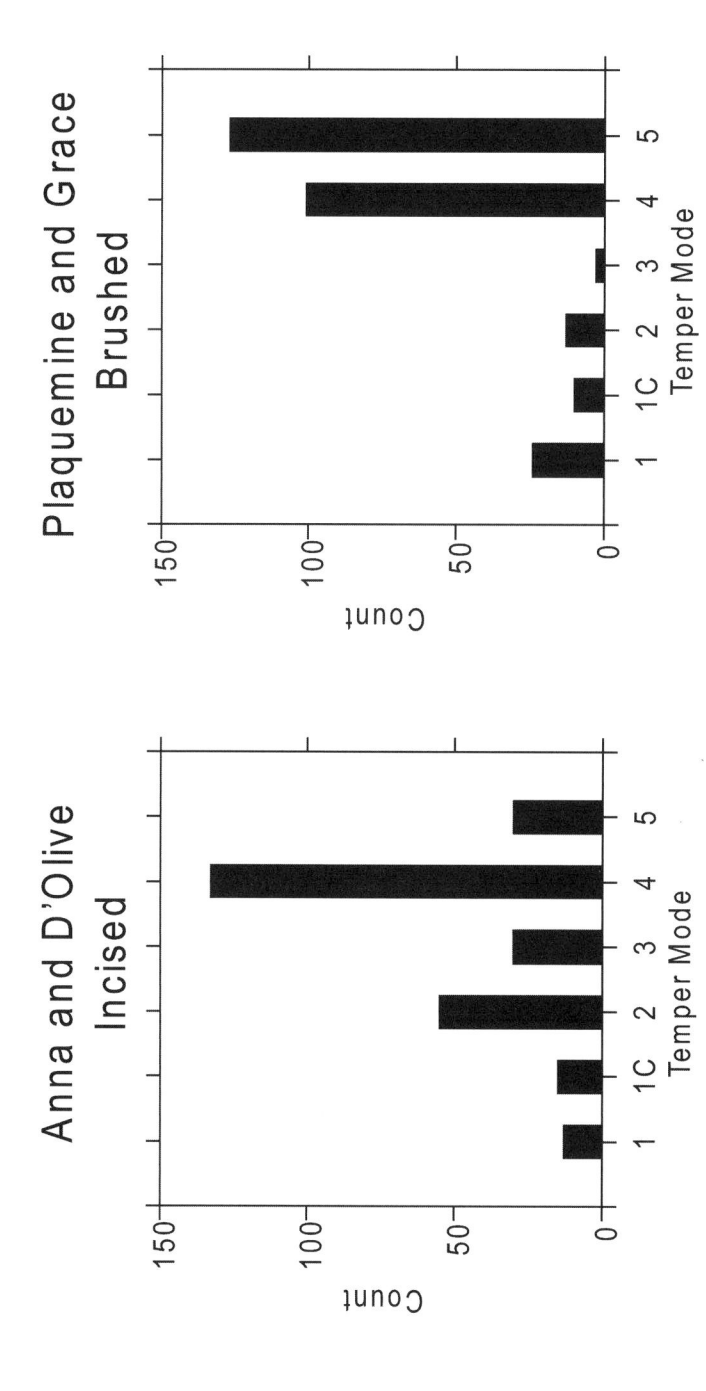

Figure 4.8. Histogram of temper modes for brushed and interior incised vessels.

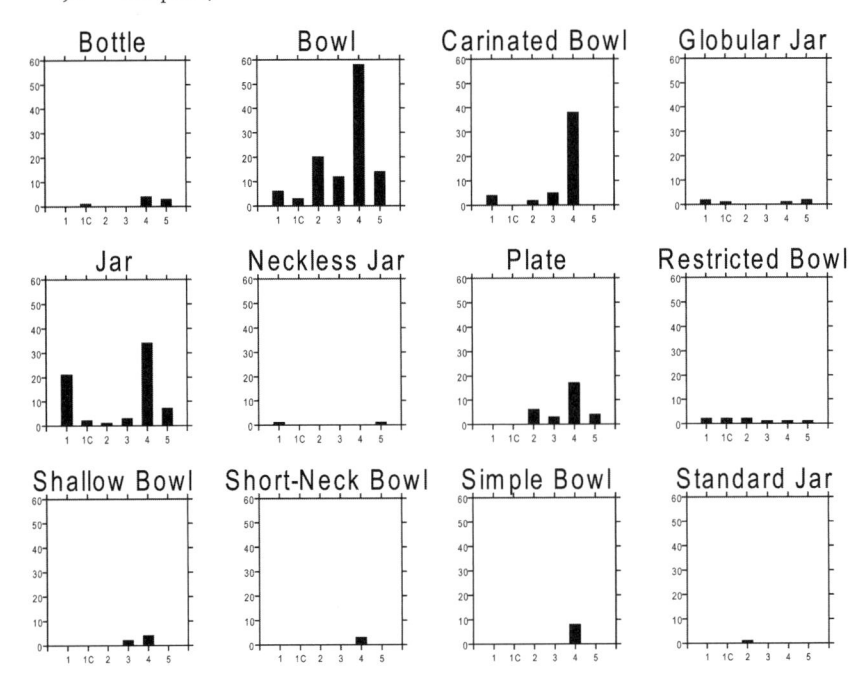

Figure 4.9. Histograms showing the number of each vessel shape having each temper mode. Since only decorated sherds were analyzed for temper mode, this graph is not complete and should not be interpreted as such.

The primary observation is that forms traditionally associated with Plaquemine culture are frequently executed on traditional Plaquemine pastes while vessel forms traditionally associated with the Mississippian are executed on the standard Middle Mississippian shell-tempered paste. For example, the plates and carinated bowls are largely made on Addis wares while the standard jar is mostly made on shell-tempered paste.

Finally, Table 4.5 shows the percentage of temper used for each vessel category (relationship between vessel shapes and category will be discussed below). The table indicates that shell tempering is preferred in almost 80 percent of the cooking/storage vessels, with coarse shell tempering being used in 54 percent. In contrast, Addis and Mississippi Plain are used about equally in serving vessels.

Paste Conclusions

Collectively, these data indicate that when matching paste with vessel form and decoration the Pearl River potters were open to wide varieties of combinations. With the ability to manufacture both shell- and grog-tempered

Table 4.5. Percentages of temper by vessel category

	Percentage of Sherds			
Temper	Serving/ Cooking	Storage/ Cooking	Unknown Function	Total
Addis	35.98	21.45	25.26	29.49
Baytown	.18	.00	.00	.09
Bell	5.64	18.81	9.90	10.15
Greenville	23.28	5.28	8.19	14.79
Mississippi Plain	34.92	54.46	56.66	45.49
Total	100.00	100.00	100.00	100.00

vessels, they were willing to use both for many different functions. However, their choices were far from random.

- They used shell temper for the majority of all their ceramics but used grog temper for the majority of the decorated ceramics.
- They tended to execute decorated ceramics on the pastes that were culturally associated with those decorations.
- They primarily used shell tempering for vessels intended for storage/cooking functions.
- Vessels with the clearest serving functions, plates, were almost exclusively executed on grog temper.

These decisions may have been motivated by a variety of considerations. To begin with, there may have been a functional explanation. Grog and shell have different physical and chemical properties and as temper they react differently to mechanical and thermal stresses. Shell tempering, particularly coarse-shell tempering, is especially good at maintaining strength even after thermal shock (Steponaitis 1983:37–45). The disadvantage is that it is platy and more prone to laminar fractures (Rice 1987:407) when compared to grog. Grog, by contrast, does not have the same thermal expansion properties, but its blocky and angular structure may make the vessel more resistant to certain mechanical stresses. Because they are relatively uncommon in the Mississippian world, far less is known about the physical properties of the mixed grog-and-shell–tempered vessels frequently manufactured and used by the Pearl River potters.

The Pearl River potters may have also had cultural reasons for their selection of temper. The Lower Mississippi Survey archaeologists constructed a model that emphasizes the cultural dichotomy between Plaquemine and Mississippian (Brain 1989; Williams and Brain 1983). The main diagnostic feature of this dichotomy is the presence or absence of shell tempering. Although they are not clear on this point, an extreme interpretation of their model would posit that tempering, presumably along with other more visible features, is an emblematic stylistic (Hegmon 1992; Wiessner 1983, 1984, 1989) means of expressing cultural identity. If this were the case, we should certainly expect the potters of the Middle Pearl to have been cognizant of the cultural meaning of temper selection and that they may have been signaling their cultural identity with their choices. However, as discussed above, there are many places in the Plaquemine world where the shell- and grog-tempering dichotomy does not appear to express a simple cultural boundary (Hally 1972; Kidder 1998b, 2007; Rees and Livingood 2007). While the Middle Pearl potters must certainly have been aware of the tempering differences between their neighbors to the east and their neighbors to the west, it is entirely unclear whether they viewed temper selection as a means to signal their identity. One could make an argument that, since they tended to reserve certain decorative motifs for Addis-tempered vessels, they may have thought the choice of temper did convey cultural meaning. In this case it might have been communicating their shared identity with the Lower Valley communities, whom they were emulating or to whom they were related. However, their tendency to mix tempers with great frequency suggests this is unlikely. Temper is a low visibility attribute in pottery (Carr 1995a, 1995b) and, given the weight of the evidence, it seems unlikely that temper was a major means of emblematically expressing cultural identity.

There may also have been historically contingent reasons for the temper selection. Based on the preponderance of Lower Valley decorated types and the absence of known sites from the Pearl River dating to the preceding phase, we can assume that the pottery-making traditions of the Pearl River potters originated in the Lower Valley. The simplest explanation would be to postulate a migration from somewhere in the Lower Valley to the Middle Pearl, but there are not enough data to know whether the situation was more complex. For example, there may have been multiple groups with diverse origins that coalesced on the Middle Pearl or there may have been a process of intermarriage. One should also mention that given the lack of survey coverage on the Pearl further Coles Creek age sites may yet be found, forcing us to reevaluate these hypotheses.

The Middle Pearl is also remarkable for its unusual mix of grog and shell traditions. While similar assemblages are not entirely absent from the Lower Valley, they are not especially common. For example, the Transylvania site and the Lake Providence sites in the Tensas River valley (Hally 1972; Weinstein 2005) both contain large numbers of Mississippian related ceramics. So the Middle Pearl potters may have originated from a community with a tradition of mixed temper or they may have originated from a community with a homogenous grog-tempered tradition and learned to incorporate new tempering and vessel forms when they arrived on the Pearl. If the latter is the case, what we see archaeologically may be a transitional phase as the community experimented with the incorporation of different tempers and evaluated these combinations on functional and aesthetic grounds. That is, the pattern is historically contingent on the cultural background of the potters, the traditions with which they were familiar, and the traditions to which they were exposed.

In fact, it is the presence of both experimentation with temper and a lack of experimentation with decorative techniques or vessel form that seems the most revealing. As discussed below there are no novel vessel forms or decorative techniques to report from the Middle Pearl. However, the potters appeared quite willing to establish novel temper mixes, and this seems to indicate that individual potters were less culturally circumscribed in their choices in this regard than they were with respect to other attributes. This is different from what we know of potters historically. Typically, temper is more resistant to change over time than decisions about form or decoration. This holds true for many parts of the Southeast, where residents in many areas only ever used two or three tempering agents in almost two millennia of pottery production but made a dozen or more vessel forms and scores of decorations. However, the Winstead phase potters lived between two pottery-making traditions at a time of transition with respect to temper (see Feathers 2006). Their choices about temper and about other pottery attributes indicate that they were actively engaging the different traditions to which they were exposed.

Ceramic Chronology

A total of 810 decorated sherds from the Lowe-Steen and Pevey sites are associated with dated phases. Of these, 767 (94.6 percent; Table 4.6) are consistent with an Anna or Winterville phase assignment had the sherds been found in the Lower Valley (Brown 1998; Williams and Brain 1983). Within the Middle Pearl River, these are assigned to the Winstead phase, which is the local phase contemporary with the Anna and Winterville phases (Livingood 1999). A total of 27 sherds (3.3 percent) would be diagnostic of the earlier Gordon/Crippen Point phase (Table 4.7) and 16 sherds (1.9 percent) are consistent with a later phase (Table 4.8), which has been tentatively labeled the Pevey phase along the Middle Pearl River (Livingood 1999).

The Pevey and Lowe-Steen sites very clearly have a primary occupa-

Table 4.6. Decorated sherds found at the Pevey and Lowe-Steen sites that are consistent with a Winstead phase date

Type-Variety	No. of Sherds
Anna Incised, *var. Anna*	275
Barton Incised, *var. Estill*	4
Carter Engraved, *var. Carter*	58
Carter Engraved, *var. Sara*	10
Chicot Red, *var. Fairchild*	2
D'Olive Incised, *var. unspecified*	41
Grace Brushed, *var. Grace*	43
Hollyknowe Pinched, *var. Patmos*	7
L'Eau Noire Incised, *var. L'Eau Noire*	46
Leland Incised, *var. Bethlehem*	13
Mazique Incised, *var. Manchac*	4
Moundville Incised, *var. Moundville*	3
Parkin Punctated, *var. Hollandale*	5
Parkin Punctated, *var. Transylvania*	1
Plaquemine Brushed, *var. Plaquemine*	255

Table 4.7. Decorated sherds that are associated with Gordon or Crippen Point phases in the Lower Mississippi Valley

Type-Variety	Pevey Site	Lowe-Steen Site
Avoyelles Punctated, *var. Dupree*	2	0
Coles Creek Incised, *var. Hardy*	4	0
Coles Creek Incised, *var. unspecified*	5	0
Evansville Punctated, *var. Sharkey*	7	0
Harrison Bayou Incised, *var. Harrison Bayou*	7	2

tion in the Winstead phase. Of the two sites, Pevey has the more diverse assemblage with 25 of 27 possible pre–Winstead phase sherds (Table 4.7) and all of the likely post–Winstead phase sherds (Table 4.8). All of the pre–Winstead phase sherds were found in secondary contexts. This suggests that the pre–Winstead phase occupation was minor and was disturbed by Winstead phase earth moving, that the sherds in question were made during the

Table 4.8. Decorated sherds found at the Pevey site that might be indicative of a post–Winstead phase occupation

Type-Variety	No. of Sherds
Barton Incised, *var. Midnight*	2
Fatherland Incised, *var. Pine Ridge*	1
Leland Incised, *var. Foster*	1
Leland Incised, *var. Leland*	4
Maddox Engraved, *var. Silver City*	5
Owens Punctated, *var. Poor Joe*	1
Owens Punctated, *var. unspecified* (*Menard?*)	2

Winstead phase, or that these vessels were heirlooms. Given that there are presently no known Gordon/Crippen Point equivalent sites documented in Lawrence County, all explanations seem equally likely.

Fifteen of the 16 sherds with possible post–Winstead phase associations are from the upper levels of Unit E (two Barton Incised, *var. Midnight,* one Leland Incised, *var. Foster,* three Maddox Engraved, *var. Silver City,* one Owens Punctated, *var. Poor Joe*), Unit M (one Fatherland Incised, *var. Pine Ridge,* three Leland Incised, *var. Leland,* one Maddox Engraved, *var. Silver City,* two Owens Punctated, *var. Menard*), and Unit SE (one Maddox Engraved, *var. Silver City*). A single sherd of Leland Incised, *var. Leland* was recovered from the base of Unit H while cleaning the walls and floors for a photograph. While we do not know the stratigraphic level of this sherd, it is likely to have originated from one of the upper levels. All of these types are generally thought to date no earlier than the Foster or Lake George phase if they were found in the Lower Mississippi Valley, with the exception of Owens Punctated, *var. Menard,* which is thought to first appear in the Emerald or Wasp Lake phase.

Of all of the possible post–Winstead phase sherds, the two Owens Punctated, *var. Menard* sherds are the most anomalous because of their late date. One of the sherds was found in Feature 1, which also contained some Anna Incised, *var. Anna,* Avoyelles Punctated, *var. Dupree,* Grace Brushed, *var. Grace,* Plaquemine Brushed, *var. Plaquemine,* L'Eau Noire Incised, *var. L'Eau Noire,* and Mound Place Incised, *var. B.* The other sherd was found in the west half of the unit in level 2 with a similar assemblage and two Owens Punctated, *var. unspecified* sherds. It seems likely that these sherds have been misidentified and they are not actually examples of *Menard,* although they do fit the classification comfortably. With only two sherds, there is no reason to modify the variety specification or create a new variety, and these sherds are being reclassified as Owens Punctated, *var. unspecified.*

The other 14 sherds are possibly indicative of a post–Winstead date to the Pevey site. All of the sherds occur at the terminal levels of their respective units. Therefore, unlike with the pre–Winstead phase sherds, a case could be made for a small post–Winstead phase occupation of the site. In an earlier work, it was even proposed that this later phase be called the Pevey phase (Livingood 1999). However, all of these sherds that are possibly diagnostic of a post-Winstead phase are outnumbered in their excavated contexts by sherds such as Anna Incised, *var. Anna,* Carter Engraved, *var. Carter,* Grace Brushed, *var. Grace,* and Leland Incised, *var. Bethlehem,* which are thought to have an association with only the Winstead phase or its equivalent. Therefore, two scenarios are possible. In the first scenario, Pevey had only one single occupation that lasted long enough in some parts of the site to see the introduction of new vessel forms that were to predominate during the following century. In the second scenario, Pevey was occupied mostly during the Winstead phase, but it was revisited during a subsequent period by people who left only trace evidence that became slightly mixed into Winstead phase contexts by postdepositional processes. In either case, Pevey is primarily a Winstead phase site.

Therefore, based on ceramic evidence it seems likely that both the Pevey and Lowe-Steen sites were occupied during the Winstead phase, which is equivalent to the Anna or Winterville phases in the Lower Mississippi Valley. Based on a more diverse assemblage, it appears the Pevey site was occupied during the entire span of the Winstead phase since the residents appear to have made a small number of vessels associated with earlier or later phases. The Lowe-Steen site seems to have been occupied for a shorter time and was most likely abandoned before the Pevey site was.

Thirteen decorated sherds were recovered from the Phillips Farm site (22Lw593), but only one of those was classifiable. This single Plaquemine Brushed, *var. Plaquemine* sherd could have a Winstead phase date, but it could also be associated with an earlier or later phase. The single radiocarbon date from the site (discussed in Chapter 6) is the only other clue to the temporal assignment of this site.

Vessel Form

A total of 1,152 rim sherds were examined in the course of the ceramic analysis (Table 4.9). Vessel form categories were derived primarily from Steponaitis (1983:67). In addition to those forms, this study used the categories of deep bowl, carinated bowl, plate, and shallow bowl or plate. These are all forms that are diagnostic of the Plaquemine. Vessels that were recognizable

Table 4.9. Total number of sherds representative of vessel shape, by site

Vessel Category	Vessel Form	Lw510	Lw511	Lw593	Lw644	Lw660	Lw661
Bottle	Bottle	12	1				
Bowl	Bowl, generic	209	92	1		3	1
Bowl	Carinated bowl	36	26				
Bowl	Deep bowl	14	2				
Bowl	Flaring-rim bowl	7					
Bowl	Outslanting bowl	3					
Bowl	Restricted bowl	16	3				
Bowl	Shallow bowl or plate	26	5				
Bowl	Short-neck bowl	19	15				
Bowl	Simple bowl	10	5				
Jar	Globular jar	10					
Jar	Jar, generic	117	57				
Jar	Neckless jar	21	3				
Jar	Standard jar	50	1				
Plate	Plate	65	2				
Unknown	Unknown	266	42	7	1	2	2
Total		881	254	8	1	5	3

as bowls or jars, but not as a specific form of bowl or jar, were coded as a generic form.

Overall, the assemblage of vessel forms has the greatest similarity to contemporaneous Lower Valley assemblages. While there are a few examples of standard Middle Mississippian forms such as the standard jar and globular bowl, far more of the vessels are plates, shallow bowls, and vertical-walled vessels typical of the Plaquemine.

One of the goals of this section is to determine whether there are obvious differences in the types of activities taking place at different locations within the Pevey and Lowe-Steen sites. To evaluate this using ceramics, archaeologists have typically looked at the likely function of ceramic vessels at the location based on the vessels' shape and size.

Following the work of Hally (1984, 1986), Blitz (1993a), and Wells (2005: 312), bowls and plates are hypothesized to have a serving/cooking role. Their open design makes them unlikely candidates for storage since contents could have easily been spilled or evaporated. Jars are assigned storage/cooking func-

Figure 4.10

Unit: B, C, E, G, H, I, K, M, SE, SJ, T

Storage/Cooking (top), Serving/Cooking (bottom); scale 0%–100%

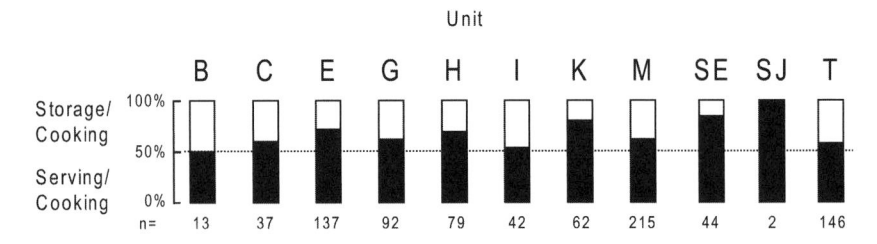

n = 13, 37, 137, 92, 79, 42, 62, 215, 44, 2, 146

Figure 4.10. Graph showing the proportion of serving and storage vessels for the units of 22Lw510.

Figure 4.11

Unit: 1136R876, 956R1003, 975R1007, Feature 4

Storage/Cooking (top), Serving/Cooking (bottom); scale 0%–100%

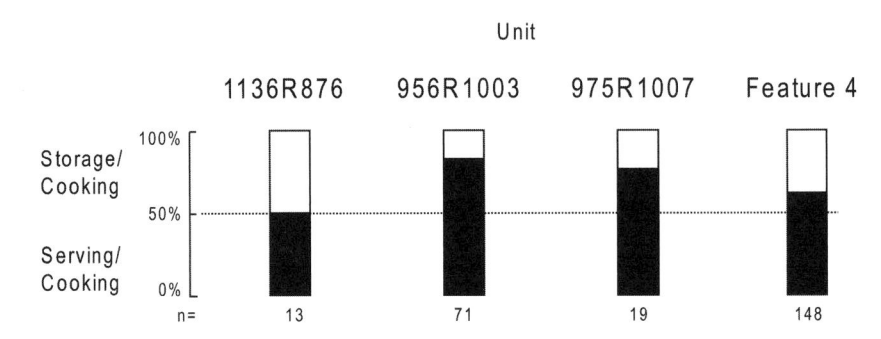

n = 13, 71, 19, 148

Figure 4.11. Graph showing the proportion of serving and storage vessels for the units of 22Lw511.

tions. Bottles could have been used either for serving or for storage. Because this assemblage of bottles is largely undecorated (as in Wells 2005:312), they are assigned a storage function. It is likely that the aboriginal use of these vessel forms was more complex than just two categories of use. For example, some of the small plates and bowls may have had ritual purposes and some of the larger bowls may have had storage functions (Steponaitis and Knight 2004). However, these assignments are a first approximation given our current information.

Figure 4.10 shows the proportion of serving/cooking and storage/cooking vessels per unit for the Pevey site, and Figure 4.11 shows the same for the Lowe-Steen site. The arrangement of mounds at Pevey is suggestive that there was a central plan that dictated the use of space, and such a central plan may have also involved specialized functions for the mounds and their attendant structures. Given the current scarcity of excavation, the best way to hazard a guess for the function of any mounds comes from the ceramic evidence. Since we currently only have 1-×-2-m or 2-×-2-m units from each mound and several occupation levels are represented by few sherds, it was decided to lump all levels from each unit together for analysis. Any distinctions found at this level of abstraction will indicate long-term trends. In particular, we are interested in detecting whether broad areas of the site, such as the western mounds and the eastern mounds, or the contexts around Mound E, had enduring and detectable differences.

All of the units have at least 50 percent of the known vessels being used for serving/cooking. At the Pevey site, the units with the highest proportion of storage/cooking vessels are B, C, I, M, and T. Excluding Unit SJ, with a sample of only two, the E, K, and SE units all have the highest proportion of serving/cooking vessels. Since Unit SE, on the summit of Mound E, is the most likely to have served as the residence of the chief, the unusually high proportion of probable serving vessels makes the unique nature of this area apparent. Even the midden on the north flank of Mound E (Unit E) contains an above-average proportion of serving/cooking vessels. The terrace unit (Unit T) to the east of Mound E contains a relatively large number of storage/cooking vessels, which may support the supposition that this area was used for feasting. The vessels in this case would have been used to transport food from other areas of the site to this area for the events or used to prepare the food on-site. Likewise, Unit M, on the flats to the west of Mound E, may have had a similar role, given the large number of ceramics and the relatively high proportion of storage vessels. The ceramic data are less clear about the apparent function of the other mounds.

At the Lowe-Steen site, the sample sizes are generally smaller, making comparisons less reliable. Still, Unit 975R1007 on the flank of Mound A and 956R1003 to the south have the highest proportion of serving/cooking ware, while Feature 4 and 1136R876 on Mound B have more storage/cooking vessels. This may reflect the more socially restricted nature of the Mound A area and the relatively more public and more domestic role of the other end of the plaza from Mound A.

Another tool for determining differences in the nature of the occupation of an area is to examine vessel size. For example, at the Mississippi period Lubbub Creek site, Blitz (1993a, 1993b:91–93) found that mound contexts, on average, had larger vessels than village contexts, and he linked this pattern to feasting and storage activities taking place at the mound locations (Blitz 1993b:93). Specifically, the mound contexts did not contain the smallest vessels, presumably intended for household use, thereby skewing the distributions and the average.

For this project, vessel rim diameters were measured to the nearest centimeter using the standard concentric circle bull's-eye forms. Figures 4.12 and 4.13 show the rim diameters for specific nongeneric forms of bowls and jars. Figure 4.14 presents box-and-whisker plots of vessel orifice diameter

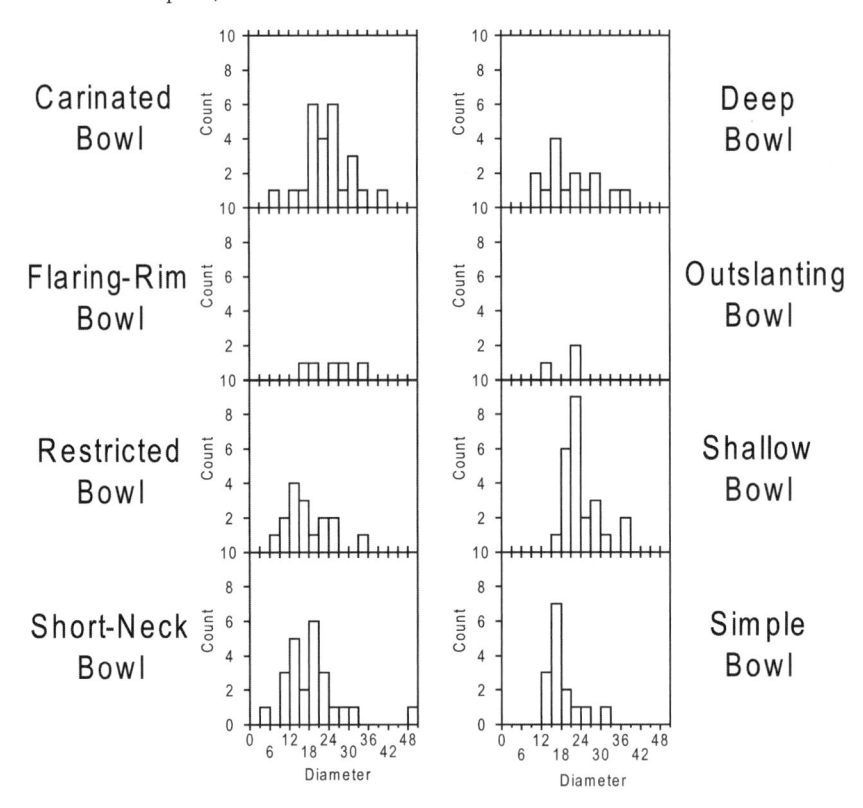

Figure 4.12. Histograms of rim diameters, all nongeneric bowls.

for each of the excavation units at the Pevey site. The findings show that for bowls, vessel size was relatively uniform across the site. Both Units C and I have a better representation of the largest bowls and have the largest median. Units G and T each have two extremely large outlier bowls. SJ has the smallest bowls, but with only two specimens the sample size is too small to be informative. Otherwise, the units have similar-looking size profiles.

There is more diversity within the category of jars, which may be attributable to the smaller sample sizes. Units E, G, and T are very similar, with medians in the 15- to 18-cm range and similar distributions. Units I and M are similar in their slightly higher median diameters than the previous group but the distributions are skewed toward larger jars. The other units all have larger diameter jars but, with the exception of Unit H, all have sample sizes too small to be significant. Figure 4.15 shows the same box-and-whisker plots for the vessel categories at the Lowe-Steen site.

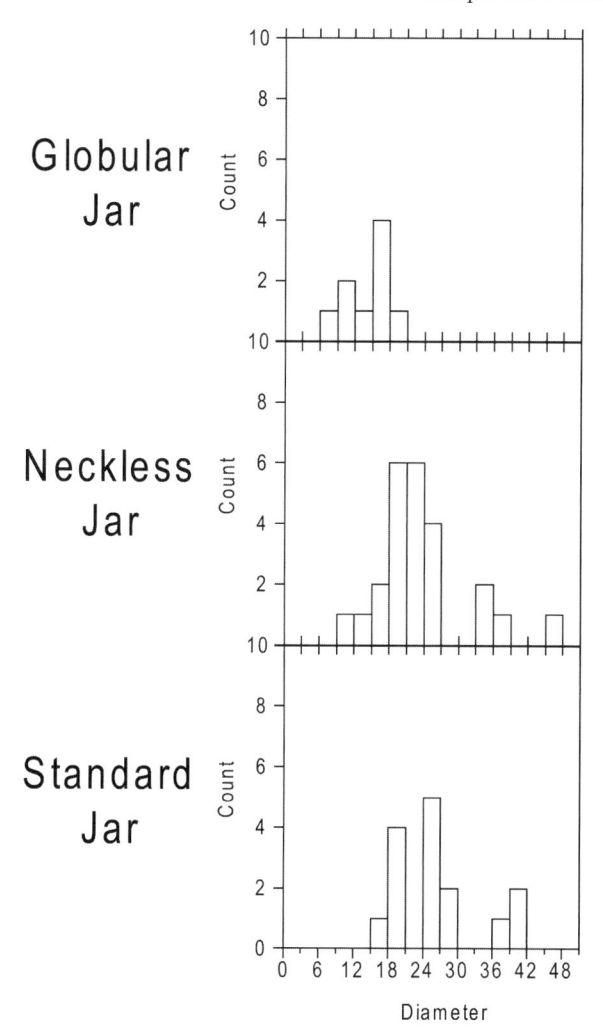

Figure 4.13. Histograms of rim diameters of jars, excluding generic jars.

Overall, these plots show that the units are not appreciably different from one another in vessel size. At Lubbub Creek, Blitz (1993a, 1993b) found few differences between mound and village contexts when considering vessel form or decoration, but he did find a difference between vessel sizes. At Pevey and Lowe-Steen, the sizes appear to be relatively uniform when comparing mound and between-mound contexts, while the proportion of vessel types and decorations appear to vary somewhat.

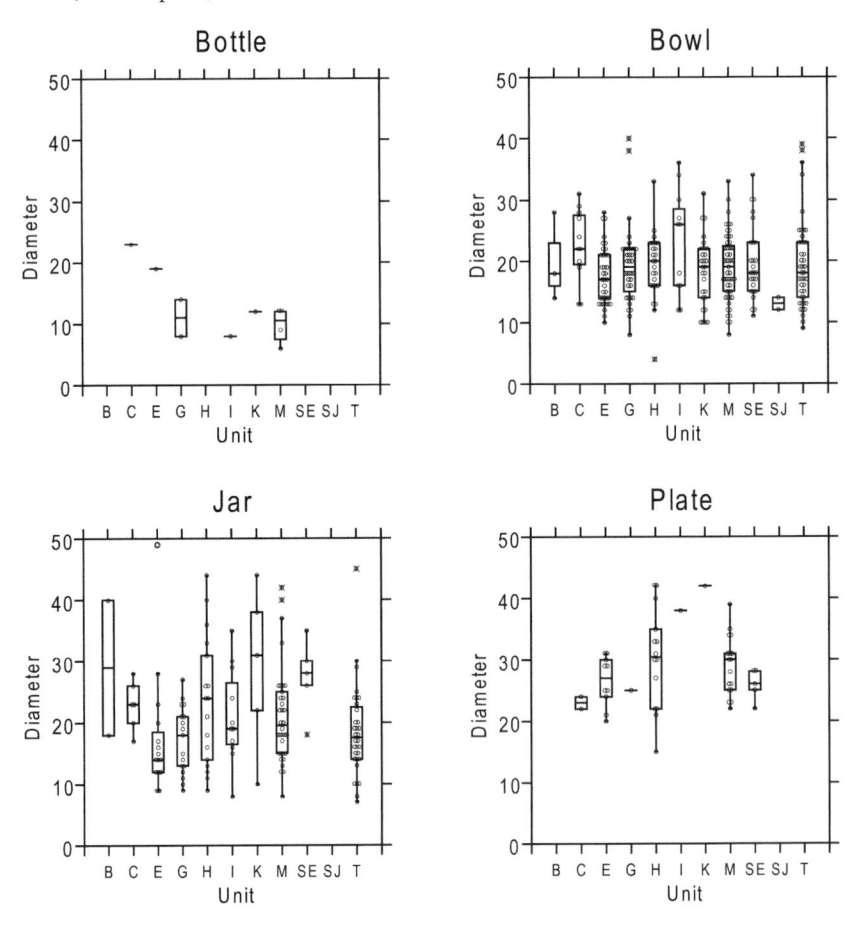

Figure 4.14. Box-and-whisker plots of vessel orifice diameter by vessel type and unit for site 22Lw510. Open dots show the values of individual vessels; outliers are indicated by x's.

Summary

Analysis of ceramics recovered from the Pevey and Lowe-Steen sites was carried out through a microscopic examination of 29 thin sections using a digital image analysis approach. This analysis identified six temper modes and demonstrated that they do not overlap well with the plainware varieties that have been established for Lower Mississippi Valley ceramics. A further analysis of temper indicated that Middle Pearl potters frequently combined grog and shell, but tended to use shell temper for storage/cooking vessels and grog temper for plates. The ceramics were also used to construct a chro-

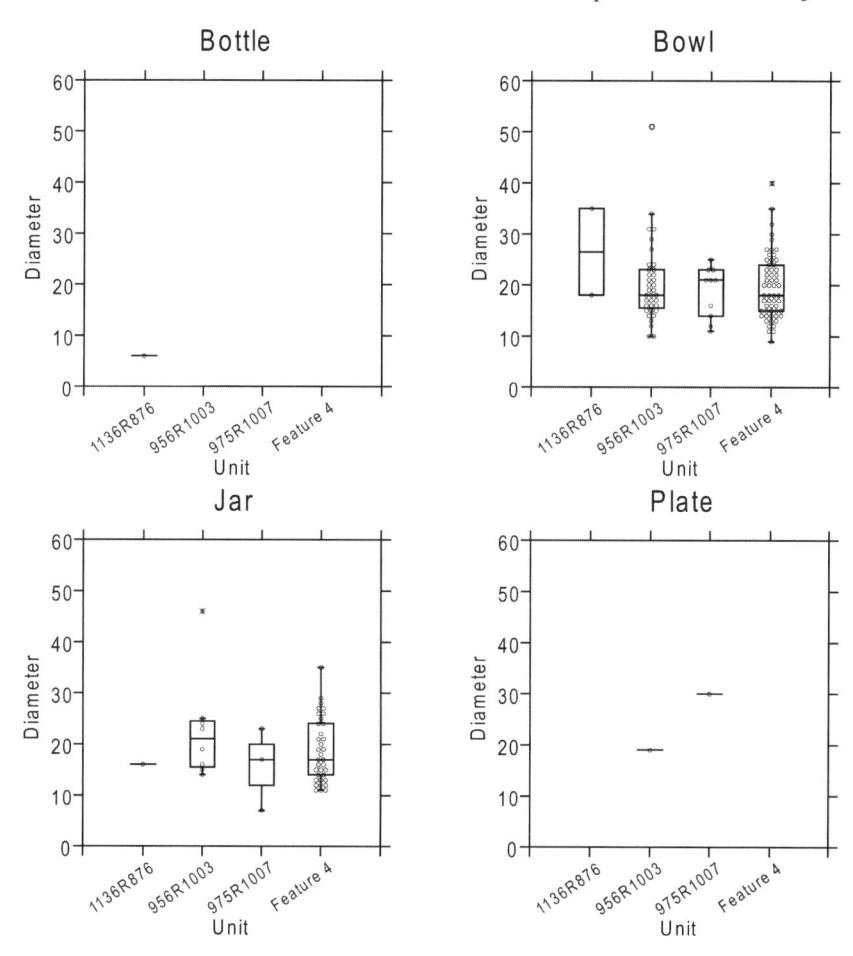

Figure 4.15. Box-and-whisker plots of vessel orifice diameter by vessel type and unit for site 22Lw511. Open dots show the values of individual vessels; outliers are indicated by x's.

nology, which indicated that the major occupation of both Pevey and Lowe-Steen was coeval with the Anna phase (A.D. 1200–1350).

Finally, an examination of the distribution of vessel types over the Pevey site confirmed earlier hypotheses. It indicated that Mound E (Units SE and E) had a higher proportion of serving vessels, confirming that it was probably the home of a chief and may have served other important ritual functions. Additionally, most of the plates at the site, the vessel type with the clearest serving or ritual role, were found in Units E, H, and M, the units in the eastern half of the site.

5
Analyses of Foodways and of Other Artifact Classes

Analysis of all nonceramic artifacts from Pevey and Lowe-Steen is discussed with special attention paid to evidence that may serve to interpret the differential functions of the mounds at Pevey. The nonlocal artifact materials found at these mounds are also documented to understand the types of exchange networks that the prehistoric residents may have been involved with.

Plant Remains

During the 1993 and 1994 excavations of the Pevey and Lowe-Steen sites, 10-liter soil samples were taken from each hearth, midden deposit, or pit. All this feature fill was processed through a flotation tank to recover carbonized plant remains or was water-screened through ½-inch, ¼-inch, and 1/16-inch screens. Thirteen samples from the Pevey site and one sample from the Lowe-Steen site were chosen for paleobotanical analysis (Table 5.1); one of the samples was analyzed by Jeff Takacs (1994) and the rest by E. Marco Brewer (1994, 1995). The results of the analysis of the Pevey samples were then compiled and reported by Marco Brewer (1995).

The most abundant plant food taxon from these samples is maize, at 57 percent of all remains as measured by raw taxa counts (Tables 5.2 and 5.3) (Brewer 1995:17). Maize was found in all samples except the one from Mound E, Level 8. The greatest concentration of maize was from Mound I, Level 7, which contained cupules, kernels, and pieces of stalk. Brewer (1995:17) suggests this Mound I context might represent a smudge pit (Binford 1967). Since the other Mound I sample also has a high abundance of maize, it is more likely this location was important for the processing of maize. The next highest abundance of maize was from the Unit T samples.

Several probable domesticates and cultigens were recovered from the Pevey site sample. One sumpweed achene was recovered from the Unit H2 sample,

Table 5.1. Summary of flotation samples from Pevey site

Site	Unit	Provenience	Provenience No.	Analytical Unit	Sample Volume (liters)	Wood Charcoal Weight (g)	Plant Weight (g)
22Lw510	C	Level 12N	214	6	10	2.55	2.61
22Lw510	SE	Level 3	359	1	10	0.36	0.37
22Lw510	SE	Level 8E	375	5	20	0.22	0.24
22Lw510	G	Level 9, Fea. 1	248	5	30	11.29	11.45
22Lw510	G	Level 9A	249	5	20	12.67	12.74
22Lw510	H	Level 6, Fea. 1	276	4	10	20.98	33.05
22Lw510	H2	Level 1, Fea. 1	310	2	10	9.53	69.82
22Lw510	I	East ½, Level 7	139	1	10	1.24	14.58
22Lw510	I	East ½, Level 9, Fea. 1	142	3	10	13.58	26.02
22Lw510	M	Level 1, Fea. 1	153	1	10	8.93	9.06
22Lw510	T	East ½, Level 1	165	1-2	10	7.08	9.17
22Lw510	T	West ½, Level 2	163	2	10	10.69	15.18
22Lw510	T2	Level 1	175	1-2	10	5.44	17.72
22Lw511	Fea. 4	Fea. 4	1	1	10?	5.68	5.87

Note: Table based on Brewer (1994, 1995:14).

Table 5.2. Plants identified among the Pevey samples

Common Name	Taxonomic Name	Item Name
Corn kernel	*Zea mays*	Kernel
Corn cupule	*Zea mays*	Cupule
Corn stalk	*Zea mays*	Corn stalk
Chenopod	*Chenopodium berlandieri*	Seed
Sunflower	*Helianthus annuus*	Seed
Sumpweed	*Iva annua*	Seed
Amaranth	*Amaranthus* sp.	Seed
Little barley	*Hordeum pusillum*	Seed
Maygrass	*Phalaris caroliniana*	Seed
Acorn	*Quercus* sp.	Nutshell
Acorn meat	*Quercus* sp.	Nut meat
Hickory	*Carya* sp.	Nutshell
Elderberry	*Sambucus* sp.	Seed
Fruit seed		Seed
Grape	*Vitis* sp.	Seed
Persimmon	*Diospyros virginiana*	Seed
Sumac	*Rhus* sp.	Seed
Bulrush	*Scirpus* sp.	Seed
Carpetweed	*Mollugo* sp.	Seed
Digitaria cf.	*Digitaria* sp.	Seed
Smartweed	*Polygonum* cf. *pensylvanicum*	Seed
Cane	*Arundinaria* sp.	Cane
Pine cone	*Pinus* sp.	Cone
Unidentifiable		Seed

Note: Reproduced from Brewer (1995:17).

but it was too fragmentary to evaluate whether its overall size was large enough to be considered a domesticate. Two partial halves of a single sunflower achene were found in the Mound G, Level 9 sample. Based on the size of the achene, it appears to be domesticated (Brewer 1995:20). Chenopod was recovered in 6 of the 13 samples, with the largest concentration from the Mound G, Level 9 hearth (Brewer 1995:19–21). Amaranth was recovered in small quantities from two locations. Little barley was found in two hearths: Mound C, Level 12 and Mound G, Level 9. Maygrass was found in small quantities in 5 of the 13 samples. Interestingly, these are the same five samples in which the majority of the maize was found. Brewer (1995:23) suggests there may be an interesting relationship between the production or consumption of maize and maygrass (Brewer 1995:21–23).

Table 5.3. Raw taxa counts from Pevey samples

Plant Taxa	C.L12	E.L3	E.L8e	G.L9	G.L9a	H.L6	H2.L1	I.L7	I.L9	M.L1	T.L1	T.L2	T2.L1	Lw511 F4
Corn kernel	0	0	0	2	2	5	15	16	10	3	23	10	17	6
Corn cupule	7	4	0	0	14	10	12	1,259	114	4	3	415	251	1
Corn stalk	0	0	0	0	0	0	0	544	0	0	0	0	0	0
Chenopod	0	0	0	5	1	0	0	1	2	1	0	1	0	0
Sumpweed	0	0	0	0	0	0	1	0	0	0	0	0	0	0
Sunflower	0	0	1	0	1	0	0	0	0	0	0	0	0	0
Amaranth	0	0	0	1	1	0	0	0	0	0	0	0	0	0
Little barley	2	0	0	1	0	0	0	0	0	0	0	0	0	0
Maygrass	0	0	0	0	0	0	0	10	1	0	1	2	1	0
Acorn	0	0	1	17	11	1,191	5	0	25	3	10	1	1	0
Acorn meat	0	0	0	0	0	7	0	0	0	0	0	0	0	0
Hickory	5	0	0	4	1	81	33	5	3	1	16	4	4	17
Elderberry	0	0	1	0	0	0	0	0	0	0	0	0	0	0
Fruit seed	0	0	0	0	0	0	0	1	1	0	0	0	0	0
Grape	0	0	0	0	0	0	0	1	0	0	0	0	0	0
Persimmon	0	0	0	0	0	0	0	0	2	0	0	0	0	0
Bulrush	0	0	0	0	0	0	1	0	0	0	0	0	0	0
Carpetweed	0	0	0	5	0	1	0	0	0	0	0	0	0	0
Digitaria cf.	91	0	88	3	0	0	0	0	0	0	0	0	0	0
Smartweed	0	0	1	0	0	0	0	0	0	0	0	0	0	0
Sumac	0	0	0	1	0	0	0	0	0	0	0	3	0	0
Pine cone	0	0	0	0	0	0	0	0	0	0	5	0	0	0
Cane	0	0	0	3	2	136	0	0	21	0	1	0	0	3
Unidentified	8	0	7	3	1	8	9	0	3	1	5	2	0	8

Note: Adapted from Brewer (1995:18) and Brewer (1994).

Interestingly, seeds from *Digitaria* cf. were unusually abundant at the Pevey site. They represent 5 percent of the total food remains, which is more than all the other starch seeds combined. Brewer (1995:24) notes that *Digitaria*, sometimes called "hungry rice," is not frequently recovered archaeologically in the Southeast, and its abundance suggests it may have been used for food. It also could have had a nonsubsistence use such as bedding, thatch, or fuel (Brewer 1995:23–24).

Nuts appear to be the second most important food for the Pevey residents. Nutshell represents 37 percent of the plant remains. Acorn represents 33 percent of the food total while hickory is 4 percent of the total (based on counts). Since hickory shell is more likely to be preserved than acorn, it has been suggested (Lopinot 1982; Yarnell and Black 1985) to multiply the acorn shell weight by 50 in order to approximate the actual percent of acorn relative to hickory. If this were done in the Pevey sample, acorn would outweigh hickory by 400 g to 4 g, meaning it is 100 times more important (Brewer 1995:25–26). Acorns are high in carbohydrates, fat, and calories but, when compared to other significant food sources utilized by maize agriculturalists, it is not especially productive or nutritious. As a nut, hickory is a much more efficient source of calories and nutrients, primarily because it contains twice as much fat by weight as acorns and because it contains more of 9 out of 10 essential amino acids (Gardner 1997; Smith 1978b). It is likely acorns would only have been exploited when hickory was not available. Lysine is the only amino acid that acorns have in more abundance than maize. Since maize is particularly deficient in lysine, a combined diet of acorns and maize would have helped the Pevey residents obtain a more complete plant protein (Gardner 1997; Petruso and Wickens 1984).

In an analysis of a single sample from Lowe-Steen Feature 4, Brewer (1994) found that hickory nutshell was the most abundant plant type in the sample at 79 percent. Maize kernel fragments, a cupule, and a glume represented 21 percent of the sample. The eight other seeds in the sample could not be identified.

Scarry and Steponaitis (1997) demonstrated that the ratios of nutshells and cupules, which represent food processing, to kernels, which represent food consumption and cooking, can be useful tools for understanding the food-related activities at a location (see also Scarry 2003a). They found that Moundville farmsteads had higher levels of processing debris than mound centers or elite residences but that the number of consumables remained about the same. Table 5.4 shows the counts of maize cupules and kernels for the samples, sorted by the ratio between the two. Interestingly, the Unit T, Level 2 and the Unit T2, Level 1 samples contained high amounts of cupules and the Unit T, Level 1 sample contained high numbers of kernels (Brewer

Table 5.4. Kernel and cupule counts for the samples, sorted by ratio of kernels to cupules

Unit/Provenience	Maize Kernel	Maize Cupule	Kernel to Cupule Ratio
G.L9	2	0	N/A
T.L1	23	3	7.67
Lw511 F4	6	1	6.00
H2.L1	15	12	1.25
M.L1	3	4	.75
H.L6	5	10	.50
G.L9a	2	14	.14
I.L9	10	114	.09
T2.L1	17	251	.07
T.L2	10	415	.02
I.L7	16	1,259	.01
C.L12	0	7	.00
E.L3	0	4	.00

1995:18). These findings indicate this might have been the location of maize processing. Table 5.5 shows the counts for hickory and corn cupules, sorted by that ratio. This table indicates nut processing might have been more significant than maize processing at Unit H and at Feature 4 at Lowe-Steen. Hickory was also more abundant than corn cupules in Unit T, Level 1 and in Unit G, Level 9a but not in other proveniences from those units. All of the other contexts show evidence of a bias toward maize processing.

Brewer (1995) contrasted the Pevey plant remains with plant remains from the Moundville I phase samples from Moundville (Scarry 1986), the Summerville I and Summerville II/III phase samples from Lubbub Creek (Blitz 1993a; Caddell 1983), and the Old Hoover mound and village sites (Lorenz 1992). In addition, results were compared to findings from the Routh phase at Hedgeland (Roberts 2004) and Mounds A and C at Bottle Creek (Scarry 2003a, 2003b). These Bottle Creek samples were selected because they appear to primarily date to the Bottle Creek I phase, although they also date to earlier and later phases (Table 5.6; see Chapter 7 for a map showing these sites).

Brewer (1995:33) and Caddell (1983) note that 96 percent of the Summerville II/III plant remains are maize, but this number is unduly influenced by a single one of the 31 samples. This one feature contained over 22,000 maize

Table 5.5. Corn cupule and hickory counts for the samples, sorted by ratio of cupules to hickory

Unit/Provenience	Maize Cupule	Hickory	Ratio of Cupules to Hickory
G.L9	0	4	.00
Lw511 F4	1	17	.06
H.L6	10	81	.12
T.L1	3	16	.19
H2.L1	12	33	.36
C.L12	7	5	1.40
M.L1	4	1	4.00
G.L9a	14	1	14.00
I.L9	114	3	38.00
T2.L1	251	4	62.75
T.L2	415	4	103.75
I.L7	1,259	5	251.80
E.L3	4	0	N/A

remains, of which most were kernels. If this sample were removed from consideration, nutshells would outnumber maize fragments by a 7:1 ratio. This result would be more similar to the Old Hoover assemblage, which Brewer (1995:32) suggests is suspiciously low and may not be as reliable since it is based on only three flotation samples. Lorenz (1992) argues that the Old Hoover polity was located on marginal soils and was less politically complex and had fewer regional connections than most other contemporary polities. Its residents may have intentionally chosen a more reliable subsistence pattern that relied on nuts and other seedy plants, a pattern that was typical before the Mississippi period (Yarnell and Black 1985:97). Bottle Creek also has an unusually high percentage of maize. This is related to a pair of midden samples from Mound C that have an anomalously high amount of maize when compared with the other samples from the site.

With these caveats in mind, it is clear that the Pevey site is fairly typical when compared with most of its neighbors: 57 percent of the food remains at Pevey were maize, compared with 66 percent at the Summerville I phase Lubbub Creek site, 45 percent at Moundville I, and 41 percent at Hedgeland. When comparing the ratio of cupules to kernels, it appears that Pevey looks similar to Lubbub Creek and Hedgeland in having a higher ratio of cupules to kernels. This likely indicates that primary processing was taking place at these locations. In contrast, the Moundville and Bottle Creek samples in-

Table 5.6. Percentages of plant food taxa from Pevey and other sites

Common Name	Pevey (n = 13)	Old Hoover (n = 3)	Summerville I (n = 44)	Summerville II/III (n = 37)	Moundville I (n = 32)	Hedgeland (n = 2)	Bottle Creek (n = 20)
Corn kernel	3	8	4	83	27	14	61
Corn cupule	54	8	62	13	18	28	35
Corn totals	57	16	66	96	45	41	95
Bean	0	<1	<1	<1	1	0	0
Chenopod	<1	0	0	0	2	1	<1
Sunflower	<1	1	3	0	0	1	0
Amaranth	<1	0	0	<1	<1	1	0
Domesticate totals	0	1	3	0	3	4	<1
Knotweed	0	1	0	0	<1	0	<1
Little barley	<1	2	0	0	0	0	<1
Maygrass	<1	<1	<1	<1	1	0	<1
Cultigen totals	<1	3	<1	<1	1	0	<1
Acorn	33	1	3	<1	33	49	2
Black walnut	0	5	0	0	<1	0	0
Hickory	4	55	21	4	9	1	<1
Pecan	0	18	0	0	0	0	0
Juglandaceae	0	0	0	0	0	1	0
Nut totals	37	79	24	4	42	51	3
Persimmon	<1	0	3	<1	5	<1	<1

Continued on the next page

Table 5.6. Continued

Common Name	Pevey (n = 13)	Old Hoover (n = 3)	Summerville I (n = 44)	Summerville II/III (n = 37)	Moundville I (n = 32)	Hedgeland (n = 2)	Bottle Creek (n = 20)
Fruit totals	0	0	3	0	5	1	<1
Digitaria cf.	5	0	0	0	0	0	0
Pokeweed	0	0	0	0	1	0	0
Poacea	0	0	2	<1	0	0	0
Grass family	0	0	0	0	1	4	0
Miscellaneous totals	5	0	2	0	2	4	2

Note: Table from Brewer (1995:32).

dicate corn was being provided to the mounds in an already processed form (Scarry 2003a, 2003b; Scarry and Steponaitis 1997).

At Pevey, nuts were second in importance to maize. This is also true at Moundville, Lubbub Creek during Summerville I, and Bottle Creek. However, at Old Hoover, Lubbub Creek during Summerville II/III (assuming the anomalous feature is ignored), and Hedgeland nuts appear to be the primary food source (Brewer 1995:35–36). Domesticates and cultigens such as amaranth, chenopod, knotweed, little barley, and sunflower played a small role at all of these sites. Collectively they made up no more than 4 percent of the samples. Persimmon was the only fruit with significant abundance at any of the sites. It represented 3 percent of the Summerville I and 5 percent of the Moundville samples.

Faunal Remains

Animal bone and mussel shell were found in some proveniences at Lowe-Steen and Pevey. The faunal remains from Units E and M were analyzed by Simone Rowe, and the data and results are presented in Appendix 2. Rowe examined these remains for evidence of elite faunal exploitation such as (1) a diverse sample of birds, (2) the presence or rate of unusual prey, (3) evidence of feasting, and (4) evidence of provisioning. Rowe finds little evidence in any of these categories for elite faunal exploitation. Interestingly, she does find evidence for bone grease processing at Unit E, which she argues is consistent with scarcity in food supply. Given that much of the E assemblage dates to the terminal Winstead phase, this would suggest that the final residents at Pevey were experiencing food scarcity.

Lithic Analysis

All analyzed lithics were recorded individually with a minimum of five attributes: weight, size category, material, amount of cortex, and lithic type (form and attributes adapted from Byram 1996). All lithic types were determined from a sorting tree (Figure 5.1) adapted from work by Andrefsky (1998:Figures 4.7 and V.1; Andrefsky et al. 1994:101). This sorting tree categorized all lithic types into 14 categories using simple binary decisions. This was an excellent tool for sorting a large number of lithics in a consistent manner with the assistance of several dedicated but inexperienced student analysts.

The sorting tree (Figure 5.1) first has analysts separate ground stone, unmodified stone, and chipped stone. Ground stone was weighed, coded as "other," and set aside for further analysis. Unmodified stone was discarded. Chipped stone was sorted into one of 12 categories. The first means of sorting chipped stone was to separate objective pieces, or pieces with evidence of modification, from debitage. Objective pieces are classified as tools in

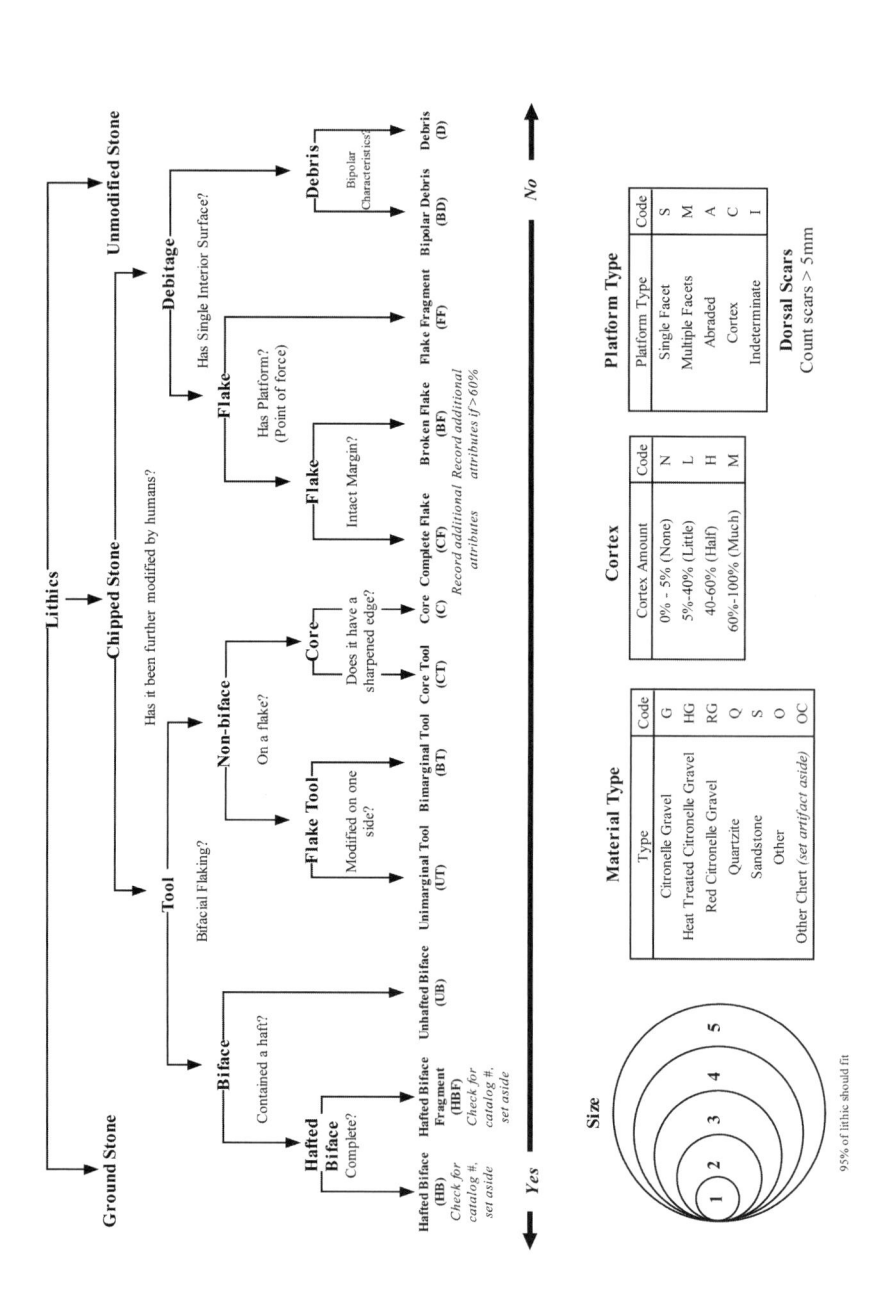

Figure 5.1. The flow chart used for sorting and analyzing lithics.

this nomenclature. Debitage with a single smooth ventral surface is called a flake. Flakes with intact margins and platforms are coded as complete flakes, flakes with intact platforms but incomplete margins are broken flakes, and flakes without a platform are flake fragments. Nonflake debitage is categorized as bipolar debris or debris based on the presence or absence of bipolar characteristics. Tools are first sorted into bifaces and nonbifaces. Nonbifaces that are on a flake are sorted into unimarginal or bimarginal tools based on the presence of modifications on one face or two. Nonbifaces that are not flakes are coded as cores and are called core tools if there is flaked edge. Bifaces are sorted into unhafted bifaces, hafted biface fragments, and hafted bifaces based on the presence of a haft. All hafted bifaces and hafted biface fragments were set aside for further analysis and are discussed below.

A total of 13,801 lithic pieces were analyzed in this study. Some lithics from proveniences with low research potential were not analyzed. This included some proveniences in Survey Block 6 that were pre-Mississippian sites in the vicinity of the Phillips Farm site and it also included the Phillips Farm site, which had 12,604 lithic pieces from several different time periods.

The most common lithic material is Citronelle gravel. This comes from the Citronelle Formation, a band of secondarily deposited gravels extending from Illinois to Texas and Florida (Stallings 1989:38). In Mississippi, sources of this material are found in the Loess Bluffs and along the Gulf Coast as far north as Jackson (Stallings 1989:38). This formation provides chert, quartzite, and sandstone pebbles and cobbles ranging in size from a few millimeters to several centimeters in gravel bars within streams and in numerous gravel quarries (Stallings 1989:38). Cortex is found on all of the chert and quartz and may be up to 6 mm thick on chert samples (Stallings 1989:41). The most common interior colors are tans, browns, yellows, and grays, but red and olive hues have also been noted (Stallings 1989:48). When heat treated, Citronelle gravel turns red or pink and may occasionally have some purple (Collins 1984; Stallings 1989:49). The presence of natural red coloration makes it very difficult to determine precisely the frequency of heat treating. For this reason, all Citronelle gravel with clear incidences of heat treating such as pot-lid fractures were coded together. All red-colored Citronelle gravel lacking obvious morphological signs of heat treating were coded separately from the rest of the Citronelle gravel. Some percentage of this red gravel was likely heat treated and some percentage is just naturally red.

Only one piece of nonlocal chert has been documented at Pevey, and it is represented by a complete flake from Unit H. Three pieces of nonlocal chert have been documented from Lowe-Steen in the form of two flake fragments and a unimarginal tool. These nonlocal cherts may have been ob-

118   Chapter 5

Table 5.7. Counts of lithic types from the Pevey and Lowe-Steen sites classified by debitage, tool, or other

Site	Unit	Debitage	Tool	Other	Total Lithics	Percentage of Tools
22Lw510	B	27	4		31	12.90
22Lw510	C	151	17		168	10.12
22Lw510	E	116	16		132	12.12
22Lw510	G	612	47	1	660	7.12
22Lw510	H	433	53	1	487	10.88
22Lw510	I	214	11		225	4.89
22Lw510	J	23	5		28	17.86
22Lw510	K	304	28		332	8.43
22Lw510	M	225	41		266	15.41
22Lw510	SE	95	9		104	8.65
22Lw510	SJ	244	24		268	8.96
22Lw510	T	130	29		159	18.24
22Lw511	1136R876	306	18		324	5.56
22Lw511	956R1003	139	24		163	14.72
22Lw511	975R1007	147	12		159	7.55
22Lw511	Feature 4	2,249	67	2	2,318*	2.89
Total		5,415	405	4	5,824	6.95

*Due to time constraints, 1,812 lithics from Feature 4 were not analyzed and are not included in this total.

tained through Mississippi period exchange, but it is also possible they were transported to the region by earlier Archaic or Woodland period residents and collected by Mississippians.

Analysis of lithics from the Pevey site is discussed below. Presentation of data from the analysis of lithics from the other contexts can be found elsewhere (Livingood 2006). Table 5.7 reports the counts of lithics from Pevey classified by the first level of sorting used in the analysis and reports the percentage of lithics from each unit that were classified as tools. Table 5.8 shows the highest level of classification. At the Pevey site, Unit I is remarkable for having a very high ratio of debitage to tools. The majority of this debitage is flakes and this likely indicates tool production or tool sharpening was occurring there. Interestingly, the high ratio of debitage to tools holds for analytical units 1 (2 percent tools) and 3 (3 percent tools) in Excavation Unit I but not as strongly for analytical unit 2 (12 percent tools). On the other extreme, Units J, M, and T are remarkable for a high ratio of tools to debitage.

Table 5.8. Totals of analyzed lithic types by excavation unit for the Pevey site

Unit	BD	BF	BT	C	CF	CT	D	FF	HB	HBF	UB	UT	Other	Total
B		3		2	13		1	10				2		31
C		26		10	71		11	43	1	1	1	4		168
E	1	11		10	38	1	8	58			1	4		132
G	1	137		27	282	1	17	175	3		12	4	1	660
H	2	55	2	31	206	3	18	152	1	1	8	7	1	487
I		29		5	82	1	19	84	1	1	3			225
J		7		5	7		1	8						28
K	1	58		13	139	2	7	99	1	1	5	6		332
M		38		26	76	2	11	100			3	10		266
SE		14		7	42	1	15	24				1		104
SJ		43	3	8	122	1	2	77	1	3	4	4		268
T		16	1	14	44	3	6	64		4	1	6		159
Total	5	437	6	158	1,122	15	116	894	8	11	38	48	2	2,860

Note: Tool codes are those in Figure 5.1.

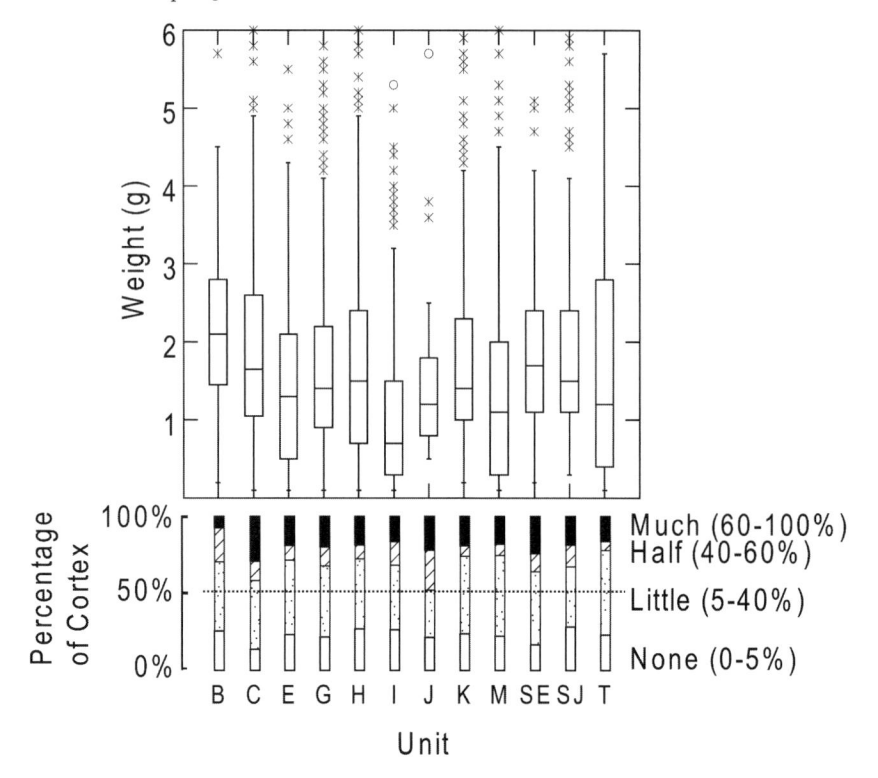

Figure 5.2. Plot of debitage from the Pevey units. The top part of the figure is a box-and-whisker plot of debitage weight. The scale is artificially truncated at 6 g in order to better show the median and quartiles. The bottom graph shows the relative percent of different cortex amounts. For example, Unit J shows approximately equal proportions of debitage with no cortex, little cortex, half cortex, or much cortex.

Unit J is suspect since the sample size of 28 lithics is so small. However, Units M and T both have significant numbers of tools and they are present at a high level in every analytical unit for which there are a respectable number of lithics (n > 7). Coupled with the unusual ceramic assemblages and the unusual kernel to cupule ratio at Unit T, it is clear these non-mound excavation blocks were the location of some atypical activities at the site.

Figure 5.2 shows the weight and cortex characteristics of the debitage from the Pevey site. The graphs show that Units T and M, which were primarily midden contexts, have very few pieces of debitage with extensive cortex coverage. This could suggest that larger cobbles were being utilized, but since there is little reason for differential selection of cobble size by mound, it is more likely that a greater amount of late-stage reductions was taking place. However, since the number of dorsal scars is relatively low and the platform thicknesses are relatively high, this suggests large expedient flakes were being made at these units. Therefore, it appears that a significant number of formal and expedient tools were being used for the activities at Units T and M. Other units with unusual debitage profiles are B and J. Unit B has especially heavy lithics with much higher than average numbers of dorsal scars that suggest tool manufacturing. The debitage from J has more cortex and fewer dorsal scars than average, suggesting the early reduction of stone cobbles. These assemblages suggest that outlying areas were more involved in basic tool production than the mound area. However, Units J and B are both shallow units. The majority of excavated soil was plow zone, so it is possible that the lithics from these units are from non-Winstead phases. The rest of the mound contexts appear to have roughly similar-looking lithic assemblages.

Only two drills were found at the Pevey site. One was found in Mound G, analytical unit 2 and the other in Mound I, analytical unit 3. Sandstone was extremely common at the site and the environs and may have been used as abraders, but there were no examples of microdrills or other debris commonly associated with craft production. One likely hammerstone was recorded from Unit H, analytical unit 2. Another small ground stone object was found in the mound fill of Unit G.

All projectile points were sorted according to McGahey's *Mississippi Projectile Point Guide* (2000). There were 11 identifiable hafted bifaces recovered from the Pevey site, and they date to either the Woodland or the Late Archaic (Livingood 2006). The only arrowheads that might date to the Mississippi period that were recovered during the survey and excavations were a Collins and a Scallorn point from 22Lw660. Pevey residents were likely following a pattern common to the Plaquemine in which very few formal lithic arrow points were produced. These prehistoric hunters and warriors likely used expedient flakes, cane, bone, or gar scales, all of which were noted by European explorers (Swanton 1949:571–582). There may have been some form of functional typology, such as the one recorded for the historic Natchez, whereby cane was used for hunting birds and small fish, bone for large mammals and large fish, and gar scales for war (Swanton 1911:58–59).

Hematite

Hematite is a locally available mineral that may have been ground to use as a pigment. It is found in many of the units. In addition, red ochre was found at the base of Unit C and would have been used as a pigment.

Mica

Two sheets of mica measuring approximately 4 × 3 cm and 2.5 × 1.5 cm were recovered from Feature 4 at Lowe-Steen. In addition, small fragments of mica were found in the flotation sample (Brewer 1994), possibly indicating

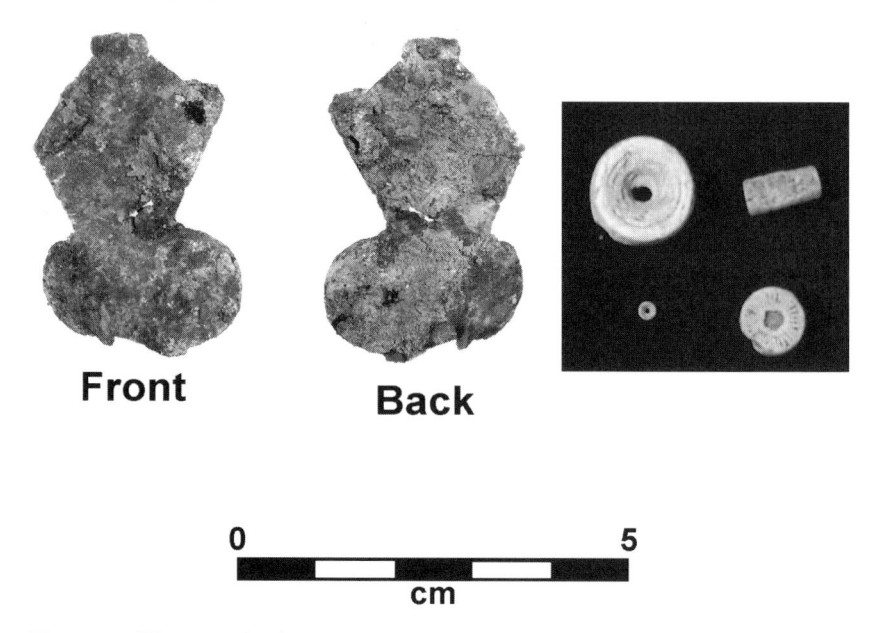

Figure 5.3. Photograph of copper foil and beads and crinoid stems from Pevey. The copper foil, from Unit M, is in the shape of a bilobed arrow or mace/baton ornament. The upper left bead is a crinoid bead from Unit G. The others are from Unit H.

postdepositional damage or that mica was being worked at this location for use in ornaments or paint.

Copper

A single fragment of copper foil was found in analytical unit 2 of Unit M (Figure 5.3). The piece appears to be a fragment of a bilobed arrow but could also be a mace or baton. In either case, this is one of the only artifacts that depicts an object from the corpus of images traditionally glossed as the Southeastern Ceremonial Complex (King 2007; Knight 2006; Knight et al. 2001; Reilly and Garber 2007). Copper artifacts are fairly rare in the Lower Mississippi Valley (Goodman 1984), but in the study area they have been found at the Pocahontas sites, Lubbub Creek, and most extensively at Moundville (Blitz 1993a; Goodman 1984; Steponaitis 1991). The ultimate source for the copper was likely the southern Appalachians, but it could have come from the Great Lakes (Goad 1978). There is no way to determine whether the Pevey community received the copper as a finished ornament or whether they created it themselves.

The bilobed arrow was emblematic of the Mississippi period and was especially common around the thirteenth century (Muller 2007:22). The image has been identified as representing "a conventionalized bow and arrow composite that operates as an instrument of soul flight, by which the bearer magically projects soul essence into the upper world" (Knight et al. 2001:137), as well as an atlatl and a sexual reference (Muller 2007:22). It is also highly associated with the Birdman imagery (J. Brown 2007:100). Maces or batons are associated with the Mississippian corpus related to war (Dye 2007:155) but also can be found in the ritual objects associated with Birdman (J. Brown 2007:86).

Beads

Three fossil beads were found in Unit H, analytical unit 2. Crinoid-stem beads were found in Unit C, analytical unit 6 and Unit G, analytical unit 7 (Figure 5.3) that may have been used by the Pevey residents or may represent accidental fossil inclusions.

Summary

Analysis of the paleobotanical remains from Pevey and Lowe-Steen included contrasting the findings with remains at other nearby contemporaneous sites. The samples show that maize was the most significant plant food and that it was found in abundances similar to those of Lubbub Creek, Moundville, and Hedgeland. The second most significant plant food was acorns, similar in abundance to those at Moundville and Hedgeland. The distribution data and comparison of maize kernel to cupule ratios indicate that maize processing may have been performed at Mound I and the Unit T terrace but that there is little evidence for extensive provisioning at any of the mound areas. The faunal analysis of areas M and E further supports this interpretation and also suggests that the Winstead phase residents of Pevey may have been stressed and were resorting to bone grease processing.

An examination of the lithics shows that three units in particular stand out for unusual assemblage characteristics. Unit I has a very high number of flakes compared with tools, whereas Units T and M have large numbers of tools and late-stage reduction flakes.

An inventory of extralocal artifacts from Pevey and Lowe-Steen includes one piece of nonlocal chert from Pevey and three from Lowe-Steen, one piece of copper foil in the shape of a bilobed arrow or mace from Pevey, and two mica sheets from Lowe-Steen. These were all likely obtained from their neighbors through a process of exchange.

6
Interpretations of the Middle Pearl Mississippian

With the archaeological and survey data that we have available for the Pevey site, covered in the preceding four chapters, we can now review these findings paying special attention to the elements of data that are needed to make regional comparisons. An analysis of interpolity interactions in the study area follows this review and uses these data to propose a geographic limit at which large polities could influence smaller ones. This chapter will also examine whether these data support the Choctaw Genesis hypothesis.

Pevey Site Interpretations

The mounds at Pevey are arranged in two parallel rows. It is possible that the residents of Pevey might have conceptualized the mounds as pairs and that the physical arrangement of the mounds at Pevey might be indicative of the way the community determined social divisions. The mound pairs at Pevey might be E/G, D/H, C/I, B/K, and A?/J. (As discussed in Chapter 2, there is currently no evidence of a Mound A at the location designated by Baxter Mann. However, based on the symmetry of the site, it is certainly possible that a mound may have been located in that vicinity and is no longer visible today because of modern alterations to the area.) Mound pairs have been best documented at Moundville, where there were sets of mortuary and residential mounds, with each pair representative of a different clan or lineage (Knight 1998; Peebles 1971, 1983). Unfortunately, there are not enough data to sufficiently test this hypothesis for Pevey. There are no clear assemblage differences between the mounds of the northern row (A?, B, C, D, and E) and the mounds of the southern row (J, K, I, H, and G) or between alternating sets of mounds.

There are some mounds at Pevey with distinctive archaeological evidence. Unit E appears to be a midden associated with Mound E. Together with

Unit SE from the summit of Mound E, the assemblage has a high proportion of serving vessels, which would be consistent with an elite household as well as other public ceremonial functions, but if this were an elite household there is no evidence of provisioning in the botanical or faunal remains. There is also no evidence of central storage in or around Mound E, as is common with some chiefly residences. However, given the small scale of excavations compared to the size of the mound such absence is interpretively negligible. The other off-mound contexts near Mound E were distinctive and significantly different from the mound contexts. For example, Unit M, an off-mound unit near Mound E, contained a large and diverse assemblage of ceramics. It also contained a single piece of copper foil in the shape of a bilobed arrow or mace. Unit T, on the terrace to the east of Mound E, contained an abundance of maize and skewed corn cupule to kernel ratios, suggesting maize processing. There were also a limited number of decorated sherds and a high percentage of lithic tools. This evidence indicates the Unit T area was being used for events in which feasting took place.

The mounds in the eastern half of the site have more exotic assemblages than those in the western half. Beads were recovered from Units C, G, and H. Mound G had the most exotic ceramics, including a Moundville Incised, *var. Moundville* vessel that is a likely candidate to have been imported, as well as a Carter Engraved, *var. Shell Bluff* vessel that is a paragon of fine ceramic manufacture. In contrast, the mounds in the westernmost part of the site have fewer exotic artifacts. Mounds B and I have the smallest percentage of decorated sherds. Also, Mound I has ethnobotanical evidence indicating a whole maize plant was burned there either for use in a smudge pit or in maize processing. These artifacts confirm that the larger mounds and the spaces around them were host to more high-status activities and public/ceremonial roles. Collectively, these data indicate degrees of internal ranking existed within the Pevey community.

Architectural Evidence

In an analysis of Plaquemine architecture Brown (1985a) discussed five types of structures. There are circular wall-trench structures, circular structures with individually set posts, rectangular wall-trench structures, rectangular structures with individually set posts, and rectangular structures combining wall trenches and individually set posts (Brown 1985a:273–276). Brown noted distinct spatial and temporal patterns to these architectural styles. Circular wall-trench construction was used in the southern Plaquemine region, primarily during the late Coles Creek period. Circular individually set post construction was used in the transition between Coles Creek and Plaquemine in the southern part of the Plaquemine area. Rectangular wall-trench structures

Table 6.1. Summary of architectural patterns found in excavation

Site	Provenience	Architecture
22Lw510	G, analytical unit 7	Two linear trenches, one with postholes.
22Lw510	H, analytical unit 6	Linear trench with postholes.
22Lw510	SJ, analytical unit 2	Few postholes, uncertain patterning.
22Lw510	M, analytical unit 4	Rectangular wall trench with postholes.
22Lw510	SE, analytical unit 6	Linear wall trench with postholes.
22Lw510	SE, analytical unit 7	Trenches, some with postholes. Some postholes without trenches.
22Lw510	T, analytical unit 3	Postholes with uncertain patterning.
22Lw511	1136R876	Numerous posthole features, uncertain patterning.
22Lw593	Structure 1	Postholes without trenches for circular or rectangular structure.

began to be used in the Anna and Winterville phases and were constructed up until the historic period. Rectangular individually set post architecture was primarily used in the Lower Yazoo but was also found in the Natchez Bluffs during later phases. Finally, rectangular structures that combine parallel walls of wall trenches and individually set posts are rare and were only documented at Winterville, Lake George, and Fatherland (Brown 1985a: 276–279).

Individual 2-×-2-m excavation units are excellent for understanding chronology in an efficient manner, but they are not well suited for studying architecture, as they provide only small windows on architectural patterns. Table 6.1 provides a summary of the architectural evidence from Pevey and Lowe-Steen. Unit M intersected the corner of a rectangular wall-trench structure, and it was the only unit to have enough evidence to definitively place a structure in one of Brown's architectural categories. Several other units, including G, H, and SE, had patterning consistent with a rectangular wall-trench structure. Units G and SE also had lines of postholes not associated with a wall trench. Other units had postholes arranged in unknown patterns, and there is not even enough evidence to indicate whether those postholes formed walls or whether they served another purpose. In sum, the evidence suggests that rectangular wall-trench structures were the preferred pattern but that rectangular structures with individually set posts may also have been used.

The Phillips Farm structure employed individually set posts, but it is not clear whether they were used for a circular or a rectangular structure. Since the ceramics do not provide a good means of assessing the date of the site, the architecture may provide some clues. If we extrapolate Brown's chronology to the Pearl River, a circular structure would suggest a pre-Winstead or early Winstead date. A rectangular structure could indicate a range of dates from a pre-Winstead period to the historic. Given the single radiocarbon date from Phillips Farm and the relative proximity of the site to the Natchez region, a rectangular structure seems most likely and would be consistent with these other data.

Chronology

The ceramics data indicate that the occupations at both Pevey and Lowe-Steen can be classified as belonging to a single phase. This phase has been designated the Winstead phase (Livingood 1999) and, based on ceramic similarities, is largely contemporary with the Anna phase in the Natchez Bluffs or the Winterville phase in the Lower Yazoo. Using the temporal phase assignments established for the ceramics from outside the Pearl River drainage, the Pevey and Lowe-Steen sites have a few ceramics that are possibly indictive of a pre-Winstead occupation. These sherds include Avoyelles Punctated, *var. Dupree,* Coles Creek Incised, *var. Hardy,* Coles Creek Incised, *var. unspecified,* Evansville Punctated, *var. Sharkey,* and Harrison Bayou Incised, *var. Harrison Bayou.* None of these sherds were recovered from intact archaeological deposits, which suggests that there was a pre–Winstead phase occupation that was disturbed by Winstead phase earth-moving activities or that these are transitional forms made during the early Winstead phase occupation. There are also several sherds from the Pevey site that may indicate a post–Winstead phase occupation. These include Barton Incised, *var. Midnight,* Fatherland Incised, *var. Pine Ridge,* Leland Incised, *var. Foster,* Leland Incised, *var. Leland,* Maddox Engraved, *var. Silver City,* and Owens Punctated, *var. Poor Joe.* These were found in terminal deposits from Units E, SE, and M. However, there are only 14 of these sherds, and they were all found in contexts with sherds that primarily suggest Winstead phase occupation. Therefore, they seem to represent transitional ceramic forms made during the end of the Winstead phase rather than an identifiable second phase of settlement. If later work confirms there was a discontinuity in site occupation, it might be appropriate to use the label Pevey phase, suggested previously (Livingood 1999), to categorize the latest occupation. However, at the moment there is little evidence of discontinuity and for purposes of labeling and classification it seems preferable to think of the Pevey site as a single-phase occupation. The Lowe-Steen site completely lacks these late Winstead phase ceramics, suggesting it was abandoned before the Pevey

128   Chapter 6

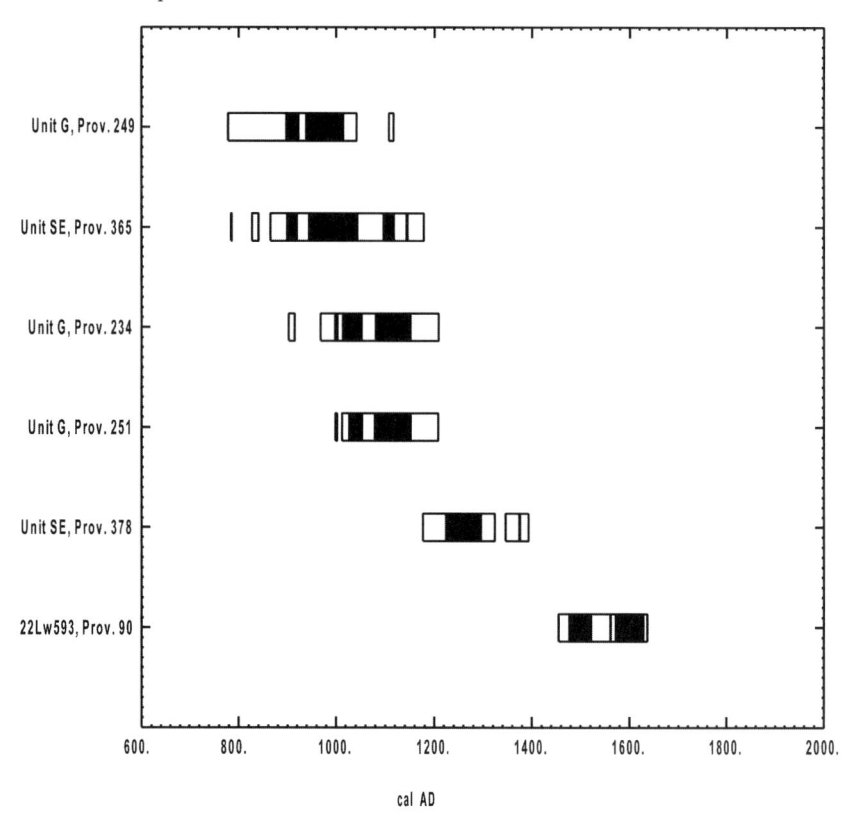

Figure 6.1. Box plots produced with Calib 5.0.2 showing the calibrated date ranges of the samples. The black bars represent 1-sigma ranges and the white bars represent 2-sigma ranges.

site. The Phillips Farm site had only one identifiable ceramic, a Plaquemine Brushed, *var. Plaquemine* sherd, which is consistent with a Winstead phase date but could also date to an earlier or later phase.

Six radiocarbon samples were tested (Figure 6.1). Two samples originated from the Mound E summit in Unit SE at the Pevey site, three from the base of Mound G at the Pevey site, and one from Feature 5 at the Phillips Farm site. The expectation was that the Mound G samples would provide an early date for the site and the Mound E samples would provide a terminal date. Table 6.2 presents the date information. Calibrations were done with Calib 5.0.2 (Stuiver et al. 2005) using the IntCal04 calibration tables (Reimer et al. 2004). All the Mound G dates produced uncalibrated radiocarbon dates between 950 and 1080 b.p. If we pool the probabilities of the Mound G samples, this provides 1-sigma calibrated date ranges of a.d. 993–1043, 1105–1118, or

1114–1146. One of the Mound E samples has an unexpectedly early date that is comparable to the Mound G dates (Figure 6.1). The other has a date with a 1-sigma range of A.D. 1222–1298 or 1372–1378, with the first range as the more probable.

Five radiocarbon dates with these age ranges leave a lot of room for interpretation. They are also challenging to compare directly with older calibrated dates because the 1998 (Stuiver et al. 1998) and 2004 (Reimer et al. 2004) radiocarbon calibrations occasionally provide significantly different results than earlier calibration tables. The structures at the base of Mound G are the most securely dated since there are three samples with tightly clustered dates. However, the radiocarbon data provide no information about when most of the mound construction was conducted, and a single terminal radiocarbon date provides a great deal of latitude for interpretation. Based on the radiocarbon dates alone the most probable date for the site would be A.D. 1025–1275. However, when the radiocarbon dates, the ceramic evidence, the architectural evidence, and the dates from sites in other regions are considered together, the best estimate for the Winstead phase is A.D. 1100–1350. These dates would indicate that the Winstead phase overlaps with the Anna phase to the east, Moundville I and the early part of Moundville II at Moundville, and Summerville I and Summerville II/III at Lubbub Creek.

There is a single date from the Phillips Farm site that has a 1-sigma date range of A.D. 1475–1631. As single radiocarbon dates often do, this date creates more questions than it answers. It is clearly far outside the range of the Winstead phase and would seem to suggest that the Phillips Farm site is a post–Winstead phase site. The lone diagnostic ceramic from the Phillips Farm site, a Plaquemine Brushed, *var. Plaquemine* sherd, is generally thought to date to the Gordon (A.D. 1000–1200), Anna (A.D. 1200–1350), or Foster phase (A.D. 1350–1500) in the Natchez Bluffs (Brown 1998:63). The overlap would suggest a ca. A.D. 1500 date. Unfortunately, with only a single radiocarbon date, it is impossible to confirm whether the date is reliable. There is also no way to know whether the Feature 5 context from which the radiocarbon sample was excavated is contemporary with the structure at the Phillips Farm site. The ceramics from Feature 5 include 2 Addis Plain, *var. Addis*, 2 Bell Plain, 43 Mississippi Plain, and 1 unclassified decorated on Mississippi Plain paste. Shell-tempered sherds represent 96 percent of the Feature 5 assemblage, which is far above the 68 percent for the Pevey site. If Feature 5 is excluded from the Phillips Farm assemblage, shell tempering drops to 34 percent of the total, so an argument could be made based on the ceramics that Feature 5 is intrusive and is not representative of the rest of the Phillips Farm site. If the radiocarbon date is reliable and it is associated with the rest of the site it would become necessary to create a new phase designation. I had

Table 6.2. List of radiocarbon samples

Site	Context	Provenience No.	Laboratory No.	Date Type	Conventional Uncalibrated Radiocarbon Date (B.P.)	Calibrated (1 sigma) (A.D.)	Calibrated (2 sigma) (A.D.)
22Lw510	Mound E, Unit SE, E ½, Level 6	365	Beta-168437	Radiometric, standard	1030 ± 70	897:921 943:1045 1094:1120 1141:1147	784:786 827:840 864:1178
22Lw510	Mound E, Unit SE, E ½, Level 10, Feature 1	378	Beta-168438	Radiometric, standard	730 ± 60	1222:1298 1372:1378	1176:1324 1345:1393
22Lw510	Mound G, West ½, Level 8, Zone A	234	Beta-168439	Radiometric, standard	980 ± 60	996:1006 1012:1054 1078:1153	903:915 968:1209
22Lw510	Mound G, Level 9, Zone A	249	Beta-168440	Radiometric, standard	1080 ± 60	895:925 936:1017	778:1042 1107:1117
22Lw510	Mound G, Level 10, Zone A	251	Beta-168441	Radiometric, standard	950 ± 50	1025:1055 1076:1154	998:1003 1013:1208
22Lw593	Feature 5, S ½ Level 1	90	Beta-168442	AMS	350 ± 40	1475:1524 1558:1564 1570:1631	1455:1637

earlier suggested the name "Pevey" for this post-Winstead phase (Livingood 1999), but this may have to be changed if future work confirms the Pevey site does not actually date to the Pevey phase and the only known site in the putative phase is the Phillips Farm site. Currently, there are not enough data to be certain whether the Phillips Farm site is a Winstead phase site, a post–Winstead phase site, or has components in both.

The Pevey Polity

The Lowe-Steen site is located 18 km north of the Pevey site. Lowe-Steen, with two mounds, has significantly fewer than the Pevey site's nine mounds. Both sites were settled at the beginning of the Winstead phase, but only the Pevey site was occupied during the end of the phase.

In his analysis of Mississippian sites in the southern Appalachians, Hally (1993) found that contemporaneous Mississippian mounds were almost always located less than 18 km or more than 33 km from each other. As discussed previously, this patterning emerges because secondary centers must be within a certain distance of the primary center in order for a chief to control it effectively. Without internal administrative specialization (Wright 1984), this effective distance appears to be the length of a half day's walk from the administrative center (Hally 2006; Spencer 1982, 1987; Wright 1977). As they are situated 18 km apart, were occupied concurrently, and possess similar material culture, we can infer the Pevey and Lowe-Steen sites were part of the same polity. Given the discrepancies in size and the fact that the Lowe-Steen site was established later and abandoned earlier than Pevey, it seems probable that Lowe-Steen is a secondary center to Pevey. It appears that near the end of the Winstead phase most of the Pevey community abandoned the polity. Only a small number remained, and they occupied the core part of the Pevey site until they too abandoned the region shortly thereafter. Furthermore, there is evidence from the faunal remains at the flank of Mound E from the terminal Winstead phase that these remaining residents were practicing bone grease processing, which might indicate resource stress.

Choctaw Ethnogenesis

As discussed in Chapter 2, Tim Mooney originally investigated the Pevey and Lowe-Steen sites to test whether they were likely candidates for the source population of the Sixtowns band of the Choctaw, which was proposed as an element of Pat Galloway's (1995) Choctaw Genesis hypothesis. Based on the current archaeological evidence, Galloway's hypotheses do not have to be rejected, but they do need to be amended. Galloway originally suggested that the residents of Pevey and Lowe-Steen might have abandoned these sites subsequent to moving to the Choctaw homeland, but the chronological data clearly indicate that Pevey and Lowe-Steen were abandoned more than two centuries before the formation of the historic Choctaw. Unfortunately, we currently have no definitive way to track where the people of Pevey and Lowe-Steen went after they abandoned their homes or to determine whether they are direct ancestors of the Choctaw. However, following Galloway we can build a new set of hypotheses for testing. It still seems probable that the residents of the Middle Pearl, including those at the Blaine site (Baca 2001) to the north of Lowe-Steen, are ancestors of the Sixtowns band of the Choctaw. We know of a few small sites along the Pearl River and the headwaters of the Leaf River in southern Mississippi that may be post–Winstead phase missing links. One of those sites is Phillips Farm. Another is the Sims site (22Fo582) on the Leaf River (Jackson 2001). The ceramics from Sims are predominately shell tempered, but the decorated forms are primarily on Addis paste. Most of the decorated sherds are Fatherland Incised, but there are also examples of Chicot Red and Anna Incised. This selection of temper and decoration is consistent with post–Winstead phase potters (Jackson 2001). Since survey coverage for much of the Pearl and Leaf rivers is poor, we do not know how typical the Sims or Phillips Farm sites may be of late prehistoric Mississippian settlements in the area.

Thus, the amended Choctaw Genesis hypothesis as it applies to the Sixtowns band is that the Sixtowns ancestors probably did live at the Pevey site and the other mounds along the Middle Pearl including Blaine and Lowe-Steen, which were all established and used sometime after A.D. 1100. Sometime before or around A.D. 1350 these mounds were abandoned, although a small remnant population may have continued to use the Mound E precinct for a few decades after most residents left. With the dissolution of a centralized social hierarchy, people scattered across the landscape and probably settled along the Middle Pearl and the upper tributaries of the Leaf River drainages. This reorganization also occurred among other groups to the east that would eventually join the Choctaw confederacy. Although it has been considered a collapse by some it may also represent an adaptation to a different social landscape and a change from a focus on bottomland maize agriculture to a more broad-spectrum diet. Following Galloway then, these dispersed farmsteads partially relocated and coalesced as the Sixtowns band in the sixteenth and seventeenth centuries, which marked a return to an aggregated settlement pattern.

One of Galloway's most important contributions in her book was showing how several of the traits that became a normative part of Choctaw culture were only practiced by a minority of the original proto-Choctaw peoples.

For example, the Choctaw burial practices that involved extended processing and defleshing of the bodies were likely derived from the cultural repertoire of the eastern groups (Galloway 1995:344). Galloway suggests that the tradition of cross-moiety handling of burial processing may have served as a useful tool to bring solidarity and cooperation to the newly formed Choctaw. Additionally, the Choctaw language was probably imported by the Eastern band because of its similarity to Chickasaw (Galloway 1995:345) and the pottery decoration tradition may have been significantly adapted from the Western communities.

In addition to the negotiation of language, mortuary practice, and pottery traditions, I can provide one additional area that needs attention and research. The worldview of the historic Choctaw puts the sun as very central to their ideology, so much so that early writers often incorrectly assumed that they worshiped the sun (Swanton 1928). The sun was important enough among the Choctaw that it played a central role in the language as a keystone for many idioms (LeRoy Sealy, personal communication 2007). One very striking feature of the ceramic assemblage at the Pevey site is that it contained a remarkable number of plates, a large number of which have stylized depictions of the sun. There is also a single sherd found by a collector in Simpson County (adjacent to Lawrence County) with a naturalistic sunburst pattern executed on Addis paste. The sun is a much more common motif in the Lower Mississippi Valley than among Mississippian peoples to the east. Further work needs to be done from the archaeological and ethnohistoric side to understand this concept and the role it played in Choctaw worldview, but it seems likely this is one more element of the coalescent Choctaw worldview that may have been contributed by the Western groups, including the Sixtowns band.

Future Directions for Research on the Middle Pearl Mississippian

There have been only three significant episodes of field research on Lawrence County Mississippian: Mann's (1988) work in the early 1980s, the University of North Carolina Field Schools in 1992 and 1993, and my work in 1999 and 2000. There is still much left to do and many questions to be asked. Given the failure of my survey project to find a significant number of Mississippian hamlets it is possible that the residents of the Pevey polity were unusually nucleated or that they were few in number. However, since little of the floodplain terraces has been effectively surveyed, this has yet to be confirmed. All of the mound excavations were test units, which means we have very little knowledge about architecture. Also, given the apparent use of cremation, we lack the caches of high-status goods that typically accompany Mississippian burials. It is unknown whether these goods were less frequent at the Pevey and Lowe-Steen sites than among their eastern neighbors or whether such goods simply have not been found by archaeologists. We also do not know much about off-mound habitation and land use at Pevey. A question for future research is the size and extent of these settlements between the mounds, along the terrace north of Pevey, and south of Mill Creek. Finally, there are numerous questions about the use of space and mounds at Pevey. There is evidence, summarized in the next chapter, of internal differentiation at Pevey between the relatively low-status western mounds and the higher-status eastern mounds, and the extent and nature of such a differentiation is an important question. There is also the tantalizing possibility that the paired arrangement of mounds may be significant, possibly indicative of a segmentary social system such as that found at Moundville (Knight 1998; Wilson 2008).

# 7
Regional Analysis and Interpolity Competition

Little is known about the nature, the extent, or the geographic extent of interpolity competition in the Mississippian Southeast. The area between the Lower Mississippi Valley and Black Warrior Valley makes a good study area for this question because there is evidence for interpolity interaction and exchange across this region and because the late prehistoric people of this locality seem to have shared common ideas about the importance of monumental mound building. Previously, this work discussed in detail the archaeology of the Pevey polity at the center of the study area. We can now compare the Middle Pearl with its neighbors in the Mississippi, Big Black, and Mobile river drainages (Figure 7.1) in order to demonstrate that there is a distance threshold at which interpolity competition appears to have a qualitatively smaller effect.

Pearl River

Almost nothing was known about the Pearl River Mississippian before the 1980s, and very little work has been conducted since (Heartfield, Price, and Greene, Inc. 1982; Moore 1987). Current evidence indicates that Pearl River occupation during the Mississippi period was limited to the Middle Pearl River. The Upper Pearl seems to have been mostly unoccupied during this time, but after the sixteenth century it was settled by the historic Choctaw. The most famous site on the Upper Pearl is the Nanih Waiya mound, which by oral history is the ancestral home of the Choctaw. Current research (Carleton 1999) suggests the mound was a Middle Woodland flat-top mound that was reoccupied during the historic period.

There is one other mound site on the Pearl River that was likely occupied during the same time as the Pevey and Lowe-Steen sites. The Blaine site (22Hi544) is located 85 km north of the Pevey site and 66 km north of

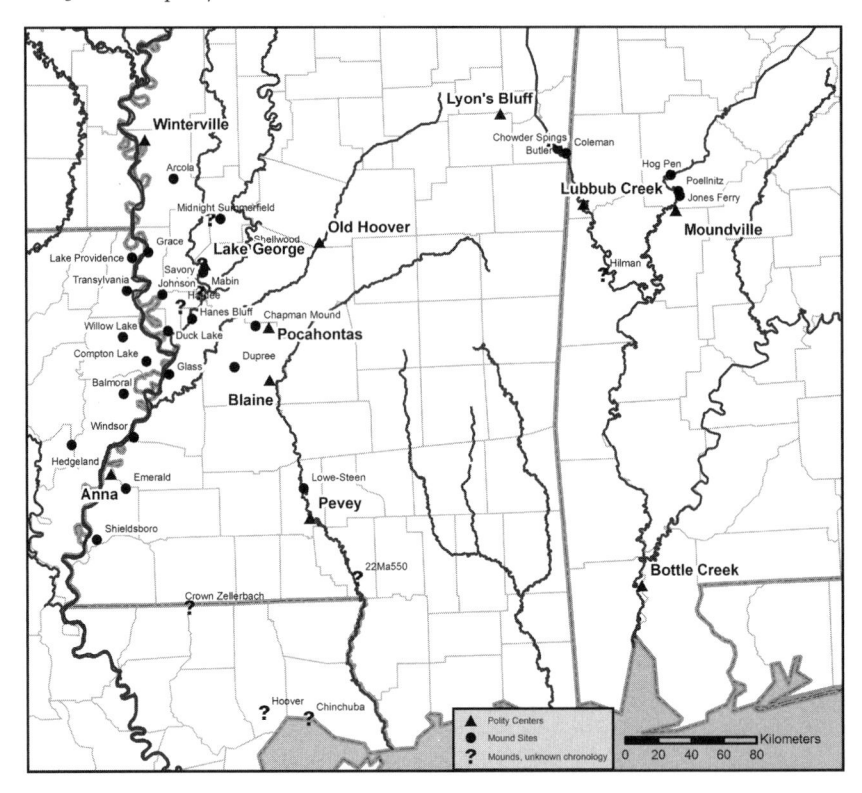

Figure 7.1. Map showing mound sites in the regional analysis that were in use at approximately A.D. 1250. Triangles indicate likely centers of polities, and question marks indicate mound sites with uncertain dates (Baca 2001; Blitz 1993b; Blitz and Mann 2000; Brown 2003; Hally 1972; Jeter and Williams 1989; Jones and Shuman 1986, 1988; Lorenz 1992; Phillips 1970; Prentice 2000; Shaffer and Steponaitis 1982; Welch 1990; Williams and Brain 1983).

the Lowe-Steen site. The single flat-top mound was destroyed by developers in 1998 (Baca 2001). Keith Baca and Doug Sims of the Mississippi Department of Archives and History (MDAH) were unable to halt the destruction, but they were able to recover some artifacts and charcoal samples from the mound while it was being bulldozed. The mound was 5 m high (Baca 2001:5) and oriented to the cardinal directions. Three radiocarbon samples and 59 sherds were recovered during the demolition. Coarse-shell tempering was present in 71 percent of the sample sherds, and the three decorated sherds were identified as Coles Creek Incised, *var. Hardy,* Anna Incised, *var. Anna,* and Carter Engraved, *var. Carter* (Baca 2001:8–9). The radiocarbon samples provided a 1-sigma calibrated date range of A.D. 1000–1400. Based on these limited data, the Blaine mound site appears to be very similar to the Pevey and Lowe-Steen sites in all confirmable respects. Specifically, there are similar ratios of shell- and grog-tempered vessels, there are similar decorated forms, and the mounds date to the same general time period. While it is tempting to use the Winstead phase designation as the cultural and temporal label for the Blaine site, it is important to note that Blaine is only 33 km south of the Pocahontas platform mound and approximately 22 km away from some of the two dozen Mississippian burial mounds that have been linked with Pocahontas, such as Dupree and Flowood (Steponaitis 1991). There are currently far too few data to infer the political and cultural relationship between Blaine and these sites. Part of the problem is that there are over 20 mounds documented in Hinds County, home to both Pocahontas and Blaine, but most have received very little research.

Forty-five kilometers south of the Pevey site, the 22Ma550 site reportedly has one platform mound and from one to three other small mounds (MDAH files). It is not known whether the site dates to the Mississippi or Woodland period.

Gulf Coast

The region of the Gulf Coast between the Pearl River and Chotawhatchee Bay in Florida was home to the Pensacola culture during the late prehistoric period (Bense 1989). Archaeologists have long recognized that the pottery of this culture is a combination of Lower Mississippi Valley forms and Mississippian forms. Most mound sites appear in this region after A.D. 1250.

On the Mississippi Gulf coast, Pinola phase potters (A.D. 1200–1350) made some choices similar to those made by Winstead phase potters. They produced grog-, shell-, and grog-and-shell–tempered vessels (Blitz and Mann 2000:56). Like the Pevey residents, they combined both the new practice of shell tempering and the traditional shell-and-grog–tempering technologies with native vessel forms. Stylistically, they utilized some Moundville Incised forms and D'Olive Incised forms that are traditionally associated with sites to the east as well as Plaquemine forms such as Carter Engraved, *var. Shell Bluff,* Barton Incised, Parkin Punctated, and Winterville Incised. They also adopted the plate form, which was common in the Southeast in the twelfth and thirteenth centuries (Blitz and Mann 2000:55–59).

After A.D. 1250, most Pensacola political centers were single-mound simple chiefdoms located around different bay systems along the coast (Bense 1989; Blitz and Mann 2000:102). The one spectacular exception is the Bottle Creek site, located on the Mobile-Tensaw Delta. It had at least 18 mounds (Brown 2003) and was the center of the largest polity in the Pensacola area. Although the site was settled earlier, its major occupation and mound construction occurred between A.D. 1250 and A.D. 1550, which means that most of the mound construction at Bottle Creek occurred late in the Winstead phase. There is one possible three-mound secondary center, although it has not yet been investigated (Brown 2003:9). As Fuller (2003) indicates, during the early history of Bottle Creek there were large numbers of ceramics with Lower Valley and Moundville stylistic connections.

North of Lake Pontchartrain and east of the Mississippi River are three mound sites that may or may not be contemporary with the Winstead phase. Eighty-nine kilometers southwest of Pevey is the single-mound Crown Zellerbach/Cavenham Industries site (16-SH-75) on the Amite River. The site has been mapped, surface collected, and cored (Jones and Shuman 1988: 115–116), but few artifacts have been recovered. The site may date to the Plaquemine period. On the north shore of Lake Pontchartrain, there is the single-mound Chinchuba site (16-ST-25), excavated over a century ago (Bushnell 1909). Based on the published photographs, the ceramics appear to be examples of L'Eau Noire Incised, Mazique Incised, and Harrison Bayou Incised and may indicate the site was occupied contemporaneously with the Winstead phase (Jones and Shuman 1988:152). The nearby Hoover site (16-TA-5) is the largest mound site in the Florida parishes of southeast Louisiana, with five or six mounds (Coastal Environments, Inc. 1983). The site has received some excavation, and the ceramics indicate that the site was primarily occupied during the Late Coles Creek period but may have had a minor Plaquemine component (Jones and Shuman 1988:157–163).

Black Warrior

Moundville is the best-studied site in the study area and one of the best-understood sites in North America. Moundville is composed of 32 mounds on a natural terrace overlooking the Black Warrior River. Following the chronology and social history produced by Knight and Steponaitis (1998), the region was dominated by nucleated villages during the West Jefferson phase. Around A.D. 1050, dispersed farmsteads became more common and people began to shift away from horticulture based on wild plants to a diet increasingly dominated by maize. Some people began to settle on the eventual site of Moundville and constructed two small mounds long before other nearby communities were building mounds. Sometime during late Moundville I, at approximately A.D. 1200, the site and the region were dramatically transformed. Within a short time, all of the mounds at Moundville were constructed according to a distinct plan. During this time, a palisade was constructed for the first time and people began to live in and around the central site. Beyond Moundville, at least three single-mound secondary centers were built. In addition, there is extensive evidence that nonlocal chert, greenstone, mica, copper, and marine shell were being imported in significant quantities.

Around A.D. 1300, the Moundville center is vacated, as most of its population moved to outlying settlements. The few people who remained residents of the central site were probably members of the elite provisioned by outlying communities. The mounds were primarily used as a mortuary facility during this time, and elite burials began to be interred with extremely elaborate goods. This system began to collapse by A.D. 1450, long after the Pevey and Lowe-Steen sites were abandoned.

The Moundville Incised sherds at Pevey may indicate some direct connections between Pevey and Moundville. In particular, the substantial fragment of a Moundville Incised, *var. Moundville* vessel looks very much like an import from Moundville or an exact replica (Steponaitis, personal communication 1998). However, these types of vessels were also being used and likely produced by communities along the Tombigbee River and the Gulf Coast. Regardless, *var. Moundville* vessels date from Moundville I to early Moundville II and are consistent with interpolity contacts that are likely to have taken place after Moundville's political consolidation.

Tombigbee

There is a string of sites located along the central Tombigbee River to the west of Moundville. The best studied of these is the Lubbub Creek site (Blitz 1993a). The Lyon's Bluff site located near the Tombigbee drainage has had extensive excavations, but little has been published (Brookes 2000; Galloway 2000; Lolley 2000; Marshall 1977, 1986). The other mound sites of Butler, Chowder Springs, Coleman, and Hilman have received very little archaeological attention, and only two of the sites can even be dated (Blitz 1993a:Table 5; Welch 1990). All of the sites appear to be single-mound Mississippian centers, with the possible exception of Chowder Springs with one Mississippian mound and one associated mound of unknown age (Blitz 1993: Table 5). The Lubbub Creek site was surrounded by dispersed farmsteads. Both the Lubbub Creek and Lyon's Bluff sites appear to have been occupied for most of the Mississippi period. Mound B at Chowder Springs was used during the Early Mississippian Summerville I phase, and the Coleman site was used during both Summerville I and early Summerville II/III. As discussed previously, a comparison of the nonlocal goods from Lubbub Creek and Moundville burials (Blitz 1993) indicated a subtle decline in some nonlocal goods at Lubbub Creek after Moundville became a complex chiefdom. In other words, the rise of Moundville came at the expense of Lubbub Creek.

Big Black

Lorenz (1992, 1996) analyzed the Old Hoover polity on the Central Big Black River. He examined excavation and survey data from the central single-mound site and several outlying farmsteads. This site is located on the Big Black River, 70 km upriver from the Pocahontas site and was occupied during the same period as Pocahontas, Lubbub Creek, and Moundville. The Old Hoover polity is comparatively lacking in evidence for social hierarchy. It also apparently did not interact in any way in a prestige goods exchange network since it is completely lacking in nonlocal artifacts except for some nonlocal stone. Lorenz (1992, 1996) argued that the best ethnographic analogue for the Old Hoover site is a Melanesian Big Man society. The platform mound, which is sometimes treated as prima facie evidence of a Mississippian chiefdom, is instead interpreted as a locus of community activity. The mound contexts contained a greater proportion of large ceramic vessels, which is interpreted as evidence for community feasts, but otherwise did not differ from the farmsteads in most respects. Lorenz (1992:342) argued that the low population density and lack of political centralization of the Old Hoover polity was related to the relatively poor soils of the Big Black drainage. The residents of Old Hoover did not utilize maize in the same way as most of their contemporaries but relied instead on a diet primarily composed of acorn and hickory (see Chapter 5). Unlike Pocahontas and Lubbub Creek, which saw modest to large decreases in access to nonlocal goods after A.D. 1200, Old Hoover appears never to have attempted to participate meaningfully in a regional exchange network. However, the fact that the Old Hoover residents elected to build a platform mound, as many of their neighbors were doing ca. A.D. 1200, is evidence that they were communicating and interacting with them on some level. They adopted or emulated this widespread architectural form, and, according to Lorenz, they invested it with their own set of meanings. Old Hoover provides an example of a polity that did not participate in any form of prestige goods exchange.

The other polity near the Big Black was Pocahontas, unusual in the study area because its residents made extensive use of Mississippi period conical burial mounds (Shaffer and Steponaitis 1982, 1983; Steponaitis 1991). The polity was apparently centered on a single platform mound at the Pocahontas site. Steponaitis (1991) argued that the Pocahontas polity had reasonably good access to nonlocal exchange goods before A.D. 1200 but that after political consolidation at some of the major sites in the region, the number of nonlocal goods declined by 80 percent.

Lower Mississippi Valley

The Lower Mississippi Valley is a unique physiographic and cultural setting. Throughout much of its history, it was home to more complex sociopolitical structures than were regularly found throughout the Southeast at the same time (Steponaitis 1998). Mound building is a tradition that goes back to at least 3500 B.P. with the Watson Brake site and other Archaic mounds (Gibson 1994; Russo 1994; Saunders and Allen 1994; Saunders et al. 1998; Saunders et al. 2005; R. Saunders 1994). Although the tradition would pass in and out of favor over time, mound construction was ultimately practiced almost continuously somewhere in the Lower and Central Mississippi valleys for approximately 1,500 years before the arrival of Europeans. More significantly, hierarchical social structures definitively emerged in the Mississippi Valley around A.D. 700 during the Coles Creek period (Barker 1999; Jeter and Williams 1989; Kidder 2004; Phillips 1970; Wells 1998). Thus, by the thirteenth century when Moundville, Bottle Creek, and other Gulf Coastal Plain chiefdoms were just starting, the Lower Valley had been host to hierarchical societies for centuries.

Jeter and Williams (1989) and Rees and Livingood (2007) review the intellectual history of the Plaquemine, the name given to the indigenous Mississippi period culture of the Lower Valley. Most researchers in the past three decades have tended to view Plaquemine as "Mississippianized Coles Creek" (Brain 1978; Brown 1985b; Williams and Brain 1983). This means it has been traditionally interpreted as an indigenous outgrowth of Coles Creek culture with the addition of cultural elements introduced from the rest of the Mississippian world. This is undoubtedly accurate, but much of the recent research has begun to focus on the theme of continuity and change and the theme of diversity across the Plaquemine world (Kidder 1998b, 2007; Rees and Livingood, eds. 2007).

The second theme is especially important for this discussion. As noted by others (Jeter and Williams 1989), some of the Lower Valley research that focused on single sites tended to extrapolate conclusions about those sites to the rest of the region or to the entire Plaquemine. In contrast, research that focused on survey (Hally 1972; Phillips 1970) tended to recognize more diversity. As our data set of excavated sites has grown (Beasley 2007; Brown 1985b; Fritz and Kidder 1993; Kidder 1993, 2007; Lewis 2008; Ryan 2004; Weinstein 2005) it is increasingly apparent that there was tremendous diversity across the Plaquemine with respect to almost every aspect of culture, including settlement patterns, ceramics, burial patterns, and subsistence (Jeter and Williams 1989; Kidder 2007). Even within regions such as the Tensas Basin, some communities were apparently using maize extensively while others were primarily utilizing seedy crops and nuts (cf. Fritz and Kidder 1993; Kidder 1992; Roberts 2004).

Some of this diversity may be related to the migration of communities into the Lower Valley during the Plaquemine. Ian Brown (2007) has suggested that the Plaquemine period residents of the Natchez Bluffs may be an example of a migrant community. Boudreaux (1997) provided a similar argument for the Cotton Mounds on the Big Black, and Hally (1972) argued that the Transylvania site may also be intrusive. Likely, further investigations will cause some of these migration events to be reinterpreted while others may be confirmed as examples of migration in the Mississippi period Southeast (Blitz and Lorenz 2002).

Another possible explanation is that diversity may have already been present in the Lower Valley by A.D. 1200. Archaeologists and historians acknowledge that the historic Lower Valley had almost unprecedented degrees of ethnic and linguistic diversity (Galloway 1998b, 2002; Giardino 1985; Jeter 2002; Kidder 1993; Swanton 1911). There may be no way to know precisely when and how these signs of diversity emerged, but it seems reasonable that the origins extend back to before the Plaquemine period. Linguistic and ethnic diversity would help to explain several of the patterns that archaeologists recognize. First, it would help account for the degree of diversity in material culture and in burial practices. Second, in the Chattahoochee River example (Blitz and Lorenz 2002), it appeared an immigrant community situated itself between two established communities that were markedly different in material culture. Theoretically, it would be more challenging for a sizable immigrant community to settle among more culturally homogenous populations. Therefore, an ethnically diverse Lower Valley would provide a setting in which immigration into a well-settled river valley would be more likely. Third, Lower Valley archaeologists have long recognized the "Cahokia horizon" in the Lower Valley when Ramey Incised vessels and other imports made an appearance (Brain 1989; Williams and Brain 1983). It is clear that not all communities participated in these exchange networks equally. Some centers such as Lake Providence (Wells and Weinstein 2007), Lake George (Williams and Brain 1983), or Winterville (Brain 1989; Jackson 2006, 2007) may have embraced these contacts while others may have avoided the networks. It is possible that intercommunity rivalries, reflected perhaps in ethnic and linguistic diversity, may have led different groups to choose very divergent strategies. However, ethnic and linguistic boundaries are challenging to detect archaeologically. The presence or absence of late prehistoric diversity is best regarded as a hypothesis that needs further investigation.

For the purposes of this book, of primary interest are the largest Plaquemine polities that were contemporaneous with Pevey and were the most likely to have exercised political influence over sites in the study area. These include the 26-mound Lake George and 23-mound Winterville sites in the Yazoo and the eight-mound Anna site in the Natchez Bluffs. These sites were all occupied for extended periods of time, including a period contemporary with the Winstead phase. There are numerous multi-mound and single-mound sites in the Lower Mississippi Valley, and, unfortunately, it is very difficult to produce a complete and accurate list of the sites that may have been major political actors during the Winstead phase. Although the Yazoo (Phillips 1970) and Upper Tensas (Hally 1972) have been extensively surveyed and reported, most mound sites are multicomponent and known only through survey. A large number of mound sites were constructed prior to the Mississippian then reused later, and it is unclear from the survey collections how significant the later phases of occupation were for the site history. This means Figure 7.1 is only a partial map of sites suspected to be contemporary with the Winstead phase.

Mapping the Polities

Figure 7.2 shows the polity boundaries across the interior of the study area at approximately A.D. 1250. The map shows Hally circles of 18-km radius around the presumed polity centers. It is important to note that no attempt has been made to indicate all of the polity boundaries for the Lower Mississippi Valley because such a project is complicated by the lack of reliable data about which sites were significant administrative centers or population concentrations at a given point in time. Also, the distance of 18 km is applicable for much of the Southeast because it represents the approximate distance that can be traveled in a half day's walk. The Lower Mississippi Valley is a unique environmental setting, and it is likely that the distance that could have been traversed in half a day varied by locale and season. Furthermore, it has been suggested that Lower and Central Mississippi Valley polities may not have utilized the 10- to 20-km buffer zones that were common to the rest of the Southeast (Rees 1997), making it more difficult to identify clusters of sites. All of these problems indicate that identifying Lower Valley polities is much more difficult than in other areas and will require future research. Fortunately for purposes of this study, identifying the polity boundaries along the Lower Valley is unnecessary.

The rest of the study area corresponds well to theoretical expectations. All platform mound sites known to be occupied at A.D. 1250 are located either less than 18 km or more than 30 km from each other. One unusual case involves the Blaine and Pocahontas sites, which are located just 31 km away from each other. Also, the conical Dupree mound, which Steponaitis (1991) associated with the Pocahontas site, is not obviously associated with the Pocahontas or Blaine polities based on our expectations of distance. These relationships will need to be explored with further research, and it is possible that a better chronology may help clarify our understanding of the political relationships.

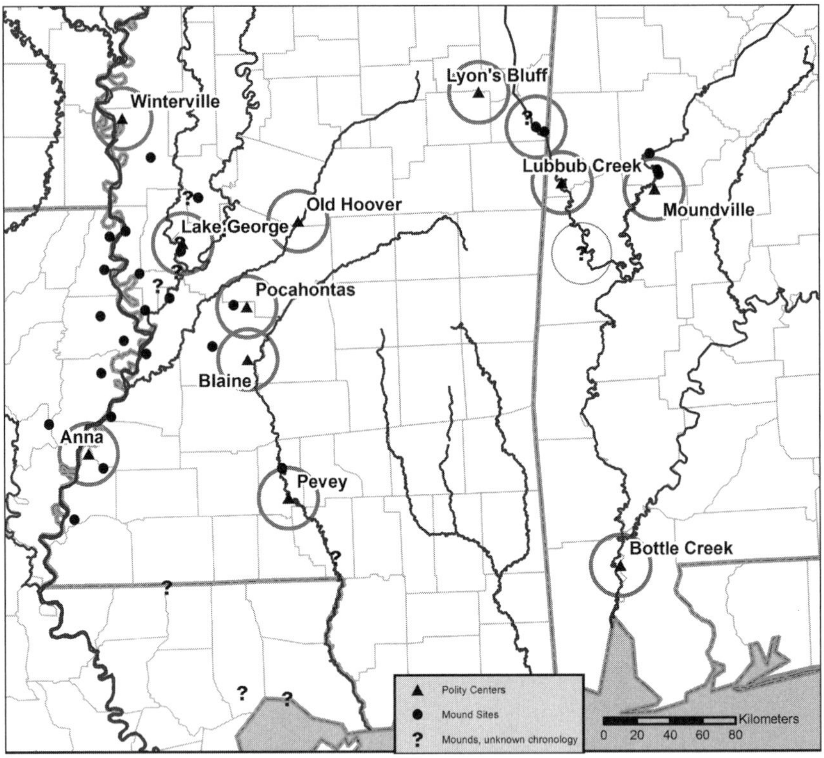

Figure 7.2. Map showing the Hally circles (18 km) around presumed polity centers dating to approximately A.D. 1250. The lines are thought to be a good representation of polity extent. As discussed in the text, the polity boundaries are not intended to be complete for the Lower Valley.

Interpolity Interactions

The goal of this study is to look for evidence of a geographic limit to the influence of large polities. This assumes that the types of interpolity relationships discussed in Chapter 1 that were observed in the historic period also occurred during the prehistoric. The challenge is that these relationships are very difficult to identify archaeologically. Even the confirmed historic cases such as Coosa and Cofitachequi did not leave many obvious archaeological signatures. This is further evidence that most Mississippian interpolity domination was short-lived and involved relatively small numbers of people and goods. Despite the problems with identifying such patterns, several archaeological projects in the regional study area have addressed this issue and were discussed in the introduction (Chapter 1).

To summarize, these studies contrasted the abundance of nonlocal goods per burial at Moundville, Lubbub Creek, and Pocahontas. They discovered that after A.D. 1200 the large polities had increased access to nonlocal goods at the expense of chiefdoms that did not increase appreciably in size. Steponaitis (1991) argued that larger chiefdoms could mobilize larger amounts of goods and labor and create conditions favorable for attracting and maintaining elite-to-elite exchange networks in prestige goods. This argument does not provide an explanation for why one site became a complex chiefdom while another did not, but it does suggest that after the emergence of a few complex polities in the Gulf Coastal Plain after A.D. 1200, it was extremely difficult for new polities to join their ranks.

Models of prestige goods economies suggest that restricting access to exotic goods should have consequences in other areas of internal political competition (Earle 2002). One way elites use prestige goods is as a means to legitimize their authority and as a means of exchange for access to other goods and labor, although it is unclear how common the latter was in the study area (Marcoux 2007). This research hypothesizes that changes in access to prestige goods brought about by interpolity competition will often be reflected in other measures of a group's degree of hierarchy and centralization. Furthermore, this research hypothesizes that the number of mounds at a site is an imperfect but potentially useful proxy for the type of interpolity interaction strategy that was employed. Previous research (Blitz and Livingood 2004; Livingood and Blitz 2004) has demonstrated that single-mound sites and large multi-mound sites pursued different strategies with respect to mound building. These differences are likely reflected in other areas, such as diplomacy.

Table 7.1 summarizes the data for polities in the study area, including the evidence for prestige goods exchange and political centralization, and Figure 7.3 shows a map of sites indicating the numbers of mounds per site. Based on these data, the study region includes at least five major polities as measured by site size and the presence of a three-tiered settlement hierarchy: Moundville, Bottle Creek, Winterville, Lake George, and Anna. Pevey may also fit these criteria. There are several other large multi-mound sites in the Lower Mississippi Valley that could be considered, but their role as polity centers is open to interpretation. Regardless, their presence is tangential to the argument below since none of them would be substantially closer to the sites in the interior of the study area than Winterville, Lake George, or Anna. Table 7.2 lists the distances between each of the mound sites in the interior of the study area and the closest major center.

Spanish accounts describe several paramount chiefdoms that bridged polity boundaries. The Ocute and Cofitachequi polities both demonstrate that the

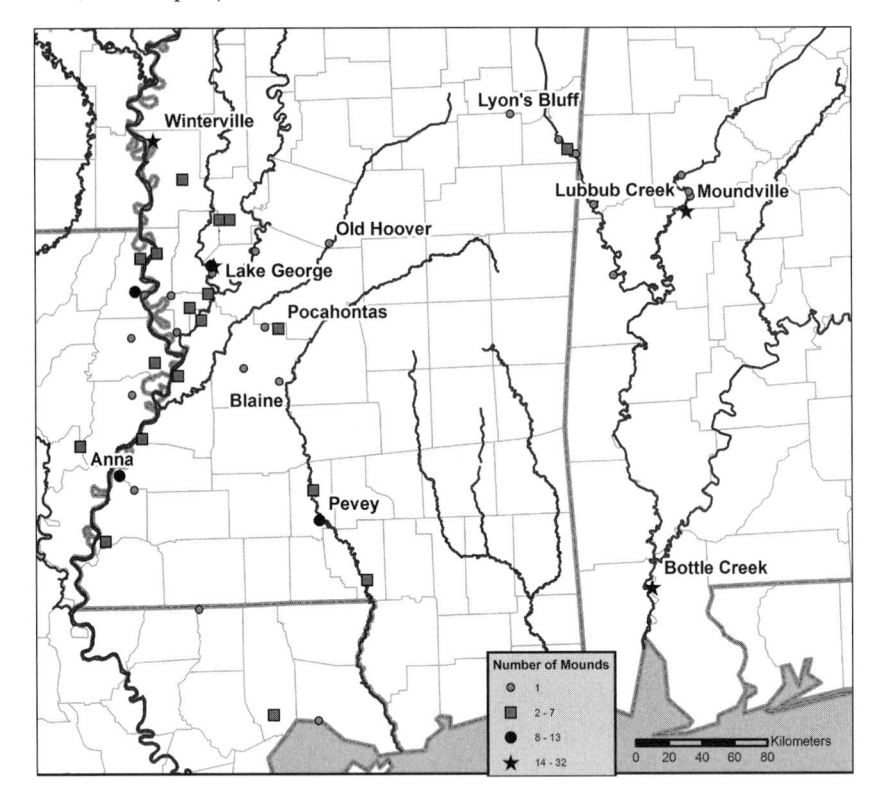

Figure 7.3. Map of mound sites in the study area that were occupied at approximately A.D. 1250, showing the number of mounds at each site.

central polity was able to exert influence at a distance of approximately 100 km. The Coosa polity was able to exert influence at a distance of 200 km. An examination of the data in Table 7.2 indicates that all of the sites in the study area that remained single-mound centers for their entire history were located less than 120 km from a major center, and most were located less than 100 km. The Pevey site, which eventually became a large nine-mound site and part of a three-tiered settlement hierarchy, was located 125 km from Anna and 163 km from Lake George. Bottle Creek, which was probably the last major center in this analysis to be constructed, was 224 km from Moundville.

Collectively, these data indicate that the approximate distance of 100 to 125 km (Figure 7.4) is the practical limit at which a large center could influence smaller chiefdoms in the Southeast. Two of the three historic examples and all of the archaeological examples in this case study indicate that it may be possible for a paramount chiefdom to operate at this distance. Coosa ap-

Table 7.1. Summary of the regions and polities in the study area, including evidence for interpolity exchange and political centralization

Region	Contemporary Mound Sites	Evidence of Interpolity Interaction	Evidence of Political Hierarchy
Middle Pearl	Pevey and Lowe-Steen, Blaine	The Pevey site has some number of extralocal goods, including ceramics, mica, chert, and copper.	The Pevey site is a nine-mound site, and the Lowe-Steen site is a two-mound secondary center. The Blaine site may be a single-mound simple chiefdom or it may have some relationship with the Pocahontas-area mounds.
Gulf Coast	Bottle Creek	The Bottle Creek site has numerous extralocal artifacts.	Bottle Creek has 14 mounds and may be the center of a complex chiefdom. The elites were provisioned with food. To the east of Bottle Creek were some simple chiefdoms with single-mound centers.
Black Warrior	Moundville	Moundville has an extensive number of extralocal goods from many places in the contemporary Southeast.	Moundville has 32 mounds and at least three secondary mound sites during Moundville II. The elites were provisioned with food and were provided with extremely prestigious burial furniture. Extralocal goods with origins from across the Southeast.
Tombigbee	Lubbub Creek, Lyon's Bluff, Hilman, Coleman, Butler, and Chowder Springs	Some extralocal goods recovered from the Lubbub Creek polity. The number of available nonlocal goods declines slightly after A.D. 1200, especially at the outlying sites.	Most of the sites appear to be simple chiefdoms with a single-mound center. The only site with data, Lubbub Creek, indicates that there were fewer distinctions between elite and nonelite contexts at Lubbub Creek than at Moundville. Elites were likely not provisioned with food.

Continued on the next page

Table 7.1. *Continued*

Region	Contemporary Mound Sites	Evidence of Interpolity Interaction	Evidence of Political Hierarchy
Big Black	Old Hoover, Pocahontas	Old Hoover has no extralocal goods other than some exotic stone. The Pocahontas sites have extralocal goods before A.D. 1200, but 80% fewer after.	Both sites are likely single-mound centers. Old Hoover has very little evidence of hierarchy and there is little differentiation between mound and farmstead contexts. Pocahontas appears to function to integrate segmentary groups.
Yazoo	Winterville, Lake George	Both sites have extensive collections of nonlocal goods, especially ceramics.	Both sites are enormous multi-mound sites that are likely to be centers of complex chiefdoms with secondary multi-mound centers. Little is known about nonelite contexts.
Natchez Bluffs	Anna	Little is known about the number of nonlocal artifacts during the Anna phase.	The Anna site is a large eight-mound site that could have been the center of a complex chiefdom.
Tensas	Hedgeland, Lake Providence, Balmoral	Extensive numbers of nonlocal goods at some sites like Lake Providence, few at others.	Several multi-mound sites. Some may have been involved in three-tiered settlement hierarchies.

Table 7.2. Distances between mound sites in the center of the research area and the closest major multi-mound centers

Site	Distance to Closest Major Mound Centers
Blaine	79 km, Lake George
	84 km, Pevey
	111 km, Anna
Bottle Creek	224 km, Moundville
Lubbub Creek	55 km, Moundville
Lyon's Bluff	119 km, Moundville
Old Hoover	72 km, Lake George
Pevey	125 km, Anna
	163 km, Lake George
	205 km, Bottle Creek
	287 km, Moundville
Pocahontas	54 km, Lake George
	115 km, Pevey

pears to be the lone example of a paramount chiefdom that could project influence beyond 100 km.

While Coosa may be an exception to this pattern, there are two factors that must be considered. First, it is noteworthy that, of the 10 polity centers that were likely subordinate to Coosa, only three were more than 100 km from the paramount center at Little Egypt, and two of these polities were downstream of the center along the Coosa River. Assuming the key variable in this analysis is travel time, also known as pheric distance, and not simply straight-line or geodesic distance, the Toqua site is the only real outlier since it is approximately 160 km from Little Egypt and would have been only indirectly accessible by water. Because of Toqua's proximity to other nearby mound sites it is possible that Toqua may have opted in to an alliance with Coosa. Another consideration is that archaeological and historic data provide overlapping but distinct data on the influence of paramount chiefdoms. In the historic cases, we understand from Spanish accounts that certain towns were "subject" to Coosa or other paramount chiefs and that they may have owed some tribute. However, we have very little sense of the time depth of these relationships. In the archaeological case from the Gulf Coastal Plain, there is long-term evidence that small polities within 100–

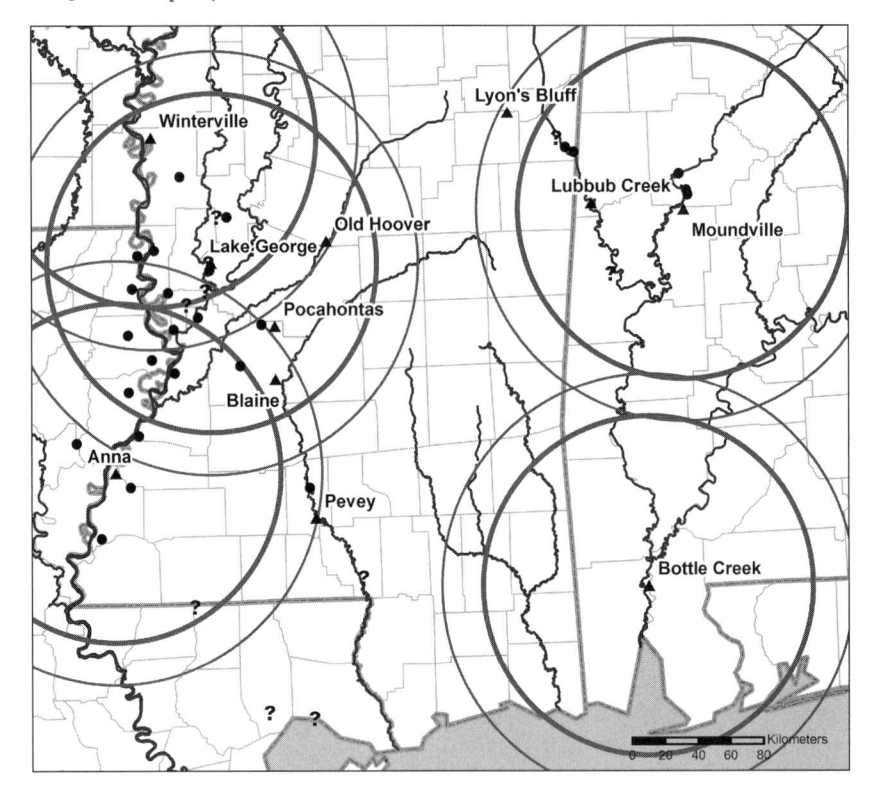

Figure 7.4. Map showing distances from the major centers in the study area. The thick circles indicate a distance of 100 km and the thin circles indicate 125 km.

125 km of very large chiefdoms never became more hierarchical or centralized while in their neighbor's shadow. We would be able to tell unambiguously if they had grown, even if only for a short period of time. Therefore, it is possible that paramount chiefdoms may have projected their influence beyond the 100- to 125-km limit for short periods of time, as was the case with Coosa, but that maintaining this influence for significant intervals may have been impossible.

What features of pre-state ranked societies would give rise to this pattern and cause 100–125 km to be a distance at which large polities are less able to affect the growth of smaller polities? Just as with the polity-size measure, the important factor is probably not the distance, but the travel time. Based on an application of the Hiker's formula, Table 7.3 shows the amount of time required to traverse 100 or 125 km on foot. Depending on the conditions of slope and the presence or absence of a trail, such a distance could take three to six days. In a separate study simulating travel time in the Southern Ap-

Table 7.3. Time required to travel 100 or 125 km on foot, based on the slope and presence of a trail

Distance to Travel	Trail — Even Terrain (5 km/h)	Trail — 5-Percent Slope (4.2 km/h)	No Trail — Even Terrain (3 km/h)	No Trail — 5-Percent Slope (2.5 km/h)
100 km	20 hours/ 2.5 days	24 hours/ 3 days	33 hours/ 4.2 days	40 hours/ 5 days
125 km	25 hours/ 3.2 days	30 hours/ 3.7 days	42 hours/ 5.2 days	50 hours/ 6.3 days

Note: The speeds were calculated from the Hiker's formula with a modifier of .6 based on absence of a trail (Gorenflo and Gale 1990; Tobler 1993). The calculation of travel days is based on an eight-hour day. The Hiker's formula is $v = 6e - 3.5|s + .05|$, where v is walking speed in kilometers per hour, s is the slope of the terrain in degrees, and e is the mathematical constant, which is the base of the natural logarithm. By this formula, a distance of 18 km could be traversed in 3.6 to 4.3 hours on foot by a reasonably healthy adult if there were a trail and most of the path had a slope of less than 5 degrees. Since most important locations in a polity were probably connected by trails, this is a safe estimate and indicates this distance could easily be covered by foot in less than half a day. If there were no trail at all, this same distance would take approximately 6 to 7.2 hours on foot. Water travel was also a viable option in many cases since Mississippian polities were usually located next to navigable rivers and streams, although travel times would have varied greatly based on the nature of the waterways, the season, the direction of travel, and the presence or absence of natural dams.

palachians (Livingood 2006, 2011) and allowing for both overland and riverine canoe travel, it was found that 3 km/hr is a typical average speed over large distances, which would suggest that 100–125 km could typically be traversed in four to five days. Counting the round trip, therefore, travel between locations that were this distant would involve the investment of one or two weeks.

Earlier, two primary mechanisms were suggested as the means by which pre-state polities might compete with each other. First, polities might compete through warfare. Certainly we should expect that the effects of coercive force would be attenuated by distance. Attacks on enemies more than 100 km away would involve an investment of at least one to two weeks, which would involve greater commitment and a greater investment of time and energy than attacks against a closer polity. Furthermore, the investment of time needed would preclude agriculturalists from undertaking such attacks during certain times of the year. Second, polities may have competed with each other for alliances and access to prestige goods networks. We would expect larger polities would overshadow nearby smaller polities in their ability to attract exchange partners and allies. In both cases, distance is likely a major factor in explaining the magnitude of the effect.

The limit of 100 km played a special role in the Aztec empire. A map of tribute relationships indicated that food was never transported from producer to center because the cost of transportation was too high (Barlow 1949). The workers would have consumed all or most of the tribute as provisions before they could reach their destination. Although the political system was much different in the Mississippian, the constraints would have been similar. Large groups of travelers face the dilemma that either they can provision their journey, which increases the organizational cost and provides a natural limit on the distance one can travel, or they can rely on hunting or raiding for provisions, which increases the travel time and is less reliable for larger groups. The evidence in this case is that costs of transport, especially if the travel is largely on foot, may have precluded regular trips of longer than 100–125 km.

When combined with the Hally distances, this research suggests there are two distance thresholds that influence regional dynamics: 18 km, which corresponds to a pheric distance in simulation of six hours or a half day's journey (Livingood 2007, 2010), and 100–125 km, which would represent a pheric distance of four to five days' travel. This parallels one of the findings of exploitable territory threshold models or optimal foraging models by researchers working under very different assumptions and in very different environments (Browman 1976; Winterhalder 1981). In these models there are multiple significant distances at which there are inflections in the net returns curve. These are indicative of distance thresholds at which there are significant increases in the social and economic costs (Browman 1976:470). In other words, under the right circumstances small quantitative changes in distance can lead to large qualitative changes in behavior and outcome. Although more economic in their analyses, these studies indicate that multiple distance thresholds are common in social models predicated on distance costs.

There have been other attempts to model polity size and the fall-off of regional influence over distance, most notably Scarry and Payne's (1986) work based on Renfrew and Level's (1979) XTENT algorithm. Their approach used very different sets of assumptions (Renfrew and Level 1979:146, 149; Scarry and Payne 1986:80–81). One key assumption was that there is a positive relationship between the size of a center and the size of the territory it controls. This research and the work of Hally suggest otherwise: at least in this study area all polities, no matter the size of their center, face similar constraints in the polity size, that is, the territory they control. Furthermore, large polities that pursue regional strategies face another threshold at which they hold influence and can negatively influence their neighbors. Such constraints exist because of the nature of organization present in these polities.

In the archaeological study region, it is possible to claim that environment may have played a role in the distribution of large and small polities rather than the effects of interpolity competition. Certainly environment may have played some role in influencing which polities became especially large. For example, the Lower Mississippi Valley was a uniquely productive setting for Mississippian subsistence technology (Fritz and Kidder 1993; Kidder 1992; Steponaitis 1998). Furthermore, Lorenz (1992) has claimed that the Old Hoover site lacked evidence for hierarchy in some part because of its especially poor environmental niche. However, environment does not appear to adequately explain why the Pevey site was significantly larger than Blaine, Pocahontas, Lubbub Creek, or Lyon's Bluff, which all would have had similar productivity. It seems much more likely that distance from a major paramountcy played a significant role.

As is frequently the case with these types of analyses, the success or failure of these models will depend on how applicable they are to other Mississippian regions and possibly to other pre-state hierarchical societies. As mentioned in the introduction to this book, one of the challenges in conducting this type of study for other regions is that this particular analysis relied upon several cultural features that may not be present in all places or times. Still, the model predicts that the effects of interpolity competition among pre-state societies will vary with distance, and that there may be a certain distance at which there is a qualitative shift in the nature of the long-term outcomes. In this study, that distance is 100–125 km or four to five days of travel, but it is entirely possible that there may be a different distance threshold elsewhere depending on the terrain, transportation technology, warfare technology, and the nature of exchange.

Appendix 1
Ceramic Types and Counts

Ceramics Recovered from Excavations at the Pevey Site, 22Lw510

Type	A 1	B 1	B 2	B 3	B 4	C 1	C 2	C 3	C 4	C 5	C 6	C 7	C 8	E 1	E 2	E 3	Unknown
Addis Plain lug																	
Addis Plain vessel base																	
Addis Plain, *var. Addis*	4	6	12	7	7	19	32	28	9		2	4	4	14	83	14	2
Addis Plain, *var. Greenville*				1	2	1						1		2	23	3	
Anna Incised, *var. Anna*							1		1		1	1		5	31		
Anna Incised, *var. Australia*																1	
Anna Incised, *var. unspecified*															1	1	
Avoyelles Punctated, *var. Dupree*															1		
Barton Incised, *var. Barton*															1		
Barton Incised, *var. Estill*																	
Barton Incised, *var. Midnight*															2		
Barton Incised, *var. unspecified*		1												1	6		
Baytown Plain																1	
Bell Plain		1				1	1							2	7	1	
Carter Engraved, *var. Carter*							3					1	1	1	4	4	
Carter Engraved, *var. Sara*																	
Carter Engraved, *var. Shell Bluff*												7		4	8		
Carter Engraved, *var. unspecified*																1	

Chicot Red, *var. Fairchild*			1	
Coles Creek Incised, *var. Hardy*				
Coles Creek Incised, *var. unspecified*	1			
D'Olive Incised, *var. unspecified*		2		3
Evansville Punctated, *var. Sharkey*				1
Evansville Punctated, *var. unspecified*				
Fatherland Incised, *var. Pine Ridge*				
Fatherland Incised, *var. unspecified*			1	
Grace Brushed, *var. Grace*				3
Harrison Bayou Incised, *var. Harrison Bayou*		1		
Hollyknowe Pinched, *var. Patmos*				1
L'Eau Noire Incised, *var. L'Eau Noire*				1
L'Eau Noire Incised, *var. unspecified*				2
Leland Incised, *var. Bethlehem*			1	2
Leland Incised, *var. Foster*				1
Leland Incised, *var. Leland*				
Leland Incised, *var. unspecified*			1	1

Continued on the next page

Type	Unit/Analytical Unit																	
	A	B				C									E			Unknown
	1	1	2	3	4	1	2	3	4	5	6	7	8	1	2	3	
Maddox Engraved, *var. Silver City*															1	2		
Maddox Engraved, *var. unspecified*																		
Mazique Incised, *var. Manchac*																	3	
Mazique Incised, *var. unspecified*																		
Mississippi Plain	3	4	25	14	47	28	71	23	52	3	22	18	47	154	408	99	2
Mississippi Plain adorno																1		
Mississippi Plain coil snake												1						
Mississippi Plain lug																		
Mississippi Plain node																2		
Mississippi Plain vessel base																1		
Mississippi Plain with handle hole scar																1		
Mississippi Plain with handle scar																		1
Mississippi Plain with node scar																1		
Mississippi Plain with pigment cover																		
Mississippi Plain with round handle																		

Mississippi Plain with strap handle				1	
Mississippi Plain with vertical node					
Mound Place Incised, *var. A*				1	1
Mound Place Incised, *var. B*		1		19	
Mound Place Incised, *var. D*				7	
Moundville Incised, *var. Moundville*					
Moundville Incised, *var. unspecified*				1	
Owens Punctated, *var. Poor Joe*			1	1	
Owens Punctated, *var. unspecified*				4	
Owens Punctated, *var. unspecified (Menard?)*					
Parkin Punctated, *var. Harris*			2		
Parkin Punctated, *var. Hollandale*					
Parkin Punctated, *var. Transylvania*		1		1	
Parkin Punctated, *var. unspecified*	5	2	1	8	
Plaquemine Brushed, *var. Plaquemine*				1	
Sand-tempered plain			1	24	3
Plaquemine			1		

Continued on the next page

Type	Unit/Analytical Unit														
	A	B			C								E			Unknown
	1	1	2	3	4	1	2	3	4	5	6	7	8	1	2	3	
Unclassified decorated on Addis Plain, *var. Addis* paste		1			1	1	5		1			1	3	5	20	7	
Unclassified decorated on Addis Plain, *var. Greenville* paste							2		1		1	1		3	8	1	
Unclassified decorated on Baytown paste															1		
Unclassified decorated on Bell Plain paste								1						3	6	1	
Unclassified decorated on Mississippi Plain paste		2	1	2		4		1			1		1	7	41	4	
Unclassified decorated on red slip on Mississippi Plain paste																	
Undecorated Addis Plain, *var. Greenville* with red slip											1				1		
Undecorated Mississippi Plain with ochre																	
Undecorated Mississippi Plain with red slip															1		
Winterville Incised, *var. unspecified*																	
Total	8	13	45	24	61	57	119	54	65	2	29	35	59	206	736	148	5

Type	G 1	G 2	G 3	G 4	G 5	G 6	G 7	G Unknown	H 1	H 2	H 3	H 4	H 5	H 6	H Unknown	I 1	I 2	I 3	I Unknown	J 1
Addis Plain lug																1				1
Addis Plain vessel base		17	8	13	2	35	21		8	204	19	3		1	1	33	6	1	3	
Addis Plain, *var. Addis*		3			1	5			1	8						5	v2			
Addis Plain, *var. Greenville*																				
Anna Incised, *var. Anna*		6	3	8	14	1	1		1	82	1				1	6		1	1	
Anna Incised, *var. Australia*			1																	
Anna Incised, *var. unspecified*				1																
Avoyelles Punctated, *var. Dupree*																				
Barton Incised, *var. Barton*			5																	
Barton Incised, *var. Estill*																				
Barton Incised, *var. Midnight*																1				
Barton Incised, *var. unspecified*																				
Baytown Plain		10	4		5	1				7	1	2				1	2			
Bell Plain				4	5	3				2						1			1	

Continued on the next page

Type	Unit/Analytical Unit																
	G								H						I			J
	1	2	3	4	5	6	7	Unknown	1	2	3	4	5	6	Unknown	1	2	3	Unknown	1
Carter Engraved, var. Carter		1	1	1	1					2						1				1
Carter Engraved, var. Sara						3				9										
Carter Engraved, var. Shell Bluff																				
Carter Engraved, var. unspecified		2	2	1						2	1	1				1	1			
Chicot Red, var. Fairchild						1														
Coles Creek Incised, var. Hardy								1												
Coles Creek Incised, var. unspecified		1	1																	
D'Olive Incised, var. unspecified		1	4	1	7	1				2						2	2			
Evansville Punctated, var. Sharkey										1										
Evansville Punctated, var. unspecified										2										
Fatherland Incised, var. Pine Ridge																				

Fatherland Incised, *var. unspecified*	1	
Grace Brushed, *var. Grace*	1	
Harrison Bayou Incised, *var. Harrison Bayou*		4
Hollyknowe Pinched, *var. Patmos*		1
L'Eau Noire Incised, *var. L'Eau Noire*		1
L'Eau Noire Incised, *var. unspecified*	1	2
Leland Incised, *var. Bethlehem*		2
Leland Incised, *var. Foster*		
Leland Incised, *var. Leland*		1
Leland Incised, *var. unspecified*		
Maddox Engraved, *var. Silver City*		
Maddox Engraved, *var. unspecified*		
Mazique Incised, *var. Manchac*		

Continued on the next page

Type	Unit/Analytical Unit																		
			G						H						I				J
	1	2	3	4	5	6	7	Unknown	1	2	3	4	5	6	Unknown	1	2	3	Unknown	1
Mazique Incised, *var. unspecified*	3																			
Mississippi Plain		70	70	88	37	65	65	5	23	569	30	3	1			261	82	46	11	1
Mississippi Plain adorno																				
Mississippi Plain coil snake																				
Mississippi Plain lug																				
Mississippi Plain node										1										
Mississippi Plain vessel base																				
Mississippi Plain with handle hole scar							1													
Mississippi Plain with handle scar																				
Mississippi Plain with node scar																				
Mississippi Plain with pigment cover										1						1				
Mississippi Plain with round handle																				
Mississippi Plain with strap handle		1																		

Mississippi Plain with vertical node					1	
Mound Place Incised, *var. A*	2	3	1		1	1
Mound Place Incised, *var. B*	1		1	2	6	1
Mound Place Incised, *var. D*			1		2	
Moundville Incised, *var. Moundville*			3			
Moundville Incised, *var. unspecified*		1	2	2	1	3
Owens Punctated, *var. Poor Joe*						
Owens Punctated, *var. unspecified*						
Owens Punctated, *var. unspecified (Menard?)*						
Parkin Punctated, *var. Harris*						
Parkin Punctated, *var. Hollandale*						
Parkin Punctated, *var. Transylvania*			1			
Parkin Punctated, *var. unspecified*					7	

Continued on the next page

Type	Unit/Analytical Unit																	
	G								H						I			J
	1	2	3	4	5	6	7	Unknown	1	2	3	4	5	6	Unknown	1	2	3	Unknown	1
Plaquemine Brushed, *var. Plaquemine*		3	4	12	1	2			2	22						1				1
Sand-tempered plain		1	1			1	1													
Unclassified decorated on Addis Plain, *var. Addis* paste		8	3	2	1	3	2	1	1	30	3	2				3		1		
Unclassified decorated on Addis Plain, *var. Greenville* paste		3				1			1	10	1	1	1							
Unclassified decorated on Baytown paste										2										
Unclassified decorated on Bell Plain paste		1		1					1	3										
Unclassified decorated on Mississippi Plain paste	1	3	8	3	6	3	2			12	1					4	1	1		
Unclassified decorated on red slip on Mississippi Plain paste																				

Undecorated Addis Plain, *var. Greenville* with red slip	4	136	120	135	75	133	93	10	40	998	61	12	2	1	2	325	97	49	16	2
Undecorated Mississippi Plain with ochre				1													1			
Undecorated Mississippi Plain with red slip																				
Winterville Incised, *var. unspecified*																				
Total	4	136	120	135	75	133	93	10	40	998	61	12	2	1	2	325	97	49	16	2

Type	K					M					SE								
	1	2	3	4	Un-known	1	2	3	4	Un-known	1	2	2-3	3	3-4	4	5	6	6-7	7	Un-known
Addis Plain lug						2															
Addis Plain vessel base						1		1													
Addis Plain, var. Addis	2	98	4	5		89	20	11	6		45	12	5	7	8	1	8	5	1	1	4
Addis Plain, var. Greenville		7			1	59	15	14			12	1		1	3		1				
Anna Incised, var. Anna		25			1	32	2	12			6	2		1			1	1			1
Anna Incised, var. Australia		2				1							1	1							
Anna Incised, var. unspecified																					
Avoyelles Punctated, var. Dupree						1															
Barton Incised, var. Barton						1															
Barton Incised, var. Estill						3															
Barton Incised, var. Midnight																					

Barton Incised, *var. unspecified*		1		4		
Baytown Plain	2			42	7 9 1	1
Bell Plain		3		4	1 2 1	
Carter Engraved, *var. Carter*		3		1		
Carter Engraved, *var. Sara*						
Carter Engraved, *var. Shell Bluff*		5		6	2 2	1
Carter Engraved, *var. unspecified*				1		
Chicot Red, *var. Fairchild*					2	
Coles Creek Incised, *var. Hardy*		1		1		
Coles Creek Incised, *var. unspecified*		2		7		
D'Olive Incised, *var. unspecified*				6		1 1
Evansville Punctated, *var. Sharkey*						
Evansville Punctated, *var. unspecified*				1		
Fatherland Incised, *var. Pine Ridge*						

Continued on the next page

Type	K				M					SE								
	1	2	3	4	Un-known	1	2	3	4	Un-known	1	2	2-3	3	3-4	4	5	6	6-7	7	Un-known
Fatherland Incised, *var. unspecified*						1		1				1			1						
Grace Brushed, *var. Grace*		5	1			4	1	2													
Harrison Bayou Incised, *var. Harrison Bayou*		2				2															
Hollyknowe Pinched, *var. Patmos*		1									1										
L'Eau Noire Incised, *var. L'Eau Noire*						41	1														
L'Eau Noire Incised, *var. unspecified*						2					1				2						
Leland Incised, *var. Bethlehem*						9	1														
Leland Incised, *var. Foster*																					
Leland Incised, *var. Leland*						3															
Leland Incised, *var. unspecified*		1				22															

Maddox Engraved, *var. Silver City*				1						
Maddox Engraved, *var. unspecified*				3	2					1
Mazique Incised, *var. Manchac*										
Mazique Incised, *var. unspecified*				2						
Mississippi Plain	2	184	13	2	827	45	106	13	2	70	49	29	14	19	3	15	6	4	8	1
Mississippi Plain adorno										
Mississippi Plain coil snake										
Mississippi Plain lug				1						
Mississippi Plain node				1						
Mississippi Plain vessel base										
Mississippi Plain with handle hole scar										
Mississippi Plain with handle scar				2						
Mississippi Plain with node scar										
Mississippi Plain with pigment cover			1							

Continued on the next page

Type	K 1	K 2	K 3	K 4	K Un-known	M 1	M 2	M 3	M 4	M Un-known	SE 1	SE 2	SE 2-3	SE 3	SE 3-4	SE 4	SE 5	SE 6	SE 6-7	SE 7	SE Un-known
Mississippi Plain with round handle																					
Mississippi Plain with strap handle																					
Mississippi Plain with vertical node																					
Mound Place Incised, *var. A*		1				3															
Mound Place Incised, *var. B*		8				17	1				1			1							
Mound Place Incised, *var. D*		2				3							1								
Moundville Incised, *var. Moundville*								1				1									
Moundville Incised, *var. unspecified*																					
Owens Punctated, *var. Poor Joe*		1				3	2				1										
Owens Punctated, *var. unspecified*												1		1							

Owens Punctated, *var. unspecified* (Menard?)		2					
Parkin Punctated, *var. Harris*		2			1		1
Parkin Punctated, *var. Hollandale*		3					
Parkin Punctated, *var. Transylvania*	4	1					
Parkin Punctated, *var. unspecified*		9			3	1	
Plaquemine Brushed, *var. Plaquemine*	16	25	9	7	3	1	1	3	1
Sand-tempered plain	1					1	1
Unclassified decorated on Addis Plain, *var. Addis* paste	3	40	49	1	3	11	3		2	2
Unclassified decorated on Addis Plain, *var. Greenville* paste	9	1	17		1	2		1	1
Unclassified decorated on Baytown paste		3	4					
Unclassified decorated on Bell Plain paste		3	3			2	1	
Unclassified decorated on Mississippi Plain paste	1	18	1	37	2	4	1	6	2	2

Continued on the next page

Type	K 1	K 2	K 3	K 4	K Unknown	M 1	M 2	M 3	M 4	M Unknown	SE 1	SE 2	SE 2-3	SE 3	SE 3-4	SE 4	SE 5	SE 6	SE 6-7	SE 7	SE Unknown
Unclassified decorated on red slip on Mississippi Plain paste						1															
Undecorated Addis Plain, *var. Greenville* with red slip		1																			
Undecorated Mississippi Plain with ochre																					
Undecorated Mississippi Plain with red slip																					
Winterville Incised, *var. unspecified*						4															
Total	10	447	21	7	2	1,376	110	180	22	3	166	76	39	27	39	4	28	16	5	12	6

Type	SJ 3	SJ 4	Unknown	T 1	T 1-2	T 2	T 2-3	T 3	T 4	Total
Addis Plain lug										5
Addis Plain vessel base					2					2
Addis Plain, *var. Addis*	3				68	28	9		3	1,065
Addis Plain, *var. Greenville*					10	1	6		3	192
Anna Incised, *var. Anna*			1		7					258
Anna Incised, *var. Australia*										7
Anna Incised, *var. unspecified*										3
Avoyelles Punctated, *var. Dupree*										2
Barton Incised, *var. Barton*										7
Barton Incised, *var. Estill*										3
Barton Incised, *var. Midnight*										2
Barton Incised, *var. unspecified*										14
Baytown Plain		2								30
Bell Plain					40	9	1	1	1	147
Carter Engraved, *var. Carter*										32
Carter Engraved, *var. Sara*										10
Carter Engraved, *var. Shell Bluff*										3
Carter Engraved, *var. unspecified*	2			1	4	16	2			72
Chicot Red, *var. Fairchild*										2
Coles Creek Incised, *var. Hardy*					1					4
Coles Creek Incised, *var. unspecified*										5

Continued on the next page

Type	SJ 3	SJ 4	SJ Unknown	T 1	T 1-2	T 2	T 2-3	T 3	T 4	Total
D'Olive Incised, *var. unspecified*										36
Evansville Punctated, *var. Sharkey*										7
Evansville Punctated, *var. unspecified*										4
Fatherland Incised, *var. Pine Ridge*										1
Fatherland Incised, *var. unspecified*										5
Grace Brushed, *var. Grace*				3	5					37
Harrison Bayou Incised, *var. Harrison Bayou*							5		3	7
Hollyknowe Pinched, *var. Patmos*					1					5
L'Eau Noire Incised, *var. L'Eau Noire*					1					46
L'Eau Noire Incised, *var. unspecified*					1					11
Leland Incised, *var. Bethlehem*										13
Leland Incised, *var. Foster*										1
Leland Incised, *var. Leland*										4
Leland Incised, *var. unspecified*										25
Maddox Engraved, *var. Silver City*										5
Maddox Engraved, *var. unspecified*										5
Mazique Incised, *var. Manchac*					3					3
Mazique Incised, *var. unspecified*										5
Mississippi Plain	12			260	973	267	244	1	56	5,675

Mississippi Plain adorno		1
Mississippi Plain coil snake		1
Mississippi Plain lug		1
Mississippi Plain node		4
Mississippi Plain vessel base		1
Mississippi Plain with handle hole scar		1
Mississippi Plain with handle scar		3
Mississippi Plain with node scar		1
Mississippi Plain with pigment cover	1	2
Mississippi Plain with round handle		3
Mississippi Plain with strap handle		3
Mississippi Plain with vertical node		1
Mound Place Incised, *var. A*		6
Mound Place Incised, *var. B*	5	70
Mound Place Incised, *var. D*	1	19
Moundville Incised, *var. Moundville*		3
Moundville Incised, *var. unspecified*		11
Owens Punctated, *var. Poor Joe*		1
Owens Punctated, *var. unspecified*		13
Owens Punctated, *var. unspecified (Menard?)*		2
Parkin Punctated, *var. Harris*		4
Parkin Punctated, *var. Hollandale*		5
Parkin Punctated, *var. Transylvania*		1
Parkin Punctated, *var. unspecified*	1	36

Continued on the next page

Type	Unit/Analytical Unit								Total
	SJ			T					
	3	4	Unknown	1	1-2	2	2-3	3	4	
Plaquemine Brushed, *var. Plaquemine*					9	2	1			163
Sand-tempered plain										10
Unclassified decorated on Addis Plain, *var. Addis* paste				3	8	1	2			232
Unclassified decorated on Addis Plain, *var. Greenville* paste		1								68
Unclassified decorated on Baytown paste					1					11
Unclassified decorated on Bell Plain paste					1					27
Unclassified decorated on Mississippi Plain paste				2	8	8	5	1		207
Unclassified decorated on red slip on Mississippi Plain paste										1
Undecorated Addis Plain, *var. Greenville* with red slip										3
Undecorated Mississippi Plain with ochre										2
Undecorated Mississippi Plain with red slip					1					1
Winterville Incised, *var. unspecified*						1				6
Total	17	3	1	270	1,151	333	276	3	66	8,684

Ceramics Recovered from the Lowe-Steen Site, 22Lw511

Type	1136R876			956R1003						975R1007						Feature 4	Total
	2	3	4	5	1	2	3	4	5	Un-known	1	2	3	3-4	4	5	1	
Addis Plain, *var. Addis*	1	12		1	12	41	1	2		1	1	2		13	32	1	198	318
Addis Plain, *var. Greenville*		3				4	1					1		5	1		8	23
Anna Incised, *var. Anna*						5	1							1	2	1	5	15
Barton Incised, *var. Barton*							2										1	3
Barton Incised, *var. Estill*		1																1
Baytown Plain													1				3	4
Bell Plain		4					2						7	1	1		4	19
Carter Engraved, *var. Carter*						2	1										23	26
Carter Engraved, *var. unspecified*						6	6						1					13
D'Olive Incised, *var. unspecified*		2				1	1											4
Grace Brushed, *var. Grace*						1	1											
Harrison Bayou Incised, *var. Harrison Bayou*												1			1		4	6
																		2

Continued on the next page

Type	1136R876			956R1003						975R1007					Feature 4	Total
	2	3	4	5	1	2	3	4	5	Un-known	1	2	3	3-4	4	5		
Hollyknowe Pinched, *var. Patmos*						2												2
Marksville Stamped, *var. unspecified*																	1	1
Mazique Incised, *var. Manchac*														1				1
Mazique Incised, *var. unspecified*																	2	2
Mississippi Plain	2	79		4	3	226	172	24	9	12	1	5	16	18	121	1	941	1,634
Mississippi Plain adorno																	1	1
Mississippi Plain lug							2											2
Mississippi Plain node						1												1
Mississippi Plain with handle scar																	3	3
Mississippi Plain with round handle							1										7	8
Mound Place Incised, *var. B*		1				7	6				1				1			16

Plaquemine Brushed, *var. Plaquemine*			1		1	6	4		1		1	2	3	4	64	87
Unclassified decorated on Addis Plain, *var. Addis* paste				1	2	3		1			1	2	1		18	30
Unclassified decorated on Mississippi Plain paste			1		18	11							2	1	10	43
Total	3	101	3	5	17	322	215	26	11	13	4	12	30	42	164	4	1,293	2,265

Ceramics Recovered from the Phillips Farm Site, 22Lw593

Type	Feature 1	Feature 5	Feature 23	N1002E1014	N1005E1013	N1006E1012	N1006E1014	N1008E1002	N1008E1004	N1008E1006	N1008E1008	N1008E1010	N1008E1012	N1008E1014	N1008E1016	N1008E1018	N1010E1014	Total
Addis Plain, *var. Addis*	2	2		14	2	3	4	6	5	10	4	2	5	9	7	2	8	85
Addis Plain, *var. Greenville*								2								1		3
Bell Plain		2																2
Mississippi Plain		43	6	16		1	6		3	7	1	1	1	3	1		1	90
Mississippi Plain with round handle															1			1
Plaquemine Brushed, *var. Plaquemine*															1			1
Sand-tempered plain			1															1
Unclassified decorated on Addis Plain, *var. Addis* paste							1			2			2		1			6
Unclassified decorated on Addis Plain, *var. Greenville* paste				2				1										3
Unclassified decorated on Mississippi Plain paste		1		2					1									4
Total	2	48	7	34	2	4	11	9	9	19	5	3	8	12	11	3	9	196

Appendix 2
Macrofaunal Analysis from Two Units at the Pevey Site

Simone B. Rowe

University of Oklahoma and Sam Noble Oklahoma Museum of Natural History

Macrofaunal remains from two of the nine mounds at the Pevey site were analyzed and compared. Units at Mound E were chosen for analysis because they are hypothesized to have been the refuse of an elite household. Mound M was chosen for comparison because its analytical units contained the largest amount of macrofaunal remains. Both sets of remains were examined for evidence of elite patterns of faunal use. Results indicate little evidence for provisioning or feasting from either set of macrofaunal remains. However, evidence for bone grease processing was found at Mound E.

Background

As detailed in earlier chapters, the Pevey site in Lawrence County, Mississippi, is located in the Piney Woods region of the Gulf Coastal Plain on a floodplain of the west bank of the Pearl River. The site forms a naturally well-demarcated zone with a sharp terrace defining both the northern and eastern borders and with Mill Creek (which drains into the Pearl River) as the south border. This area has been relatively stable geologically and environmentally for at least 5,000 years.

The site consists of nine extant mounds, arranged in two parallel rows around a central plaza, extending down a gently sloping extension of the floodplain terrace. The nine mounds make it a remarkably large site, placing it among the top 5 percent of Mississippi period mound sites by number of mounds. From pottery analysis, Livingood has ascertained a primary occupation from A.D. 1200 to A.D. 1350, with possible evidence of an earlier occupation during A.D. 1000–1200.

Faunal remains were collected from several mounds as well as from units excavated between mounds. This report compares the macrofaunal remains collected at Excavation Unit E (a midden from Mound E, the largest mound at the site and hypothesized to be the residence of elites) and Excavation Unit M (an inter-mound site). All remains discussed here are macro remains recovered in ¼-inch dry screen. Microfaunal remains recovered by water screen (down to 1/32 inch) have yet to be examined.

Methods

Identification of specimens down to the lowest possible taxon was done by direct comparison with the reference collection at the University of Oklahoma Archaeological Survey. While there are some complete bone elements, especially at Excavation Unit M, a large proportion of the remains are fragmentary and not identifiable to species or even family level. Some of the material could not even be identified to class. Additionally, damage resulting from "scrubbing" against a screen during postexcavation processing is apparent on a large proportion of the remains. In some cases this damage has obscured identifying markers as well as possibly obliterating taphonomic or cultural modifications. Many of the remains also exhibit postexcavation breaks.

Large mammalian remains lacking diagnostic markers (due to breakage or weathering) were designated "large mammal" and are referred to as "probable deer." Smaller mammal bones not identifiable to species are designated as "unidentified small mammal." Remains that are not identifiable to class are labeled "unidentified vertebrate."

Analysis in this report relies largely on the primary data of count and weight. Count is given as NISP (number of identified specimens) and weight is always in grams. Secondary data in the form of MNI (minimum number of individuals) are also given. Assessment of MNI is based on element (symmetry and portion), age (including epiphyseal fusion), and (when possible) sex.

Excavation Unit E

Mound E is the largest mound at the Pevey site. The excavation unit was placed at the northeastern base of the mound, between the foot of the mound and the edge of the floodplain terrace. The intent was to sample mound flank midden that might have accumulated during the last stage of Mound E occupation (Livingood 2006:47). Pottery analysis suggests that this area of the site was used near the end of the Pevey site occupation and that the midden contents may have been the refuse of an elite household (Livingood 2006:

Table A.2.1. Excavation Unit E: Weights and NISP of Deer and Large Mammal

Analytical Unit	Deer Weight (g)	Deer NISP	Large Mammal Weight (g)	Large Mammal NISP	Deer + Large Mammal Weight (g)	Deer + Large Mammal NISP
E1	10	4	39	11	49	15
E2	93.5	16	632.2	564	725.7	580
E3	92.5	11	75.5	100	168	111
Total	196	31	746.7	675	942.7	706

263). Following Livingood (2006) the remains from Excavation Unit E have been divided into analytical units E1, E2, and E3 (see Table A.2.1).

Although Excavation Unit E did not contain a large quantity of faunal remains (992.2 g, NISP = 781), the remains that were recovered are distinct. The vast majority (75 percent by weight) of the remains are identifiable only as pieces of large mammal bone and lack identifying markers.

Analytical Unit E1. Despite containing the least amount of faunal material (84.5 g, NISP = 71), analytical unit E1 is the most diverse of the analytical units from Excavation Unit E, with a total of five species. By weight, the unit contains 78 percent mammal remains, 2 percent shell (unidentified freshwater mussel), and 7 percent bird. Nearly half (46 percent) of the total material is identifiable only as large mammal, or probable deer, and another 13 percent can only be classified as unidentified vertebrate. Of the mammal remains, five specimens are positively identified to the species level, with a sixth element tentatively identified as skunk. The other five elements are one fox squirrel (*Sciurus niger*) and four worn deer (*Odocoileus virginianus*) elements—a distal radius and three skull fragments.

Analytical Unit E2. Analytical unit E2 is the largest from Excavation Unit E (731.7 g, NISP = 589) as well as the least diverse, with only two identified species. The faunal remains in analytical unit E2 were identified as nearly 100 percent mammal—either white-tailed deer (*O. virginianus*) or unidentified large mammal. The only nonmammal remains are a single turkey (*Meleagris gallopavo*) femur (<1 percent of the total).

Fully 86 percent of the elements examined are identifiable only as large mammal or probable deer. An additional 13 percent of the remains were identified as white-tailed deer (*O. virginianus*). Note that this is six times as much unidentifiable large mammal bone as identifiable deer bone. Of the

16 deer elements, 12 are the articular ends of limb bones. The deer-sized remains include more articular ends, long-bone shafts, and vertebrae, as well as many unidentifiable pieces of bone. None of the remains are visibly burned, although one humerus shows signs of butchering in the form of cut marks. All of the macro remains are rounded, with softened borders, which contributed to difficulty in identification.

Analytical Unit E3. Analytical unit E3 (176 g, NISP = 121) is a small unit in which 95 percent of the remains were identified as either deer (52.3 percent) or unidentified large mammal (43 percent). All of the identified elements are articular ends of deer bones. Nine of these 11 elements (82 percent) were hind limb. The remaining 5 percent of the material is turtle. Both box turtle (*Terrepene* sp.) and softshell turtle (*Amyla* sp.) are represented, giving analytical unit E3 a total of three species.

Excavation Unit M

Excavation Unit M was located on a small rise on the bluff edge between Mound E and the ravine separating Mounds D and E. A dense midden suggested by soil cores was confirmed by excavation. As a whole, Excavation Unit M contained a large amount of macrofaunal material (3,691.3 g, NISP = 1,524). Following Livingood (2006), the faunal remains from Excavation Unit M were divided into four analytical units, M1, M2, M3, and M4 (see Table A.2.2).

Analytical Unit M1. Analytical unit M1 is the largest of the three subunits, the largest analytical unit overall (2,051.5 g, NISP = 1,155), and the most diverse, with at least nine species present. The vast majority (85 percent by weight) of this material is mammal. Also present in decreasing order of prevalence are freshwater mussel (6 percent); bird (2 percent), in the form of turkey (*M. gallopavo*) and a second kind of bird, probably duck; at least two kinds of turtle (1.7 percent), including box turtle (*Terrepene* sp.) and an emydid (freshwater slider/cooter); at least two kinds of fish (.3 percent), including gar (*Lepisosteus* sp.) and catfish (*Ictalus* sp.); and an unidentified snake (>.1 percent). Twelve percent of the total material is unidentified (not deer-sized) mammal or unidentified vertebrate.

Fifty percent of the individual elements are identifiable as white-tailed deer (*O. virginianus*); if probable deer are included, this proportion increases to 76 percent. At least six individual deer are represented (MNI = 6). All portions of the deer skeleton are represented, including head and feet. Approximately 13 percent of the identifiable deer remains are visibly burned. Among the unidentifiable deer-sized mammal elements (26 percent of the total weight), there are pieces of head and teeth as well as the axial and ap-

Table A.2.2. Excavation Unit M: Weights and NISP of Deer and Large Mammal

Analytical Unit	Deer Weight (g)	Deer NISP	Large Mammal Weight (g)	Large Mammal NISP	Deer + Large Mammal Weight (g)	Deer + Large Mammal NISP
M1	1,035	86	540	237	1,575	323
M2	573	55	173	106	746	161
M3	638	45	198.5	81	836.5	126
M4	0	0	7.5	3	7.5	3
Total	2,246	186	919	427	3,165	613

pendicular skeleton. Additionally, a second mammalian species was positively identified as fox squirrel.

A portion of fetal bone was identified from analytical unit M1. From the size, it was assigned to "probable deer." This indicates hunting/habitation in the spring. This unit also contains the only evidence found so far of worked bone. A tine from a deer antler was found to have been grooved and snapped, indicating possible bead manufacture.

Analytical Unit M2. Analytical unit M2 is similar in overall composition to analytical unit M1, but with a smaller sample size (958.6 g, NISP = 278). Six species were identified.

The vast majority (78 percent by weight) of this material is mammal. Also present in decreasing order of prevalence are freshwater mussel (6 percent); bird (3.5 percent), in the form of turkey (*M. gallopavo*); box turtle (*Terrepene* sp.) (1.8 percent); and fish (.3 percent), including gar (*Lepisosteus* sp.) and catfish (*Ictalus* sp.). Unidentifiable mammal or other vertebrate comprises 6.4 percent of the total.

Sixty percent of the individual elements are identifiable as white-tailed deer (*O. virginianus*); if probable deer are included, this proportion increases to 68 percent. At least four individual deer were present (MNI = 4). All portions of skeleton are represented, including head and feet. Approximately 3 percent of the identifiable deer remains are visibly burned. Among the deer-sized mammal parts (18 percent of the total weight), there are pieces of head and teeth as well as the axial and appendicular skeleton. Four of the deer limb bones display spiral fractures and two of them are visibly burned. Less than 1 percent of the deer-sized mammal remains are visibly burned.

Analytical Unit M3. Analytical unit M3 (1,146.5 g, NISP = 435) is largely mammal (79 percent by weight) and contains eight species. In addition to deer (*O. virginianus*) and probable deer, at least two other types of mammal are present, including fox squirrel (*S. niger*) and a larger (skunk-sized) species. Also present in decreasing order of prevalence are turtle (*Terrepene* sp.) (7.5 percent); freshwater mussel (6 percent); two types of bird (3.6 percent), turkey (*M. gallopavo*) and mourning dove (*Zenaida macrouria*); and at least two kinds of fish (.8 percent) including gar (*Lepisosteus* sp.) and catfish (*Ictalus* sp.). Analytical unit M3 contains a deceptively large amount of turtle (82.5 g, NISP = 23); however, most of this is a single, nearly complete carapace in 14 cross-mendable pieces. Only one individual is therefore accounted for (MNI = 1). Additionally, 9.5 percent of the total material is unidentifiable mammal (not deer-sized) or vertebrate.

Approximately half (56 percent) of the individual elements were identified as white-tailed deer (*O. virginianus*); if probable deer are included, this proportion increases to 73 percent. At least five individual deer are represented (MNI = 5). All portions of the skeleton of the deer are present, including head and feet. None of the identifiable deer remains are visibly burned though approximately 7 percent of the deer-sized mammal parts are visibly burned.

Analytical Unit M4. Analytical unit M4 is extremely small, consisting of only a few scraps of unidentified mammal and unidentified vertebrate bone (9.5 g, NISP = 9). It will not be further discussed.

Results and Discussion

Before discussing and comparing the assemblages from each unit, it is necessary to say a word about preservation and taphonomic issues. Due to acidic soil conditions, preservation in southeastern soil is notoriously poor, and the Pevey site is no exception. The macrofaunal remains no doubt represent only a small fraction of the total from the Pevey site. A second important point to be made is that the microfaunal remains have not been analyzed, which skews the results toward large prey, particularly deer. The preponderance of deer remains from the Pevey site is no doubt misleading. This site was situated on the banks of a creek and near a major river. Riverine fauna would therefore be expected to make up a large proportion of the faunal remains. The dearth of riverine fauna requires explanation. Quitmyer (2003:131) has shown that up to 94 percent of fish vertebra are missed without analysis of microfaunal remains. The lack of fine-mesh screening probably accounts for the underrepresentation of fish remains. Small mammal and bird remains may also increase when microfaunal analyses are taken into consideration. This discussion is therefore limited to information that can be derived from the macrofaunal remains; specifically, it focuses on large mammal meat processing and consumption. It does not claim to represent the animals at the core of Pevey site economic or subsistence patterns.

The areas around Excavation Units E and M are hypothesized to have been home to elite residents or high-status activities (Livingood 2006). The macrofaunal remains were examined for evidence of elite patterns of faunal use, specifically (1) a diverse sample of birds; (2) the presence of rare, unusual, or dangerous prey; and (3) evidence of feasting, including large quantities of high-utility deer bone (e.g., no skull or feet material and a disproportionate amount of long bone) (Jackson and Scott 2003).

The proportion and patterning of deer remains can also reveal patterns of provisioning. An unprovisioned, or nonelite, household would be expected to contain all portions of deer remains, including nonchoice parts such as head and feet. By contrast, a provisioned, elite household would be expected to display the same evidence already discussed in the third criterion, namely large quantities of high-utility deer bone and no skull or feet material. Furthermore, deer hindquarters are indicative of a higher elite status than forequarters indicate (Scott 2005:423).

The data available do not show a diverse sample of birds. Two types of bird were positively identified (turkey and mourning dove). A third type of bird, thought to be a duck, was also identified. The relative paucity of bird remains does not necessarily signify that a variety of birds was not consumed. Bird bones are lighter and more fragile than mammal bones and have a higher likelihood of destruction due to taphonomic processes. It is possible that a microfaunal analysis will uncover the presence of a more diverse sampling of birds.

There is currently no evidence of rare, unusual, or dangerous prey. Among the units analyzed, the only large mammal identified is white-tailed deer, and the unidentifiable large mammal bone is also most likely to be deer. However, since rare prey is (by definition) rare, it is much less likely to be preserved in the archaeological record than more common prey such as deer. It is therefore possible that the residents did consume rare or unusual prey and that there is simply no record of it as of yet.

For each unit examined, deer bone constitutes the vast majority of the macrofaunal remains. The individual units will therefore be examined for evidence of feasting or other evidence of elite presence/use.

Excavation Unit E

When compared with the more diverse assemblages of Unit M, it becomes clear that Unit E is a distinctive assemblage. There is no record of plowing, development, or disturbance and no indication of unique soil properties or geologic processes. We can thus assume that Excavation Unit E was not subject to any unique taphonomic processes that the other excavation units did not also undergo. It is therefore necessary to ask what processes could have caused an assemblage that consists primarily of unidentifiable large mammal remains and a few articular ends of deer long bones. One human activity that could create this distinctive assemblage is bone grease processing, in which the articular ends of long bones and the vertebral centra are pulverized and boiled (Scott 2005:421). Where this process has occurred, one expects to find a large amount of mammal bone that is identifiable only as large mammal, as well as the articular ends of long bones. This is precisely the assemblage found at Excavation Unit E.

Bone grease processing is not a component of feasting; rather, it is associated with scarcity in the food supply (Scott 2005:427). If Unit E was associated with an elite household, it is reasonable to hypothesize that the residents, and by extension the entire population at the Pevey site, were undergoing a period of economic hardship and subsistence stress. Since the unit dates to the terminal Winstead phase this may also indicate that the remaining residents of Pevey were under dietary stress.

Excavation Unit M

When compared with Excavation Unit E, Excavation Unit M is a larger, more diverse assemblage. None of the analytical units from Excavation Unit M display large amounts of unidentifiable large mammal bone. For each of the four analytical units, the largest amount of material is always white-tailed deer. As in Excavation Unit E, there is no evidence of large or dangerous prey, nor is a diverse array of birds found. However, there may be some evidence of feasting.

Visibly burnt remains, consistent with roasting, are seen in Excavation Unit M. Turkey, mourning dove, fox squirrel, and deer are all visibly burned. Additionally, we see charred deer bones, many with spiral fractures and/or cut and butchering marks. It is notable, however, that all of the analytical units from Excavation Unit M (discounting the very small subunit M4) have the remains of all portions of deer skeleton, including head and feet. The presence of nonchoice meat cuts suggests that the households around Excavation Unit M were self-provisioning (Jackson and Scott 2003:563).

The proportions of deer remains in Excavation Unit M thus reveal no evidence of provisioning; rather the remains from Excavation Unit M are consistent with a self-provisioning household that may have engaged in some feasting activity. However, the evidence for feasting is limited to evidence indicating butchering and roasting, which may merely be the result of everyday processing and cooking.

Summary/Conclusions

The macrofaunal remains from Excavation Units E and M alone cannot confirm the existence of an elite presence around Mound E or Excavation Unit M. The faunal remains examined from Excavation Unit E are indicative of bone grease processing, which is not usually associated with elite households. The faunal remains from Excavation Unit M appear to represent self-provisioning households that may have engaged in some roasting/feasting activities.

Future research goals for the faunal remains at the Pevey site include analysis of the macro remains from the remaining excavation units as well as analysis of all the micro remains.

References Cited

Anderson, David G.
1994a Factional Competition and the Political Evolution of Mississippian Chiefdoms in the Southeastern United States. In *Factional Competition and Political Development in the New World,* edited by E. M. Brumfiel and J. W. Fox, pp. 61–76. Cambridge University Press, Cambridge.
1994b *The Savannah River Chiefdoms: Political Change in the Late Prehistoric Southeast.* University of Alabama Press, Tuscaloosa.
1996 Fluctuations between Simple and Complex Chiefdoms: Cycling in the Late Prehistoric Southeast. In *Political Structure and Change in the Prehistoric Southeastern United States,* edited by J. F. Scarry, pp. 231–252. University of Florida Press, Gainesville.
1999 Examining Chiefdoms in the Southeast: An Application of Multiscalar Analysis. In *Great Towns and Regional Polities: In the Prehistoric American Southwest and Southeast,* edited by J. Neitzel, pp. 215–241. University of New Mexico Press, Albuquerque.

Andrefsky, William, Jr.
1998 *Lithics: Macroscopic Approaches to Analysis.* Cambridge University Press, Cambridge.

Andrefsky, William, Jr., and Marilyn J. Bender (editors)
1988 *The Piñon Canyon Maneuver Site Manual for the Conduct of Laboratory and Analytical Studies and Handling of Materials.* Prepared for the National Park Service, Rocky Mountain Region and U.S. Department of the Army, Fort Carson, Colorado.

Andrefsky, William, Jr., Elizabeth G. Wilmerding, and Steven R. Samuels
1994 *Archaeological Testing at Three Sites along the North Umpqua Drainage, Douglas County, Oregon.* Project Report 23, Center for Northwest Anthropology, Washington State University, Pullman.

Arnold, Dean E.
- 1985 *Ceramic Theory and Cultural Process.* Cambridge University Press, Cambridge.

Baca, Keith A.
- 2001 Destruction of the Blaine Mound, A Mississippian Period Site in the Central Pearl Valley, Mississippi. *Mississippi Archaeology* 36(1):1–16.

Barker, Alex W.
- 1999 *Chiefdoms and the Economics of Perversity.* Ph.D. dissertation, Department of Anthropology, University of Michigan, Ann Arbor. University Microfilms, Ann Arbor.
- 2008 Chiefdoms. In *Handbook of Archaeological Theories,* edited by R. A. Bentley, H. D. G. Maschner, and C. Chippindale, pp. 515–532. Altamira, New York.

Barlow, Robert
- 1949 *The Extent of the Empire of the Culhua-Mexica.* Ibero Americana No. 28. University of California Press, Berkeley.

Bauer, Brian S., and R. Alan Covey
- 2002 Processes of State Formation in the Inca Heartland (Cuzco, Peru). *American Anthropologist* 104:846–864.

Beasley, Virgil Roy, III
- 2007 Feasting on the Bluffs: Anna Site Excavations in the Natchez Bluffs of Mississippi. In *Plaquemine Archaeology,* edited by M. A. Rees and P. C. Livingood, pp. 127–144. University of Alabama Press, Tuscaloosa.

Beck, Robin A., Jr.
- 2003 Consolidation and Hierarchy: Chiefdom Variability in the Mississippian Southeast. *American Antiquity* 68:641–661.
- 2006 Persuasive Politics and Domination at Cahokia and Moundville. In *Leadership and Polity in Mississippian Society,* edited by B. M. Butler and P. D. Welch, pp. 19–42. Occasional Paper No. 33. Center for Archaeological Investigations, Southern Illinois University, Carbondale.

Bense, Judith A.
- 1989 *The Pensacola Archaeological Survey,* Vol. 1. Pensacola Archaeological Society Publication No. 2. Pensacola, Florida.

Binford, Lewis R.
- 1967 Smudge Pits and Hide Smoking: The Use of Analogy in Archaeological Reasoning. *American Antiquity* 32:1–10.

Blandino, Betty
- 1997 *Coiled Pottery: Traditional and Contemporary Ways.* Rev. ed. A & C Black, London.

Blitz, John H.
1993a *Ancient Chiefdoms of the Tombigbee.* University of Alabama Press, Tuscaloosa.
1993b Big Pots for Big Shots: Feasting and Storage in a Mississippian Community. *American Antiquity* 58:80–95.
1999 Mississippian Chiefdoms and the Fission-Fusion Process. *American Antiquity* 62:577–592.

Blitz, John H., and Patrick C. Livingood
2004 Sociopolitical Implications of Mississippian Mound Volume. *American Antiquity* 69:291–301.

Blitz, John H., and Karl G. Lorenz
2002 The Early Mississippian Frontier in the Lower Chattahoochee-Apalachicola River Valley. *Southeastern Archaeology* 21:117–135.

Blitz, John H., and Cyril B. Mann
2000 *Fisherfolk, Farmers and Frenchmen.* Mississippi Department of Archives and History, Jackson.

Bogan, A. E., and Richard R. Polhemus
1987 Faunal Analysis. In *The Toqua Site—40MR6: A Late Mississippian Dallas Phase Town,* edited by R. R. Polhemus, pp. 971–1111. Report submitted to the Tennessee Valley Authority by the Department of Anthropology, University of Tennessee, Knoxville. Report of Investigations 41, Department of Anthropology, University of Tennessee, Knoxville.

Boudreaux, Edmond A.
1997 Test Excavations at the Cotton Mounds (22Wr614), a Mississippi Period Site in the Lower Big Black River Valley, Warren County, Mississippi. Unpublished Master's thesis, Department of Anthropology, University of Alabama, Tuscaloosa.

Brain, Jeffrey P.
1978 Late Prehistoric Settlement Patterning in the Yazoo Basin and Natchez Bluffs Regions of the Lower State: Mississippi Valley. In *Mississippian Settlement Patterns,* edited by B. D. Smith, pp. 331–368. Academic Press, New York.
1989 *Winterville.* Mississippi Department of Archives and History, Jackson.

Brain, Jeffrey P., Ian W. Brown, and Vincas P. Steponaitis
1994 Archaeology of the Natchez Bluffs. Manuscript on file at the Research Laboratories of Archaeology, University of North Carolina, Chapel Hill.

Brain, Jeffrey P., and James L. Phillips
1996 *Shell Gorgets: Styles of the Late Prehistoric and Protohistoric Southeast.* Peabody Museum Press, Cambridge, Massachusetts.

Brewer, E. Marco

1994   Analysis of Plant Remains from the Lowe-Steen (22Lw511) and the Potts' Tract Site (9Mu103). Unpublished manuscript available from Patrick Livingood.

1995   Subsistence Patterns in Central Mississippi and Alabama: The Pearl Mounds Site (22Lw510), Lawrence Co., Mississippi. Senior honors thesis, Department of Anthropology, University of North Carolina, Chapel Hill.

Bronitsky, Gordon, and Robert Hamer

1986   Experiments in Ceramic Technology: The Effects of Various Tempering Materials on Impact and Thermal-Shock Resistance. *American Antiquity* 51:89–101.

Brookes, Samuel O.

ca. 1980s   Comments on Lithics from Mill Creek. Unpublished manuscript on file with the Mississippi Department of Archives and History, Jackson.

2000   Archaeology from Memory: Lyon's Bluff, 1968. *Mississippi Archaeology* 35(1):15–22.

Browman, D. L.

1976   Demographic Correlations of the Wari Conquest of Junin. *American Antiquity* 41:465–477.

Brown, Ian W.

1985a   Plaquemine Architectural Patterns in the Natchez Bluffs and Surrounding Regions of the Lower Mississippi Valley. *Midcontinental Journal of Archaeology* 10:251–305.

1985b   *Natchez Indian Archaeology: Culture Change and Stability in the Lower Mississippi Valley.* Archaeological Report No. 15. Mississippi Department of Archives and History, Jackson.

1998   *Decorated Pottery of the Lower Mississippi Valley: A Sorting Manual.* Mississippi Archaeological Association and Mississippi Department of Archives and History, Jackson.

2003   Introduction to the Bottle Creek Site. In *Bottle Creek: A Pensacola Culture Site in South Alabama*, edited by I. W. Brown, pp. 1–26. University of Alabama Press, Tuscaloosa.

2007   Plaquemine Culture in the Natchez Bluffs Region of Mississippi. In *Plaquemine Archaeology*, edited by M. A. Rees and P. C. Livingood, pp. 145–160. University of Alabama Press, Tuscaloosa.

Brown, James A.

2004   The Cahokian Expression: Creating Court and Cult. In *Hero, Hawk, and Open Hand: American Indian Art of the Ancient Midwest and South,*

edited by R. F. Townsend, pp. 105–123. Art Institute of Chicago, Chicago.
- 2007 On the Identity of the Birdman within Mississippian Period Art and Iconography. In *Ancient Objects and Sacred Realms: Interpretations of Mississippian Iconography,* edited by F. K. Reilly and J. Garber, pp. 56–106. University of Texas Press, Austin.

Brown, James A., Richard A. Kerber, and Howard D. Winters
- 1990 Trade and the Evolution of Exchange Relations at the Beginning of the Mississippian Period. In *The Mississippian Emergence,* edited by B. D. Smith, pp. 251–280. Smithsonian Institution Press, Washington, D.C.

Burden, E., D. Wiseman, Richard A. Weinstein, and Sherwood M. Gagliano
- 1978 *Cultural Resources Survey of the Lacassine National Wildlife Refuge, Cameron Parish, Louisiana.* Coastal Environments, Inc., Baton Rouge, Louisiana.

Bushnell, David I.
- 1909 *The Choctaw of Bayou LaCombe, St. Tammany Parish, Louisiana.* Bureau of American Ethnology Bulletin No. 48. Smithsonian Institution, Washington, D.C.

Byram, Scott
- 1996 *On-Site Lithic Analysis Manual.* Prepared for the Malheur National Forest, U.S. Department of Agriculture, John Day, Oregon.

Caddell, Gloria
- 1983 Floral Remains from the Lubbub Creek Archaeological Locality. In *Studies of Material Remains from the Lubbub Creek Archaeological Locality,* edited by C. S. Peebles, pp. 194–271. U.S. Army Corps of Engineers, Mobile, Alabama.

Carleton, Kenneth H.
- 1999 Nanih Waiya (22WI500): An Historical and Archaeological Overview. *Mississippi Archaeology* 34(2):125–155.

Carr, Christopher
- 1995a Building a Unified Middle-Range Theory of Artifact Design: Historical Perspectives and Tactics. In *Style, Society, and Person: Archaeological and Ethnological Perspectives,* edited by C. Carr and J. Neitzel, pp. 151–170. Plenum Press, New York.
- 1995b A Unified Middle-Range Theory of Artifact Design. In *Style, Society, and Person: Archaeological and Ethnological Perspectives,* edited by C. Carr and J. Neitzel, pp. 171–257. Plenum Press, New York.

Clayton, Lawrence A., Vernon James Knight Jr., and Edward C. Moore
- 1993 *The De Soto Chronicles: The Expedition of Hernando de Soto to North*

America in 1539–1543. 2 vols. University of Alabama Press, Tuscaloosa.

Coastal Environments, Inc.
1983 *An Assessment of Prehistoric Cultural Resources within the Coastal Zone of Tangipahoa Parish.* Report prepared for Tangipahoa Parish Tourist Commission. Report on file with the Louisiana Division of Archaeology, Baton Rouge.

Cobb, Charles R.
2000 *From Quarry to Cornfield: The Political Economy of Mississippian Hoe Production.* University of Alabama Press, Tuscaloosa.

Cohen, Ronald, and Alice Schlegel
1968 The Tribe as a Socio-Political Unit: A Cross-Cultural Examination. In *Essays on the Problem of Tribe,* edited by J. Helm, pp. 120–149. Proceedings of the Annual Spring Meeting of the American Ethnological Society, Seattle. University of Washington Press, Seattle.

Collins, Wilkie J.
1984 Observations on Thermal Treatment of Citronelle Gravels from Louisiana and Mississippi: An Archaeological Assessment. *Mississippi Archaeology* 19(2):7–13.

Cordell, Ann S.
2004 Petrographic Analysis of Four Addis Plain Thin Sections. Manuscript on file, Florida Museum of Natural History, Gainesville.

Cotter, John L.
1951 Stratigraphic and Area Tests at the Emerald and Anna Mound Sites. *American Antiquity* 17:18–32.
1952 The Gordon Site in Southern Mississippi. *American Antiquity* 18:110–126.

Cross, R. D., R. W. Wales, and C. T. Traylor
1974 *Atlas of Mississippi.* University Press of Mississippi, Jackson.

D'Altroy, Terence, and Timothy K. Earle
1985 Staple Finance, Wealth Finance, and Storage in the Inka Political Economy. *Current Anthropology* 26:187–206.

DeBoer, Warren R., and D. Lathrap
1979 The Making and Breaking of Shipibo-Conibo Ceramics. In *Ethnoarchaeology: Implications of Ethnography for Archaeology,* edited by C. Kramer, pp. 102–138. Columbia University Press, New York.

DePratter, Chester
1994 The Chiefdom of Cofitachequi. In *The Forgotten Centuries: Indians and Europeans in the American South, 1521–1704,* edited by C. Hudson and C. C. Tesser, pp. 197–226. University of Georgia Press, Athens.

Di Caprio, N. C., and S. Vaughn
1993 An Experimental Study in Distinguishing Grog (Chamotte) from Argillaceous Inclusions in Ceramic Thin Sections. *Archeomaterials* 7:21–40.

Diaz-Granados, Carol
2004 Marking Stone, Land, Body, and Spirit: Rock Art and Mississippian Iconography. In *Hero, Hawk, and Open Hand: American Indian Art of the Ancient Midwest and South,* edited by R. F. Townsend, pp. 139–149. Art Institute of Chicago, Chicago.

Dickson, D. Bruce
1981 The Yanomamo of the Mississippi Valley? Some Reflections on Larson (1972), Gibson (1974), and Mississippian Period Warfare in the Southeastern United States. *American Antiquity* 46:909–916.

Dye, David H.
1990 Warfare in the Sixteenth-Century Southeast: The de Soto Expedition in the Interior. In *Columbian Consequences,* Vol. 2, *Archaeological and Historical Perspectives on the Spanish Borderlands East,* edited by D. H. Thomas, pp. 211–222. Smithsonian Institution Press, Washington, D.C.
1994 The Art of War in the Sixteenth-Century Central Mississippi Valley. In *Perspectives on the Southeast: Linguistics, Archaeology, and Ethnohistory,* edited by P. B. Kwachka, pp. 44–60. University of Georgia Press, Athens.
1995 Feasting with the Enemy: Mississippian Warfare and Prestige-Goods Circulation. In *Native American Interactions: Multiscalar Analyses and Interpretations in the Eastern Woodlands,* edited by M. S. Nassaney and K. Sassaman, pp. 289–316. University of Tennessee Press, Knoxville.
2007 Ritual, Medicine, and the War Trophy Iconographic Theme in the Mississippian Southeast. In *Ancient Objects and Sacred Realms: Interpretations of Mississippian Iconography,* edited by F. K. Reilly III and J. F. Garber, pp. 152–173. University of Texas Press, Austin.
2009 *War Paths, Peace Paths: An Archaeology of Cooperation and Conflict in Native Eastern North America.* AltaMira, Lanham, Maryland.

Dye, David H., and Adam King
2007 Desecrating the Sacred Ancestor Temples: Chiefly Conflict and Violence in the American Southeast. In *North American Indigenous Warfare and Ritual,* edited by R. J. Chacon and R. G. Mendoza, pp. 160–181. University of Arizona Press, Tucson.

Earle, Timothy K.
1978 *Economic and Social Organization of a Complex Chiefdom: The Halelea*

District, Kaua'i Hawaii. Anthropological Papers No. 63. Museum of Anthropology, Ann Arbor, Michigan.

1987 Chiefdoms in Archaeological and Ethnohistorical Perspective. *Annual Review of Anthropology* 16:279–308.

1997 *How Chiefs Come to Power: The Political Economy in Prehistory.* Stanford University Press, Stanford, California.

2002 *Bronze Age Economics: The Beginnings of Political Economies.* Westview Press, Boulder, Colorado.

Emerson, Thomas E., and Randall E. Hughes

2000 Figurines, Flint Clay Sourcing, the Ozark Highlands, and Cahokian Acquisition. *American Antiquity* 65:79–101.

Emerson, Thomas E., Randall E. Hughes, Mary R. Hynes, and Sarah U. Wisseman

2003 The Sourcing and Interpretation of Cahokia-Style Figurines in the Trans-Mississippi South and Southeast. *American Antiquity* 68:287–313.

Feathers, James K.

2006 Explaining Shell-Tempered Pottery in Prehistoric Eastern North America. *Journal of Archaeological Method and Theory* 13:89–133.

Feinman, Gary, and Jill Neitzel

1984 Too Many Types: An Overview of Sedentary Prestate Societies in the Americas. In *Archaeological Method and Theory*, vol. 7, edited by M. Schiffer, pp. 39–102. Academic Press, New York.

Ford, James A.

1935a *Ceramic Decoration Sequence at an Old Indian Village near Sicily Island, Louisiana.* Anthropological Study No. 1. Department of Conservation, Louisiana Geological Survey, New Orleans.

1935b Outline of Louisiana and Mississippi Pottery Horizons. *Louisiana Conservation Review* 4(6):33–38.

1936 *Analysis of Indian Village Site Collections from Louisiana and Mississippi.* Anthropological Study No. 2. Department of Conservation, Louisiana Geological Survey, New Orleans.

1938 A Chronological Method Applicable to the Southeast. *American Antiquity* 3:260–264.

1951 *Greenhouse: A Troyville-Coles Creek Period Site in Avoyelles Parish, Louisiana.* Anthropological Papers of the American Museum of Natural History, vol. 44, pt. 1. American Museum of Natural History, New York.

Ford, James A., and Gordon R. Willey

1941 An Interpretation of the Prehistory of the Eastern United States. *American Antiquity* 43:325–363.

Frankenstein, Susan, and Michael J. Rowlands
  1978 The Internal Structure and Regional Context of Early Iron Age Society in Southwest Germany. *University of London Institute of Archaeology Bulletin* 15:73–112.
Fritz, Gayle J., and Tristram R. Kidder
  1993 Recent Investigations into Prehistoric Agriculture in the Lower Mississippi Valley. *Southeastern Archaeology* 12:1–14.
Fuller, Richard S.
  1998 Indian Pottery and Cultural Chronology of the Mobile-Tensaw Basin and Alabama Coast. *Journal of Alabama Archaeology* 44:1–51.
  2003 Out of the Moundville Shadow: The Origin and Evolution of Pensacola Culture. In *Bottle Creek: A Pensacola Culture Site in South Alabama,* edited by I. W. Brown, pp. 27–62. University of Alabama Press, Tuscaloosa.
Fuller, Richard S., and Noel R. Stowe
  1982 A Proposed Typology for Late Shell Tempered Ceramics in the Mobile Bay/Mobile-Tensaw Delta Region. In *Archaeology in Southwestern Alabama: A Collection of Papers,* edited by C. Curren, pp. 45–93. Alabama Tombigbee Regional Commission, Camden.
Galaty, Michael
  2008 Ceramic Petrography and the Classification of Mississippi's Archaeological Pottery by Fabric: A GIS Approach. In *Interstate 69 in Mississippi: A Regional Archaeological Perspective,* edited by J. Rafferty and E. Peacock, pp. 243–273. University of Alabama Press, Tuscaloosa.
Gall, Daniel G., and Vincas P. Steponaitis
  2001 Composition and Provenance of Greenstone Artifacts from Moundville. *Southeastern Archaeology* 20:99–117.
Galloway, Patricia K.
  1995 *Choctaw Genesis: 1500–1700.* University of Nebraska Press, Lincoln.
  1998a Debriefing Explorers: Amerindian Information in the Delisles' Mapping of the Southeast. In *Cartographic Encounters: Perspectives on Native American Mapmaking and Map Use,* edited by G. M. Lewis, pp. 223–240. University of Chicago Press, Chicago.
  1998b Commentary and Reflection on Long-Term Continuities and Discontinuities. In *The Natchez District in the Old, Old South,* edited by V. P. Steponaitis, pp. 67–78. Southern Research Report 11. Academic Affairs Library, University of North Carolina, Chapel Hill.
  2000 Archaeology from the Archives: The Chambers Excavations at Lyon's Bluff, 1934–35. *Mississippi Archaeology* 35(1):23–90.
  2002 Colonial Period Transformations in the Mississippi Valley: Disintegration, Alliance, Confederation, Playoff. In *The Transforma-*

tion of the Southeastern Indians, 1540–1760, edited by R. Ethridge and C. Hudson, pp. 225–248. University Press of Mississippi, Jackson.

Gardner, Paul S.
1997 The Ecological Structure and Behavioral Implications of Mast Exploitation Strategies. In *People, Plants, and Landscapes: Studies in Paleoethnobotany*, edited by K. J. Gremillion, pp. 161–178. University of Alabama Press, Tuscaloosa.

Giardino, Marco J.
1985 Ceramic Attribute Analysis and Ethnic Group Composition: An Example from Southeastern Louisiana. Unpublished Ph.D. dissertation, Department of Anthropology, Tulane University, New Orleans.

Gibson, Jon L.
1974 Aboriginal Warfare in the Prehistoric Southeast: An Alternative Perspective. *American Antiquity* 39:130–133.
1994 Before Their Time? Early Mounds in the Lower Mississippi Valley. *Southeastern Archaeology* 13:162–186.

Goad, Sharon
1978 *Exchange Networks in the Prehistoric Southeastern United States*. Ph.D. dissertation, Department of Anthropology, University of Georgia, Athens. University Microfilms, Ann Arbor.

Goodman, Claire Garber
1984 *Copper Artifacts in Late Eastern Woodlands Prehistory*. Center for American Archaeology, Evanston, Illinois.

Gorenflo, L. J., and Nathan Gale
1990 Mapping Regional Settlement in Information Space. *Journal of Anthropological Archaeology* 9:240–274.

Gougeon, Ramie A.
2006 Different but the Same: Social Integration of Households in Mississippian Chiefdoms. In *Leadership and Polity in Mississippian Society*, edited by B. M. Butler and P. D. Welch, pp. 178–196. Occasional Paper No. 33. Center for Archaeological Investigations, Southern Illinois University, Carbondale.

Hally, David J.
1972 The Plaquemine and Mississippian Occupations of the Upper Tensas Basin, Louisiana. Unpublished Ph.D. dissertation. Department of Anthropology, Harvard University, Cambridge.
1980 *Archaeological Investigation of the Little Egypt Site (9Mu102), Murray County, Georgia, 1970–72 Seasons*. Report submitted to the Heritage Conservation and Recreation Service, U.S. Department of the Interior, Atlanta.
1984 Vessel Assemblages and Food Habits: A Comparison of Two Ab-

original Southeastern Vessel Assemblages. *Southeastern Archaeology* 3:46–64.

1986   The Identification of Vessel Function: A Case Study from Northwestern Georgia. *American Antiquity* 51:267–295.

1993   The Territorial Size of Mississippian Chiefdoms. In *Archaeology of Eastern North America: Papers in Honor of Stephen Williams*, edited by J. B. Stoltman, pp. 143–168. Mississippi Department of Archives and History, Jackson.

1994   The Chiefdom of Coosa. In *The Forgotten Centuries: Indians and Europeans in the American South, 1521–1704*, edited by C. Hudson and C. C. Tesser, pp. 227–253. University of Georgia Press, Athens.

1999   The Settlement Pattern of Mississippian Chiefdoms in Northern Georgia. In *Settlement Pattern Studies in the Americas: Fifty Years since Virú*, edited by B. R. Billman and G. M. Feinman, pp. 96–115. Smithsonian Institution Press, Washington, D.C.

2006   Nature of Mississippian Regional Systems. In *Light on the Path: The Anthropology and History of the Southeastern Indians*, edited by T. J. Pluckhahn and R. Ethridge, pp. 26–42. University of Alabama Press, Tuscaloosa.

Hally, David J., Marvin T. Smith, and James B. Langford

1990   The Archaeological Reality of De Soto's Coosa. In *Columbian Consequences*, Vol. 2, *Archaeological and Historical Perspectives on the Spanish Borderlands East*, edited by D. H. Thomas, pp. 121–138. Smithsonian Institution Press, Washington, D.C.

Hammerstedt, Scott W.

2001   Late Woodland and Mississippian Settlement of the Black Warrior Valley: A Preliminary Assessment. *Journal of Alabama Archaeology* 47(1):1–45.

Heartfield, Price, and Greene, Inc.

1982   *A Cultural Resources Inventory of the Pearl River Basin, Louisiana and Mississippi.* Report prepared for the U.S. Army Corps of Engineers, Mobile District.

Hegmon, Michelle

1992   Archaeological Research on Style. *Annual Review of Anthropology* 21:517–536.

Helms, Mary W.

1979   *Ancient Panama.* University of Texas Press, Austin.

1988   *Ulysses' Sail: An Ethnographic Odyssey of Power, Knowledge, and Geographic Distance.* Princeton University Press, Princeton, New Jersey.

1993   *Craft and the Kingly Ideal: Art, Trade, and Power.* University of Texas Press, Austin.

Holstein, Harry O., and Keith J. Little
1986   *A Short-Term Archaeological Investigation of the Davis Farm Archaeological Complex, a Multicomponent Prehistoric Site in Calhoun County, Alabama.* Research Series 1. Archaeological Resource Laboratory, Jacksonville State University, Jacksonville, Alabama.

Hudson, Charles
1994   The Hernando de Soto Expedition: 1539–43. In *The Forgotten Centuries: Indians and Europeans in the American South, 1521–1704,* edited by C. Hudson and C. C. Tesser, pp. 74–103. University of Georgia Press, Athens.
1997   *Knights of Spain, Warriors of the Sun: Hernando de Soto and the South's Ancient Chiefdoms.* University of Georgia Press, Athens.

Hudson, Charles (editor)
1990   *The Juan Pardo Expeditions.* Smithsonian Institution Press, Washington, D.C.

Hudson, Charles, Marvin T. Smith, and Chester DePratter
1984   The Hernando de Soto Expedition: From Apalachee to Chiaha. *Southeastern Archaeology* 3:65–77.

Hudson, Charles, Marvin T. Smith, Chester DePratter, and Emilia Kelley
1985   Coosa: A Chiefdom in the Sixteenth Century United States. *American Antiquity* 50:723–737.
1989   The Tristan de Luna Expedition, 1559–1561. *Southeastern Archaeology* 8:31–45.

Jackson, H. Edwin
2001   Mississippian Occupation of the Leaf River Drainage in Southeast Mississippi: Investigations at the Sims Site (22FO582). Paper presented at the 58th Annual Meeting of the Southeastern Archaeological Conference, Chattanooga, Tennessee.
2006   *Interim Report: The 2005 Excavations at Winterville Mounds (22WS500), Washington County, Mississippi.* Report submitted to the Mississippi Department of Archives and History, Jackson.
2007   *Interim Report: The 2006 Excavations at Winterville Mounds (22WS500), Washington County, Mississippi.* Report submitted to the Mississippi Department of Archives and History, Jackson.

Jackson, H. Edwin, and Susan L. Scott
1995   The Faunal Record of the Southeastern Elite: The Implications of Economy, Social Relations, and Ideology. *Southeastern Archaeology* 14:103–119.
2003   Patterns of Elite Faunal Utilization at Moundville, Alabama. *American Antiquity* 68:552–572.

Jennings, J. D.
- 1952 Prehistory of the Lower Mississippi Valley. In *Archaeology of Eastern United States,* edited by J. B. Griffin, pp. 256–271. University of Chicago Press, Chicago.

Jeter, Marvin D.
- 2002 From Prehistory through Protohistory to Ethnohistory in and near the Northern Lower Mississippi Valley. In *The Transformation of the Southeastern Indians, 1540–1760,* edited by R. Ethridge and C. Hudson, pp. 177–223. University Press of Mississippi, Jackson.

Jeter, Marvin D., and G. Ishmael Williams Jr.
- 1989 Late Prehistoric Cultures, AD 1000–1500. In *Archeology and Bioarchaeology of the Lower Mississippi Valley and Trans-Mississippi South in Arkansas and Louisiana,* edited by M. D. Jeter, J. C. Rose, G. I. Williams Jr., and A. M. Harmon, pp. 171–220. Research Series No. 37. Arkansas Archeological Survey, Fayetteville, Arkansas.

Jones, Dennis, and Malcolm Shuman
- 1986 *Archaeological Atlas and Report of Prehistoric Indian Mounds in Louisiana,* Vol. I. Museum of Geoscience, Louisiana State University, Baton Rouge.
- 1988 *Archaeological Atlas and Report of Prehistoric Indian Mounds in Louisiana,* Vol. III. Museum of Geoscience, Louisiana State University, Baton Rouge.

Kidder, Tristram R.
- 1992 Timing and Consequences of the Introduction of Maize Agriculture in the Lower Mississippi Valley. *North American Archaeology* 13(1):15–41.
- 1993 The Glendora Phase: Protohistoric-Early Historic Culture Dynamics on the Lower Ouachita River. In *Archaeology of Eastern North America: Papers in Honor of Stephen Williams,* edited by J. B. Stoltman, pp. 231–260. Mississippi Department of Archives and History, Jackson.
- 1998a Rethinking Caddoan-Lower Valley Interaction. In *The Native History of the Caddo: Their Place in Southeastern Archaeology and Ethnohistory,* edited by T. K. Pertula and J. E. Bruseth, pp. 129–143. Studies in Archeology, vol. 30. Texas Archeological Research Laboratory, Austin.
- 1998b Mississippi Period Mound Groups and Communities in the Lower Mississippi Valley. In *Mississippian Towns and Sacred Spaces: Searching for an Architectural Grammar,* edited by R. B. Lewis and C. Stout, pp. 123–150. University of Alabama Press, Tuscaloosa.
- 2004 Prehistory of the Lower Mississippi Valley after 800 B.C. In *Southeast,* edited by R. D. Fogelson, pp. 545–559. Handbook of North

American Indians, vol. 14, William Sturtevant, general editor. Smithsonian Institution Press, Washington, D.C.

2007   Contemplating Plaquemine Culture. In *Plaquemine Archaeology*, edited by M. A. Rees and P. C. Livingood, pp. 196–205. University of Alabama Press, Tuscaloosa.

King, Adam

2003   *Etowah: The Political History of a Chiefdom Capital*. University of Alabama Press, Tuscaloosa.

2006   Leadership Strategies and the Nature of Mississippian Chiefdoms in Northern Georgia. In *Leadership and Polity in Mississippian Society*, edited by B. M. Butler and P. D. Welch, pp. 73–90. Occasional Paper No. 33. Center for Archaeological Investigations, Southern Illinois University, Carbondale.

King, Adam (editor)

2007   *Southeastern Ceremonial Complex: Chronology, Content, Context*. University of Alabama Press, Tuscaloosa.

Knight, Vernon James, Jr.

1998   Moundville as a Diagrammatic Ceremonial Center. In *Archaeology of the Moundville Chiefdom*, edited by V. J. Knight Jr. and V. P. Steponaitis, pp. 44–62. Smithsonian Institution Press, Washington, D.C.

2004   Characterizing Elite Midden Deposits at Moundville. *American Antiquity* 69:304–321.

2006   Farewell to the Southeastern Ceremonial Complex. *Southeastern Archaeology* 25:1–5.

Knight, Vernon James, Jr. (editor)

2009   *The Search for Mabila: The Decisive Battle between Hernando de Soto and Chief Tascalusa*. University of Alabama Press, Tuscaloosa.

Knight, Vernon James, Jr., James A. Brown, and George E. Lankford

2001   On the Subject Matter of Southeastern Ceremonial Complex Art. *Southeastern Archaeology* 20:129–153.

Knight, Vernon James, Jr., and Vincas P. Steponaitis

1998   A New History of Moundville. In *Archaeology of the Moundville Chiefdom*, edited by V. J. Knight and V. P. Steponaitis, pp. 1–25. Smithsonian Institution Press, Washington, D.C.

Knight, Vernon James, Jr., and Vincas P. Steponaitis (editors)

1998   *Archaeology of the Moundville Chiefdom*. Smithsonian Institution Press, Washington, D.C.

Kowalewski, Stephen A., and James W. Hatch

1991   The Sixteenth-Century Expansion of Settlement in the Upper Oconee Watershed, Georgia. *Southeastern Archaeology* 10:1–17.

Krause, Richard A.
1985   *The Clay Sleeps.* University of Alabama Press, Tuscaloosa.

Lafferty, Robert H., III
1994   Prehistoric Exchange in the Lower Mississippi Valley. In *Prehistoric Exchange Systems in North America,* edited by T. G. Baugh and J. E. Ericson, pp. 177–213. Plenum Press, New York.

Lankford, George E.
2004   World on a String: Some Cosmological Components of the Southeastern Ceremonial Complex. In *Hero, Hawk, and Open Hand: American Indian Art of the Ancient Midwest and South,* edited by R. F. Townsend, pp. 207–217. Art Institute of Chicago, Chicago.

Larson, Lewis H.
1972   Functional Considerations of Theory: Warfare in the Southeast during the Mississippi Period. *American Antiquity* 37:383–392.

Lewis, Clifford Thomas, III
2008   *Excavations at the Chittoloosa Site (22Wr631): Exploration of a Late Prehistoric Frontier in the Lower Big Black Region of West-Central Mississippi.* Ph.D. dissertation, Department of Anthropology, University of Alabama, Tuscaloosa. University Microfilms, Ann Arbor.

Lindauer, Owen, and John H. Blitz
1997   Higher Ground: The Archaeology of North American Platform Mounds. *Journal of Archaeological Research* 5:169–207.

Little, Kenneth
1967   The Mende Chiefdoms of Sierra Leone. In *West African Kingdoms in the Nineteenth Century,* edited by D. Forde and P. Kaberry, pp. 239–259. Oxford University Press, London.

Livingood, Patrick C.
1999   Investigation of Mississippian Mounds on the Middle Pearl River, Mississippi. Paper presented at the 56th Annual Meeting of the Southeastern Archaeological Conference, Pensacola, Florida.
2006   The Geographic Limit of Inter-Polity Interaction during the Mississippian: A View from the Pevey and Lowe-Steen Sites on the Middle Pearl River, Mississippi. Unpublished Ph.D. dissertation, Department of Anthropology, University of Michigan, Ann Arbor.
2007   No Crows Made Mounds: Do Cost-Distance Calculations of Travel Time Improve Distance-Based Models of the Mississippian? Paper presented at the 64th Annual Meeting of the Southeastern Archaeological Conference, Knoxville, Tennessee.
2011   No Crows Made Mounds: Do Cost-Distance Calculations of Travel Time Improve Distance-Based Models of the Southern Appalachian

Mississippian? In *Archaeological Approaches to Least Cost Analysis,* edited by D. White and S. Surface-Evans. University of Utah Press, Salt Lake City. In press.

Livingood, Patrick C., and John H. Blitz
2004 Timing Is Everything: The Periodicity of Mississippian Mound Construction. Paper presented at the 61st Annual Meeting of the Southeastern Archaeological Conference, St. Louis.

Livingood, Patrick C., and Ann S. Cordell
2009 Point/Counter Point: The Accuracy and Feasibility of Digital Image Techniques in the Analysis of Ceramic Thin Sections. *Journal of Archaeological Science* 36(3):867–872.

Lolley, Terry L.
2000 Archaeology at the Lyon's Bluff Site, a Mississippian and Protohistoric Settlement in Oktibbeha County, Mississippi. *Mississippi Archaeology* 35(1):1–14.

Lopinot, Neal H.
1982 Plant Remains. In *The Carrier Mills Archaeological Project,* edited by R. W. Jeffries and B. Miller, pp. 717–750. Research Paper 33. Center for Archaeological Investigations, Southern Illinois University, Carbondale.

Lorenz, Karl G.
1992 Big Men in the Big Black Valley: Small Prehistoric Community Organization in Central Mississippi. Unpublished Ph.D. dissertation, Department of Anthropology, University of Illinois, Urbana-Champaign.
1996 Small-Scale Mississippian Community Organization in the Big Black River Valley of Mississippi. *Southeastern Archaeology* 15:119–131.

McGahey, Samuel O.
2000 *Mississippi Projectile Point Guide.* Archaeological Report No. 31. Mississippi Department of Archives and History, Jackson.

McGuire, Randall H.
1983 Breaking Down Cultural Complexity: Inequality and Heterogeneity. *Advances in Archaeological Method and Theory* 6:91–141.

Mann, Cyril Baxter
1988 Archaeological Classification of Ceramics from the Pearl Mounds (22Lw510), Lawrence County, Mississippi. Unpublished Master's thesis, Department of Anthropology, University of Southern Mississippi, Hattiesburg.

Marcoux, Jon Bernard
2007 On Reconsidering Display Goods Production and Circulation in the Moundville Chiefdom. *Southeastern Archaeology* 26:232–245.

Marshall, Richard A.
1977 Lyon's Bluff Site (22OK1) Radiocarbon Dated. *Journal of Alabama Archaeology* 23:53–58.
1986 Stylistic Changes in the Mississippian House Patterns at the Lyons Bluff Site, 22Ok1, Oktibbeha County, Mississippi. *Journal of Alabama Archaeology* 32:25–38.

Maxham, Mintcy D.
2000 Rural Communities in the Black Warrior Valley, Alabama: The Role of Commoners in the Creation of the Moundville I Landscape. *American Antiquity* 62:337–354.

Mehrer, Mark W.
1995 *Cahokia's Countryside: Household Archaeology, Settlement Patterns, and Social Power.* Northern Illinois University Press, DeKalb.

Milner, George R.
1998 *The Cahokia Chiefdom: The Archaeology of a Mississippian Society.* Smithsonian Institution Press, Washington, D.C.

Milner, George R., and Sissel Schroeder
1999 Mississippian Sociopolitical Systems. In *Great Towns and Regional Polities in the Prehistoric American Southwest and Southeast,* edited by J. Neitzel, pp. 95–108. University of New Mexico Press, Albuquerque.

Moore, Bill
1987 Prehistory of the Pearl River, Louisiana and Mississippi: Report on a Literature Search. *Louisiana Archaeology* 11:190–227.

Morse, Phyllis A.
1990 The Parkin Site and the Parkin Phase. In *Towns and Temples along the Mississippi,* edited by D. H. Dye and C. A. Cox, pp. 118–134. University of Alabama Press, Tuscaloosa.

Muller, Jon
1978 The Kincaid System: Mississippian Settlement in the Environs of a Large Site. In *Mississippian Settlement Patterns,* edited by B. D. Smith, pp. 269–292. Academic Press, New York.
1986 *Archaeology of the Lower Ohio River Valley.* Academic Press, New York.
1993 Lower Ohio Valley Mississippian Revisited: An Autocritique of "The Kincaid System." In *Archaeology of Eastern North America: Papers in Honor of Stephen Williams,* edited by J. B. Stoltman, pp. 127–142. Mississippi Department of Archives and History, Jackson.
1997 *Mississippian Political Economy.* Plenum Press, New York.
2007 Prolegomena for the Analysis of the Southeastern Ceremonial Complex. In *Southeastern Ceremonial Complex: Chronology, Content, Context,* edited by A. King, pp. 15–37. University of Alabama Press, Tuscaloosa.

Neumann, Robert W.
- 1984   *An Introduction to Louisiana Archaeology.* Louisiana State University Press, Baton Rouge.

Nicklin, K.
- 1981   Pottery Production and Distribution in Southeast Nigeria. In *Production and Distribution: A Ceramic Viewpoint,* edited by H. Howard and E. Morris, pp. 169–186. BAR International Series 120. British Archaeological Reports, Oxford.

O'Shea, John M., and Alex W. Barker
- 1996   Measuring Social Complexity and Variation: A Categorical Imperative? In *Emergent Complexity: The Evolution of Intermediate Societies,* edited by J. E. Arnold, pp. 13–24. International Monographs in Prehistory, Ann Arbor, Michigan.

Pauketat, Timothy R.
- 1994   *The Ascent of Chiefs: Cahokia and Mississippian Politics in Native North America.* University of Alabama Press, Tuscaloosa.
- 2007   *Chiefdoms and Other Archaeological Delusions.* AltaMira, Lanham, Maryland.

Pauketat, Timothy R., and Thomas E. Emerson
- 1999   The Representation of Hegemony as Community at Cahokia. In *Material Symbols: Culture and Economy in Prehistory,* edited by J. E. Robb, pp. 302–317. Occasional Paper No. 26. Center for Archaeological Investigations, Southern Illinois University, Carbondale.

Payne, Claudine
- 1994   *Mississippian Capitals: An Archaeological Investigation of Precolumbian Political Structure.* Ph.D. dissertation, Department of Anthropology, University of Florida, Gainesville. University Microfilms, Ann Arbor.

Payne, Claudine, and John F. Scarry
- 1998   Town Structure at the Edge of the Mississippian World. In *Mississippian Towns and Sacred Spaces: Searching for an Architectural Grammar,* edited by R. B. Lewis and C. Stout, pp. 22–48. University of Alabama Press, Tuscaloosa.

Paynter, Robert
- 1989   The Archaeology of Equality and Inequality. *Annual Review of Anthropology* 18:369–399.

Peebles, Christopher S.
- 1971   Moundville and Surrounding Sites: Some Structural Considerations of Mortuary Practices. In *Approaches to the Social Dimensions of Mortuary Practices,* edited by J. A. Brown, pp. 68–91. Memoir 25. Society for American Archaeology, Washington, D.C.

1979 *Excavations at Moundville: 1905–1951.* University of Michigan Press, Ann Arbor.
1983 Moundville: Late Prehistoric Sociopolitical Organization in the Southeastern United States. In *The Development of Political Organization in Native North America*, edited by E. Tooker, pp. 183–201. American Ethnological Society, Washington, D.C.
1987 The Rise and Fall of the Mississippian in Western Alabama: The Moundville and Summerville Phases, A.D. 1000 to 1600. *Mississippi Archaeology* 22(1):1–31.

Peebles, Christopher S., and Susan M. Kus
1977 Some Archaeological Correlates of Ranked Societies. *American Antiquity* 42:421–448.

Petruso, Karl M., and Jere M. Wickens
1984 The Acorn in Aboriginal Subsistence in Eastern North America: A Report on Miscellaneous Experiments. In *Experiments and Observations on Aboriginal Wild Plant Food Utilization in Eastern North America*, edited by P. J. Munson, pp. 360–378. Prehistory Research Series 6, No. 2. Indiana Historical Society, Indianapolis.

Phillips, Philip
1970 *Archaeological Survey in the Lower Yazoo Basin, Mississippi, 1949–1955.* Peabody Museum of Archaeology and Ethnology, Harvard University, Cambridge, Massachusetts.

Phillips, Philip, and James A. Brown
1978 *Pre-Columbian Shell Engravings from the Craig Mound at Spiro, Oklahoma.* Peabody Museum Press, Cambridge, Massachusetts.

Phillips, Philip, James A. Ford, and James B. Griffin
1951 *Archaeological Survey in the Lower Mississippi Alluvial Valley, 1940–1947.* Peabody Museum of Archaeology and Ethnology, Harvard University, Cambridge, Massachusetts.

Pluckhahn, Thomas J., and David A. McKivergan
2002 A Critical Appraisal of Middle Mississippian Settlement and Social Organization on the Georgia Coast. *Southeastern Archaeology* 21:149–161.

Polhemus, Richard R.
1987 *The Toqua Site—40MR6: A Late Mississippian Dallas Phase Town.* Report submitted to the Tennessee Valley Authority by the Department of Anthropology, University of Tennessee, Knoxville. Report of Investigations 41. Department of Anthropology, University of Tennessee, Knoxville.

Powell, Mary Lucas
1988 *Status and Health in Prehistory: A Case Study of the Moundville Chiefdom.* Smithsonian Institution Press, Washington, D.C.

1991   Related Status and Health in the Mississippian Chiefdom at Moundville. In *What Mean These Bones? Studies in Southeastern Bioarchaeology,* edited by M. L. Powell, P. S. Bridges, and A. M. W. Mires, pp. 22–51. University of Alabama Press, Tuscaloosa.

Prentice, Guy

1985   Economic Differentiation among Mississippian Farmsteads. *Midcontinental Journal of Archaeology* 10:77–122.

2000   *Ancient Indian Architecture of the Lower Mississippi Delta Region.* The Southeast Archaeological Center, Tallahassee, Florida.

Quimby, George I.

1942   The Natchezan Culture Type. *American Antiquity* 7:255–275.

1951   The Medora Site, West Baton Rouge Parish, Louisiana. *Field Museum of Natural History, Anthropological Series* 24:81–135.

1957   The Bayou Goula Site, Iberville Parish, Louisiana. *Fieldiana Anthropology* 47(2). Chicago Natural History Museum.

Quitmyer, Irvy R.

2003   Zooarchaeological Remains from Bottle Creek. In *Bottle Creek: A Pensacola Culture Site in South Alabama,* edited by I. W. Brown, pp. 130–155. University of Alabama Press, Tuscaloosa.

Rafferty, Janet, Jeffrey Alvey, S. Homes Hogue, and Robert McCain

2004   *Archaeological Testing at the Pocahontas Mound A Site (22Hi500), Hinds County, Mississippi.* Report funded and prepared for the Mississippi Department of Transportation, Jackson.

Rees, Mark A.

1997   Coercion, Tribute and Chiefly Authority: The Regional Development of Mississippian Political Culture. *Southeastern Archaeology* 16:113–133.

Rees, Mark A., and Patrick C. Livingood

2007   Introduction and Historical Overview. In *Plaquemine Archaeology,* edited by M. A. Rees and P. C. Livingood, pp. 1–19. University of Alabama Press, Tuscaloosa.

Rees, Mark A., and Patrick C. Livingood (editors)

2007   *Plaquemine Archaeology.* University of Alabama Press, Tuscaloosa.

Reilly, F. Kent, III, and James F. Garber (editors)

2007   *Ancient Objects and Sacred Realms: Interpretations of Mississippian Iconography.* University of Texas Press, Austin.

Reimer, P. J., M. G. L. Baillie, E. Bard, A. Bayliss, J. W. Beck, C. J. H. Bertrand, P. G. Blackwell, C. E. Buck, G. S. Burr, K. B. Cutler, P. E. Damon, R. L. Edwards, R. G. Fairbanks, M. Friedrich, T. P. Guilderson, A. G. Hogg, K. A. Hughen, B. Kromer, F. G. McCormac, S. W. Manning, C. B. Ramsey, R. W. Reimer, S. Remmele, J. R. Southon,

M. Stuiver, S. Talamo, F. W. Taylor, J. van der Plicht, and C. E. Weyhenmeyer
2004 IntCa104 Terrestrial Radiocarbon Age Calibration, 26–0 ka BP. *Radiocarbon* 46:1029–1058.

Renfrew, Colin, and Eric V. Level
1979 Exploring Dominance: Predicting Polities from Centers. In *Transformations: Mathematical Approaches to Culture Change,* edited by C. Renfrew and K. L. Cooke, pp. 145–167. Academic Press, New York.

Rice, Prudence M.
1987 *Pottery Analysis: A Sourcebook.* University of Chicago Press, Chicago.

Roberts, Katherine M.
2004 Plant Remains. In *Data Recovery Excavations at the Hedgeland Site (16CT19), Catahoula Parish, Louisiana,* edited by J. Ryan, pp. 207–226. Report submitted to the U.S. Army Corps of Engineers, Vicksburg District, by Coastal Environments, Inc., Baton Rouge, Louisiana.

Roth, J. A.
1980 Analysis of Faunal Remains. In *Archaeological Investigation of the Little Egypt Site (9Mu102), Murray County, Georgia 1970–2 Seasons,* by D. J. Hally, pp. 570–591. Report submitted to the Heritage Conservation and Recreation Service, U.S. Department of the Interior, Atlanta.

Rucker, Marc D.
1976 *Archaeological Investigations of Pocahontas Mound A, Hinds County, Mississippi.* Archaeological Excavation Report No. 3. Mississippi State Highway Department, Jackson.

Russ, John C.
1999 *The Image Processing Handbook.* 3rd ed. CRC Press, Boca Raton, Florida.

Russo, Michael
1994 Brief Introduction to the Study of Archaic Mounds in the Southeast. *Southeastern Archaeology* 13:89–93.

Ryan, Joanne (editor)
2004 *Data Recovery Excavations at the Hedgeland Site (16CT19), Catahoula Parish, Louisiana.* Report submitted to the U.S. Army Corps of Engineers, Vicksburg District, by Coastal Environments, Inc., Baton Rouge, Louisiana.

Rye, Owen S.
1976 Keeping Your Temper under Control: Materials and the Manufacture of Papuan Pottery. *Archaeology and Physical Anthropology in Oceania* 11:106–137.

Saunders, Joe W., and Thurman Allen
1994   Hedgepeth Mounds, an Archaic Mound Complex in North-Central Louisiana. *American Antiquity* 59:471–489.

Saunders, Joe W., Reca Jones, Kathryn Moorhead, and Brian Davis
1998   "Watson Brake Objects," an Unusual Archaic Artifact Type from Northeast Louisiana and Southwest Mississippi. *Southeastern Archaeology* 17:72–79.

Saunders, Joe W., Rolfe D. Mandel, C. Garth Sampson, Charles M. Allen, E. Thurman Allen, Daniel A. Bush, James K. Feathers, Kristen J. Gremillion, C. T. Hallmark, H. Edwin Jackson, Jay K. Johnson, Reca Jones, Roger T. Saucier, Gary L. Stringer, and Malcolm F. Vidrine
2005   Watson Brake, a Middle Archaic Mound Complex in Northeast Louisiana. *American Antiquity* 70:631–668.

Saunders, Rebecca
1994   Case for Archaic Period Mounds in Southeastern Louisiana. *Southeastern Archaeology* 13:118–134.

Scarry, C. Margaret
1986   *Change in Plant Procurement and Production during the Emergence of the Moundville Chiefdom.* Ph.D. dissertation, Department of Anthropology, University of Michigan, Ann Arbor. University Microfilms, Ann Arbor.
1993   Agricultural Risk and the Development of the Moundville Chiefdom. In *Foraging and Farming in the Eastern Woodlands,* edited by C. M. Scarry, pp. 157–181. University of Florida Press, Gainesville.
2003a   Food Plant Remains from Excavations in Mounds A, B, C, D, and L at Bottle Creek. In *Bottle Creek: A Pensacola Culture Site in South Alabama,* edited by I. W. Brown, pp. 103–113. University of Alabama Press, Tuscaloosa.
2003b   The Use of Plants in Mound-Related Activities at Bottle Creek and Moundville. In *Bottle Creek: A Pensacola Culture Site in South Alabama,* edited by I. W. Brown, pp. 114–129. University of Alabama Press, Tuscaloosa.

Scarry, C. Margaret, and Vincas P. Steponaitis
1997   Between Farmstead and Center: The Natural and Social Landscape of Moundville. In *People, Plants, and Landscapes: Studies in Paleoethnobotany,* edited by K. J. Gremillion, pp. 107–122. University of Alabama Press, Tuscaloosa.

Scarry, John F., and Claudine Payne
1986   Mississippian Polities in the Fort Walton Area: A Model Generated from the Renfrew-Level XTENT Algorithm. *Southeastern Archaeology* 5:79–90.

Scott, Susan
- 2005 Vertebrate Fauna. In *Lake Providence: A Terminal Coles Creek Culture Mound Center, East Carroll Parish, Louisiana,* vol. 2, edited by R. A. Weinstein, pp. 411–429. Prepared for the U.S. Army Corps of Engineers, Vicksburg District, by Coastal Environments, Inc., Baton Rouge, Louisiana.

Service, Elman R.
- 1962 *Primitive Social Organization.* Random House, New York.

Shaffer, John G., and Vincas P. Steponaitis
- 1982 James A. Ford's and Moreau B. Chambers' Mound Excavations in the Big Black River Drainage, Mississippi: A Preliminary Descriptive Report. Manuscript on file at the Department of Anthropology, University of North Carolina, Chapel Hill.
- 1983 Burial Mounds from the Big Black Drainage in Mississippi: Some New Interpretations. Paper presented at the 40th Annual Meeting of the Southeastern Archaeological Conference, Columbia, South Carolina.

Shepard, Anna O.
- 1976 *Ceramics for the Archeologist.* Carnegie Institution of Washington, Washington, D.C.

Sinopoli, Carla M.
- 1991 *Approaches to Archaeological Ceramics.* Plenum Press, New York.

Skibo, James M., Kenneth C. Reid, and Michael B. Schiffer
- 1989 Organic-Tempered Pottery: An Experimental Study. *American Antiquity* 54:122–146.

Smith, Bruce D.
- 1985 Mississippian Patterns of Subsistence and Settlement. In *Alabama and the Borderlands: From Prehistory to Statehood,* edited by R. R. Badger and L. A. Clayton, pp. 64–79. University of Alabama Press, Tuscaloosa.

Smith, Bruce D. (editor)
- 1978a *Mississippian Settlement Patterns.* Academic Press, New York.
- 1978b *Prehistoric Patterns of Human Behavior: A Case Study in the Mississippi Valley.* Academic Press, New York.

Smith, Marvin T.
- 2000 *Coosa: The Rise and Fall of a Southeastern Mississippian Chiefdom.* University of Florida Press, Gainesville.

Spencer, Charles S.
- 1982 *The Cuicatlán Cañada and Monte Albán: A Study of Primary State Formation.* Academic Press, New York.
- 1987 Rethinking the Chiefdom. In *Chiefdoms in the Americas,* edited

by R. D. Drennan and C. Uribe, pp. 369–390. University Press of America, Lanham, Maryland.

1990   On the Tempo and Mode of State Formation: Neoevolutionism Reconsidered. *Journal of Anthropological Archaeology* 9:1–30.

Stallings, Richard

1989   Factors in Interpreting the Prehistoric Use of the Citronelle Gravels in Mississippi. *Mississippi Archaeology* 24(1):35–58.

Steinen, Karl T.

1992   Ambushes, Raids, and Palisades: Mississippian Warfare in the Interior Southeast. *Southeastern Archaeology* 11:132–139.

Steponaitis, Laurie Cameron

1986   *Prehistoric Settlement Patterns in the Lower Patuxent Drainage, Maryland.* Ph.D. dissertation, Department of Anthropology, State University of New York, Binghamton. University Microfilms, Ann Arbor.

Steponaitis, Vincas P.

1974   The Late Prehistory of the Natchez Region: Excavations at the Emerald and Foster Sites, Adams County, Mississippi. Unpublished Honors thesis, Harvard University, Cambridge, Massachusetts.

1978   Location Theory and Complex Chiefdoms. In *Mississippian Settlement Patterns,* edited by B. D. Smith, pp. 417–453. Academic Press, New York.

1983   *Ceramics, Chronology, and Community Patterns: An Archaeological Study at Moundville.* Academic Press, New York.

1991   Contrasting Patterns of Mississippian Development. In *Chiefdoms: Power, Economy, and Ideology,* edited by T. Earle, pp. 193–228. Academic Press, New York.

1998   Native American Cultures in the Precolonial South. In *The Natchez District in the Old, Old South,* edited by V. P. Steponaitis, pp. 1–22. Southern Research Report 11. Academic Affairs Library, University of North Carolina, Chapel Hill.

Steponaitis, Vincas P., M. James Blackman, and Hector Neff

1996   Large-Scale Patterns in the Chemical Composition of Mississippian Pottery. *American Antiquity* 61:555–572.

Steponaitis, Vincas P., and Vernon James Knight Jr.

2004   Moundville Art in Historical and Social Context. In *Hero, Hawk, and Open Hand: American Indian Art of the Ancient Midwest and South,* edited by R. F. Townsend, pp. 167–181. Art Institute of Chicago, Chicago.

Stoltman, James B.

1989   A Quantitative Approach to the Petrographic Analysis of Ceramic Thin Sections. *American Antiquity* 54:147–160.

1991 Ceramic Petrography as a Technique for Documenting Cultural Interaction: An Example from the Upper Mississippi Valley. *American Antiquity* 56:103–120.

2001 The Role of Petrography in the Study of Archaeological Ceramics. In *Earth Sciences and Archaeology,* edited by P. Goldberg, V. T. Holliday, and C. R. Ferring, pp. 297–326. Kluwer Academic/Plenum, New York.

Stubbs, John

ca. 1980 Notes on the Surface Collections Made from the Mill Creek Mounds. Manuscript on file with the Mississippi Department of Archives and History, Jackson.

Stuiver, M., P. J. Reimer, E. Bard, J. W. Beck, G. S. Burr, K. A. Hughen, B. Kromer, F. G. McCormac, J. v. d. Plicht, and M. Spurk

1998 INTCAL98 Radiocarbon Age Calibration, 24000–0 cal BP. *Radiocarbon* 40:1041–1083.

Stuiver, M., P. J. Reimer, and R. W. Reimer

2005 CALIB 5.0. Electronic document, http://Calib.qub.ac.uk/Calib/, accessed February 2006.

Swanton, John R.

1911 *Indian Tribes of the Lower Mississippi Valley and Adjacent Coast of the Gulf of Mexico.* Bureau of American Ethnology Bulletin No. 43. Government Printing Office, Washington, D.C.

1928 Sun Worship in the Southeast. *American Anthropologist* 30:206–213.

1949 *The Indians of the Southeastern United States.* Bureau of American Ethnology Bulletin No. 137. Smithsonian Institution Press, Washington, D.C.

Takacs, Jeff

1994 Maygrass for Lunch. Unpublished manuscript available from Patrick Livingood.

Tobler, Waldo

1993 Non-isotrophic Geographic Modeling. In *Three Presentations on Geographic Analysis and Modeling.* Technical Report 93-1. University of California, National Center for Geographic Information and Analysis, Santa Barbara.

U.S. Army Corps of Engineers

1970 Agricultural Requirements and Upstream Watershed Development. In *Pearl River Comprehensive Basin Study,* vol. 6, Appendix G. U.S. Army Corps of Engineers, Mobile District, Mobile, Alabama.

1975 *Final Environmental Impact Statement; Flood Control Mississippi River and Tributaries; Yazoo River Basin, Mississippi.* Report on file, U.S. Army Engineer District, Vicksburg, Mississippi.

U.S. Department of Agriculture
- 1978 *Soil Survey of Lawrence County.* U.S. Department of Agriculture, Washington, D.C.

van der Leeuw, Sander E.
- 1977 Toward a Study of the Economics of Pottery Making. In *Ex Horreo,* edited by B. L. Van Beek, R. W. Brandt, and W. G.-v. Waateringe, pp. 68–76. University of Amsterdam, Amsterdam.

Velde, Bruce, and Isabelle C. Druc
- 1998 *Archaeological Ceramic Materials.* Springer-Verlag, Berlin.

Waddell, Gene
- 2005 Cofitachequi: A Distinctive Culture, Its Identity, and Its Location. *Ethnohistory* 52(2):333–369.

Waselkov, Gregory
- 1989 Indian Maps of the Colonial Southeast. In *Powhatan's Mantle: Indians in the Colonial Southeast,* edited by P. H. Wood, G. Waselkov, and M. T. Hatley, pp. 292–343. University of Nebraska Press, Lincoln.
- 1998 Indian Maps of the Colonial Southeast: Archaeological Implications and Prospects. In *Cartographic Encounters: Perspectives on Native American Mapmaking and Map Use,* edited by G. M. Lewis, pp. 205–222. University of Chicago Press, Chicago.

Weinstein, Richard A.
- 1987 Development and Regional Variation of Plaquemine Culture in South Louisiana. In *Emergent Mississippian: Proceedings of the Sixth Mid-South Archaeological Conference,* edited by R. A. Marshall, pp. 85–106. Occasional Paper No. 87-01. Cobb Institute of Archaeology, Mississippi State University, Mississippi State.

Weinstein, Richard A. (editor)
- 2005 *Lake Providence: A Terminal Coles Creek Culture Mound Center, East Carroll Parish, Louisiana.* 2 vols. Prepared for the U.S. Army Corps of Engineers, Vicksburg District, by Coastal Environments, Inc., Baton Rouge, Louisiana.

Welch, Paul D.
- 1990 Mississippian Emergence in West-Central Alabama. In *The Mississippian Emergence,* edited by B. D. Smith, pp. 197–226. Smithsonian Institution Press, Washington, D.C.
- 1991 *Moundville's Economy.* University of Alabama Press, Tuscaloosa.
- 1998 Outlying Sites within the Moundville Chiefdom. In *Archaeology of the Moundville Chiefdom,* edited by V. J. Knight Jr. and V. P. Steponaitis, pp. 1–25. Smithsonian Institution Press, Washington, D.C.
- 2006 Interpreting Anomalous Rural Mississippian Settlements: Leadership from Below. In *Leadership and Polity in Mississippian Society,* edited by

B. M. Butler and P. D. Welch, pp. 214–235. Occasional Paper No. 33. Center for Archaeological Investigations, Southern Illinois University, Carbondale.

Welch, Paul D., and C. Margaret Scarry
1995 Status-Related Variation in Foodways in the Moundville Chiefdom. *American Antiquity* 60:397–420.

Wells, Douglas C.
1998 The Early Coles Creek Period and the Evolution of Social Inequality in the Lower Mississippi Valley. Unpublished Ph.D. dissertation, Department of Anthropology, Tulane University, New Orleans.
2005 Aboriginal Ceramics. In *Lake Providence: A Terminal Coles Creek Culture Mound Center, East Carroll Parish, Louisiana,* vol. 2, edited by R. A. Weinstein, pp. 311–390. Prepared for the U.S. Army Corps of Engineers, Vicksburg District, by Coastal Environments, Inc., Baton Rouge, Louisiana.

Wells, Douglas C., and Richard A. Weinstein
2007 Extraregional Contact and Cultural Interaction at the Coles Creek–Plaquemine Transition: Recent Data from the Lake Providence Mounds, East Carroll Parish, Louisiana. In *Plaquemine Archaeology,* edited by M. A. Rees and P. C. Livingood, pp. 38–65. University of Alabama Press, Tuscaloosa.

Whitney, Cynthia, Vincas P. Steponaitis, and John J. W. Rogers
2002 A Petrographic Study of Moundville Palettes. *Southeastern Archaeology* 21:227–234.

Wiessner, Polly
1983 Style and Social Information in Kalahari San Projectile Points. *American Antiquity* 49:253–276.
1984 Reconsidering the Behavioral Basis for Style: A Case Study among the Kalahari San. *Journal of Anthropological Archaeology* 3:190–234.
1989 Style and Changing Relations between the Individual and Society. In *The Meaning of Things: Material Culture and Symbolic Expression,* edited by I. Hodder, pp. 56–63. Unwin Hyman, London.

Williams, Mark
1994 Growth and Decline of the Oconee Province. In *The Forgotten Centuries: Indians and Europeans in the American South, 1521–1704,* edited by C. Hudson and C. C. Tesser, pp. 179–196. University of Georgia Press, Athens.

Williams, Stephen, and Jeffrey P. Brain
1983 *Excavations at the Lake George Site, Yazoo County, Mississippi, 1958–1960.* Harvard University Press, Cambridge, Massachusetts.

Wilson, Gregory D.
- 2001 Crafting Control and the Control of Crafts: Rethinking the Moundville Greenstone Industry. *Southeastern Archaeology* 20:118-128.
- 2008 *The Archaeology of Everyday Life at Early Moundville.* University of Alabama Press, Tuscaloosa.

Winterhalder, Bruce
- 1981 Optimal Foraging Strategies and Hunter-Gatherer Research in Anthropology: Theory and Models. In *Hunter-Gatherer Foraging Strategies: Ethnographic and Archaeological Analyses,* edited by B. Winterhalder and E. A. Smith, pp. 13–35. University of Chicago Press, Chicago.

Wisseman, Sarah U., Duane M. Moore, Randall E. Hughes, Mary R. Hynes, and Thomas E. Emerson
- 2002 Mineralogical Approaches to Sourcing Pipes and Figurines from the Eastern Woodlands, U.S.A. *Geoarchaeology* 17(7):689–715.

Wright, Henry T.
- 1977 Recent Research on the Origins of the State. *Annual Review of Anthropology* 6:379–397.
- 1984 Prestate Political Formations. In *On the Evolution of Complex Societies: Essays in Honor of Harry Hoijer,* edited by T. Earle, pp. 41–78. Undena, Malibu, California.

Yarnell, Richard A., and M. Jean Black
- 1985 Temporal Trends Indicated by a Survey of Archaic and Woodland Plant Food Remains from Southeastern North America. *Southeastern Archaeology* 4:93–106.

Yoffee, Norman
- 1993 Too Many Chiefs? (Or, Safe Texts for the '90s). In *Archaeological Theory: Who Sets the Agenda?,* edited by N. Yoffee and A. Sherratt, pp. 60–78. Cambridge University Press, Cambridge.

Index

16Wa8, 22
22Ha515, 22
22Hi512, 22
22Lw510. *See* Pevey Site
22Lw511. *See* Lowe-Steen Site
22Lw544, 57, 58, 62
22Lw549. *See* Smith Estate No. 1
22Lw593. *See* Phillips Farm site
22Lw641. *See* Coin Farm site
22Lw644, 57–59, 62–65, 72, 99
22Lw647, 57, 72
22Lw657, 57, 58, 61–65
22Lw660, 57, 58, 61–66, 72, 99, 121
22Lw661, 57, 58, 61–66, 72, 99
22Ma550, 137

Addis, 132; analysis of temper, 75–76, 84–89; history, 70–71; paste, 132–133
Addis Plain, *var. Addis*, 59, 61, 62, 65, 70, 75, 78, 84, 85, 87–90, 129, 156, 160, 161, 166, 168, 173, 175, 178, 179, 181, 182
Addis Plain, *var. Greenville*, 59, 65, 70, 71, 85, 87, 89, 156, 160, 166–168, 173–175, 178–179, 182
Addis Plain, *var. Junkin*, 71
Addis Plain, *var. Ratcliffe*, 71
Addis Plain, *var. St. Catherine*, 70, 71
Adobe Photoshop, 80
Agriculture, 132. *See also* plant remains
Amite River, 138

Andrefsky, William, Jr., 115
Anna Incised, *var. Anna,* 30–32, 34, 37, 39, 40, 41, 43, 45, 48–50, 58, 72, 78, 87, 88, 96–98, 136, 156, 161, 168, 175, 179
Anna Incised, *var. Australia,* 32, 156, 168, 175,
Anna Incised, *var. unspecified,* 156, 161, 168, 175
Anna phase, 21, 95, 98, 105, 126, 127, 129
Anna site, 10, 21, 27, 142, 145, 146, 148, 149
Apalachee, 62
Appalachian, 5, 122, 131
Archaic, 21, 51, 58, 59, 61, 118, 121, 141
Architecture, 14, 54, 125–127. *See also* features; structures
Arkansas River, 68
Avoyelles Punctated, *var. Dupree,* 73, 96, 97, 127, 161, 168, 175
Aztec empire, 152

Baca, Keith A., 136
Bahala Creek, 57, 59
Balmoral, 148
Barton Incised, *var. Barton,* 41, 48, 73, 156, 161, 168, 175, 179
Barton Incised, *var. Estill,* 50, 96, 156, 161, 168, 175, 179
Barton Incised, *var. Midnight,* 34, 97, 127, 156, 161, 168, 175
Barton Incised, *var. unspecified,* 156, 161, 169, 175

Index

Bayou Petre phase, 69
Baytown Plain, 62, 65, 70, 156, 161, 169, 175, 179
Baytown Plain, *var. Addis,* 70. *See also* Addis Plain
Beads, 30, 31, 40, 122, 123, 125, 187
Bear Creek, 62
Bellaire style, 17
Bell Plain, 57, 65, 70, 71, 74, 76, 78, 79, 85, 87–90, 129, 156, 160, 161, 166, 169, 173, 175, 178, 179, 182
Bell Plain, *var. Bell,* 71
Bell Plain, *var. Greenville,* 59, 65, 70, 71, 74–76, 78, 85, 87, 89, 90, 93, 156, 160, 161, 166–168, 173–175, 178, 179, 182
Bell Plain, *var. Holly Bluff,* 70, 71
Bell Plain, *var. New Madrid,* 71
Bell Plain, *var. St. Catherine,* 70, 71
Big Black River, 9, 135, 139–140, 142, 148
Big Man society, 140
Black Warrior River, 1, 9, 11, 14, 15, 18, 135, 138–139, 147
Blaine site, 132, 135, 137, 143, 147, 149, 153
Blitz, John H., 10, 15, 16, 21, 101, 103
Bottle Creek site, 1, 7, 27, 111–112, 114, 115, 137–138, 141, 145–147
Boudreaux, Edmond A., 141
Brewer, E. Marko, 106–115
Brown, Ian W., 54, 73, 125, 126, 127, 141
Burials: goods, 10, 11, 134; mortuary shrine, 11; mounds, 9, 10, 124, 139; practice, 16, 133
Butler site, 139, 147

Caddo, 17, 68
Cahokia, 4, 17, 142
Carter Engraved, 88
Carter Engraved, *var. Carter,* 30, 31, 34, 37, 41, 43, 45, 48, 50, 74, 79, 87, 88, 96, 98, 136, 156, 162, 169, 175
Carter Engraved, *var. Sara,* 43, 74, 96, 156, 162, 169, 175
Carter Engraved, *var. Shell Bluff,* 39, 41, 74, 125, 137, 156, 162, 169, 175
Carter Engraved, *var. unspecified,* 45, 48, 50, 57, 61, 74, 162, 169, 175, 179
Central Mississippi Valley, 11, 141, 143
C-14. *See* Radiocarbon
Chapman phase, 10

Chattahoochee River, 142
Chert, 117. *See also* Citronelle gravel
Chiaha, 7
Chickasaw, 6, 133
Chicot Red, *var. Fairchild,* 96, 132, 157, 162, 169, 175
Chiefdom: chiefly elites, 12–14, 145, 149; chiefly residence, 101, 105, 125; complex, 10, 11; territorial limit, 5, 131, 146; model, 2, 4–5; Mississippian, 2–18, 137, 140, 141, 147–148; paramount, 5, 6–10, 139, 145, 149, 150
Chinchuba site, 138
Choctaw, 22, 124, 131–133, 135
Chotawhatchee Bay, 137
Chowder Springs site, 139, 147
Citico style, 7
Citronelle gravel, 117
Cofitachequi polity, 6, 8, 144, 145
Coin Farm site (22Lw641), 57–59, 62–65, 72
Coleman site, 139, 147
Coles Creek: ceramics, 21; period and culture, 11, 17, 21, 68, 69, 94, 125, 138, 141
Coles Creek Incised, *var. Hardy,* 30, 37, 96, 127, 136, 157, 162, 169, 175
Coles Creek Incised, *var. unspecified,* 28, 96, 127, 157, 162, 169, 175
Collins point, 57, 62, 121
Coosa chiefdom, 6–8, 12, 15, 144, 146, 149, 150
Coosa River, 149
Copper, 10, 35, 122–123, 125, 138, 147
Cordell, Ann S., 82, 83
Cotton Mounds, 142
Crippen Point phase, 95–97
Crown Zellerbach/Cavenham Industries site, 138

Dallas phase, 62
Daub, 28, 30, 31, 34, 45, 49, 50, 54
DePratter, Chester, 6
D'Olive Incised, 75, 88, 137
D'Olive Incised, *var. unspecified,* 29, 31, 34, 39, 41, 43, 48, 50, 75, 78, 79, 86–88, 90, 96, 157, 162, 169, 176, 179
Dupree phase, 10
Dupree site, 137, 143
Dye, David H., 11

Index

Emerald phase, 21, 31, 97
Emergent Mississippian, 15
Esoteric goods. *See* prestige goods
European: colonists, 6, 141; explorers, 121
Evansville Punctated, *var. Sharkey,* 43, 75, 96, 127, 157, 162, 169, 176
Evansville Punctated, *var. unspecified,* 32, 75, 157, 162, 169, 176
Excavation Unit A, 28, 39
Excavation Unit B, 28–29, 39, 100, 101, 118–121
Excavation Unit C, 29–31, 39, 100–102, 107–115, 118–121, 125
Excavation Unit E, 32–34, 35, 39, 54, 97, 100–102, 105, 115, 118–121, 124, 127–130, 183–191
Excavation Unit G, 39–42, 100, 102, 107–115, 118–123, 125, 126
Excavation Unit H, 39, 42–43, 77, 97, 100, 102, 105–115, 117, 118–121, 123, 125, 126
Excavation Unit I, 39, 43, 77, 100–102, 107–115, 118–121, 123
Excavation Unit J, 39, 45, 118–121
Excavation Unit K, 39, 43–45, 100, 101, 118–121
Excavation Unit M, 34–35, 39, 54, 77, 97, 100–102, 105, 107–115, 118–121, 122, 125–130, 183–191
Excavation Unit 956R1003, 47–48, 100, 118–121
Excavation Unit 975R1007, 48–50, 100, 101, 118–121
Excavation Unit 1136R876, 50, 100, 101, 118–121, 126
Excavation Unit SE, 31–32, 35, 39, 54, 97, 100, 101, 105, 107–115, 118–121, 124, 126, 127–130
Excavation Unit SJ, 39, 45, 100, 101, 118–121, 126
Excavation Unit T, 35–38, 39, 54, 100–102, 106, 107–115, 118–121, 123, 125, 126
Exchange. *See* trade
Exotica. *See* prestige goods

Fatherland Incised 132
Fatherland Incised, *var. Pine Ridge,* 34, 75, 97, 127, 157, 162, 169, 176

Fatherland Incised, *var. unspecified,* 32, 41, 157, 163, 170, 176
Fatherland site, 126
Faunal remains, 115, 123, 125, 131, 183–191
Feasts, 8, 12, 38, 54, 101, 115, 125, 140, 183, 189–191
Feature 4, Lowe-Steen site, 50, 64, 77, 101, 110, 111, 118, 121
Features: excavation procedures, 27, 50, 51, 106; hearth, 30, 40, 43, 47, 50, 54, 106, 108; midden, 23, 31, 33–35, 37, 39, 40, 43–45, 47, 48, 50, 54, 64, 77, 101, 106, 112, 120, 124, 184, 186; pit, 29, 54; post, 28–31, 33, 34, 36–39, 41–45, 48, 50–52, 125, 126; term, 4
Flotation, 27, 51. *See also* plant remains
Flowood site, 137
Ford, James A., 67, 68, 88
Foster phase, 21, 31, 34, 97, 129
Fuller, Richard S., 73, 138

Galaty, Michael, 71, 85
Galloway, Patricia K., 22, 131–133
Gordon phase, 21, 95–97, 129
Gorenflo, L. J., 5
Grace Brushed, *var. Grace,* 34, 37, 41, 50, 75, 78, 79, 86–88, 90, 96–98, 157, 163, 170, 176, 179
Great Lakes, 122
Gulf Coast: archaeological region, 68, 137–139, 147; chiefdoms, 9, 141
Gulf Coastal Plain, 1, 6, 9, 19, 117, 145, 149, 183

Hally, David J., 5, 6, 8, 99, 131, 142–144, 152
Hally circles, 143–144
Hamlet, 55, 59, 133
Hammerstedt, Scott W., 62
Harrison Bayou Incised, *var. Harrison Bayou,* 43, 49, 50, 96, 127, 138, 157, 163, 170, 176, 179
Heartfield, Price, and Greene, Inc., 20, 22
Hearth. *See* features
Hedgeland, 111–115, 123, 148
Helms, Mary W., 12
Hiker's formula, 5, 150–151
Hilman site, 139, 147
Hinds County, 137

Hollyknowe Pinched, *var. Patmos,* 34, 37, 48, 75, 96, 157, 163, 170, 176, 180
Hoover site, 138

Ibibio people of Nigeria, 76
Image Analysis Toolkit, 80, 82

Jeter, Marvin D., 68, 141

Kavango potters, southern Africa, 76
Kincaid, 62
Knight, Vernon, 138

Lake Borgne, 19
Lake George phase, 97
Lake George site, 27, 126, 142, 145, 146, 148–149
Lake Pontchartrain, 138
Lake Providence site, 94, 142, 148
Lamar culture, 62
Larto Red-Filmed
Lawrence County, Mississippi, 1, 18–22, 54–59, 62, 63, 66, 97, 133, 183
Leaf River, 132
L'Eau Noire Incised, 88, 138
L'Eau Noire Incised, *var. L'Eau Noire,* 34, 37, 72, 79, 87, 88, 96, 97, 157, 163, 170, 176
L'Eau Noire Incised, *var. unspecified,* 157, 163, 170, 176
Leland Incised, *var. Bethlehem,* 34, 96, 98, 157, 163, 170, 176
Leland Incised, *var. Foster,* 97, 127, 157, 163, 170, 176
Leland Incised, *var. Leland,* 97, 127, 157, 163, 170, 176
Leland Incised, *var. unspecified,* 157, 163, 170, 176
Little Egypt site, 7, 15, 149
Livingood, Patrick C., 16, 56, 73, 141, 183
Loess Bluffs, 117
Lorenz, Karl G., 112, 139, 140, 153
Louisiana State Archaeological Survey, 68
Lower Mississippi Survey, 93
Lower Mississippi Valley, 14–16, 21–22, 67–71, 77, 89, 93, 96–98, 104, 122, 133, 135, 137, 140–143, 145, 153
Lower Ouachita River, 68
Lower Patuxent, 55

Lowe-Steen site: archaeological research, 19, 45–50; architecture, 126; ceramics, 63–65, 72, 74–77, 95–96, 99–105, 179–181; chronology, 98, 127, 139; comparison, 51, 54, 59, 131, 135–137; general description, 1, 57, 147; lithics, 117–118; faunal remains, 115; plant remains, 106, 110, 111; mica, 121; settlement pattern, 62, 131
Lubbub Creek site, 1, 10–11, 55, 62, 101, 103, 111–115, 122, 123, 129, 139–140, 145, 147, 149, 153
Lyon's Bluff site, 139, 147, 149, 153

Maddox Engraved, *var. Silver City,* 31, 34, 97, 127, 158, 163, 171, 176,
Maddox Engraved, *var. unspecified,* 158, 163, 171, 176
Maize. *See* plant remains
Mann, Cyril Baxter, 20, 21, 23, 25, 28, 67, 124, 133
Marcoux, Jon Bernard, 9
MARIS, 24, 46, 52
Marksville stage, 68
Mayersville phase, 70
Mazique Incised, *var. Manchac,* 37, 96, 158, 163, 171, 176, 180
Mazique Incised, *var. unspecified,* 78, 87, 88, 158, 164, 171, 176, 180
McGahey, Samuel O., 121
McGuire, Randall H., 17
McIntire point, 59
Medora phase, 70
Melanesian, 140
Midden. *See* features
Mill Creek, 23, 24, 26, 134
Mill Creek site, 1, 20
Milner, George R., 4
Mississippian culture: chiefdoms, 2–12, 140; culture comparison, 68–70, 92, 94, 131; polities, 4, 14, 137, 143–153; sites, 20, 22, 26–27, 34, 51, 55, 66, 131, 135–143
Mississippi Department of Archives and History, 20, 136
Mississippi period, 1, 9, 23, 26, 48, 56, 57, 58, 61, 101, 112, 118, 121, 122, 135–143, 183
Mississippi Plain, 29, 30, 57, 59, 61, 62, 64, 71, 74–76, 78–79, 84, 86–87, 89, 90, 92,

93, 129, 158–159, 160, 164–167, 171–174, 176–177, 178, 180–182
Mississippi Plain, *var. Coker,* 71
Mississippi Plain, *var. Mainfort,* 71
Mississippi Plain, *var. Yazoo,* 71
Mississippi River Valley, 1, 14, 19, 138
Mobile Bay, 22
Mobile River, 18, 135
Mobile-Tensaw Delta, 137
Mooney, Tim, 22, 31, 51, 131
Mound A, Lowe-Steen, 47–50, 54, 101
Mound A, Pevey, 23, 25, 28, 124
Mound B, Lowe-Steen, 47, 50, 54, 101
Mound B, Pevey, 23, 25, 28–29, 101, 124
Mound C, Pevey, 21, 25, 29–31, 101, 106–112, 124, 125
Mound D, Pevey, 21, 25, 34, 124
Mound E, Pevey, 21, 25, 26, 31–38, 54, 101, 105, 106–112, 123–125, 128, 130–132, 183
Mound F, Pevey, 23, 25
Mound G, Pevey, 21, 25, 38, 39–42, 54, 121, 124, 125, 128, 130
Mound H, Pevey, 21, 25, 42–43, 106–112, 124, 125
Mound I, Pevey, 21, 23, 25, 43, 106–112, 121–124
Mound J, Pevey, 23–25, 45, 124
Mound K, Pevey, 23, 25, 43–45, 101, 124
Mound Place Incised, 31, 32, 34, 41, 43, 45, 48–50, 57, 61, 73–75, 78, 88
Mound Place Incised, *var. A,* 75, 159, 165, 172, 177
Mound Place Incised, *var. B,* 97, 159, 165, 172, 177, 180
Mound Place Incised, *var. D,* 75, 159, 165, 172, 177
Mound Place Incised, *var. Moundville,* 159, 165, 172, 177
Mound Place Incised, *var. unspecified,* 75, 87, 88, 165, 172, 177
Mounds: case studies, 9–11; compared to non-mound sites, 62–65, 103, 120; construction, 12, 14, 138; date of initial construction, 16, 141; date of occupation, 15; height, 26–27; house mounds, 23; number at a site, 14, 18, 26–27; Pearl River, 22; size, 13, 26–27; spatial distribution, 5, 55, 100, 143–144, 149; use, 13, 139

Moundville, 1, 7, 9, 10–12, 14, 17, 27, 40, 55, 62, 74, 110–115, 122–124, 129, 134, 138–139, 140, 141, 145–147, 149
Moundville Incised, 40, 137
Moundville Incised, *var. Moundville,* 40, 41, 73, 96, 125, 139, 159, 165, 172, 177
Moundville Incised, *var. unspecified,* 32, 41, 43, 159, 165, 172, 177
Muller, Jon, 4

Nanih Waiya mound, 135
Napochies, 7
Natchez, 121
Natchez Bluffs, 16, 21, 22, 34, 54, 67, 68, 70, 76, 126, 127, 129, 141, 142, 148
Natchez phase and period, 21, 68
National Register of Historic Places, 20
Neitzel, Stewart, 20
Newman, J. E., 20
Nonlocal goods, 9, 11, 117, 123, 138–140. *See also* prestige goods

Oconee River, 62
Ocute polity, 6, 8, 145
Old Hoover site, 55, 111–115, 138–140, 148, 149, 153
Owens Punctated, *var. Menard,* 34, 97, 159, 165, 173, 177
Owens Punctated, *var. Poor Joe,* 97, 127, 159, 165, 172, 177
Owens Punctated, *var. unspecified,* 30, 32, 34, 73, 97, 98, 159, 165, 173, 177

Paleobotanical remains. *See* plant remains
Paleo-Indian, 59
Pardo, Juan, 6
Parkin phase, 62
Parkin Punctated, 137
Parkin Punctated, *var. Harris,* 32, 73, 159, 165, 173, 177
Parkin Punctated, *var. Hollandale,* 31, 96, 159, 165, 173, 177
Parkin Punctated, *var. Transylvania,* 73, 96, 159, 165, 173, 177
Parkin Punctated, *var. unspecified,* 159, 165, 173, 177
Pascagoula drainage, 22
Pauketat, Timothy R., 4

Payne, Claudine, 14, 26, 27, 152
Paynter, Robert, 17
Pearl Mounds, 1, 20, 21
Pearl River: archaeological investigations, 20, 22, 26, 45–46, 51, 55, 58–59, 61, 70, 83–84, 89, 92–95, 132, 135–137; Middle Pearl River, 19, 67, 76; physiographic description, 19–20
Pensacola: culture, 137; pottery, 74; region, 74, 137
Pevey phase, 95, 98, 127, 131
Pevey site: alternative names, 1, 20; architecture, 125–127; ceramic counts, 72, 96–97, 99; chronology, 95–98, 127–131; comparison with other sites, 26–27, 45, 51; description, 1, 23–28, 57; environment, 23–26; excavation units, 31–45; faunal remains, 115, 183–191; lithic analysis, 115–121; mound arrangement, 124–125; plant remains; 106–115, polity, 62–66, 131, 135–137, 143–153; previous research, 20–23; survey, 59–61
Phillips Farm site (22Lw593), 51–54, 57, 61–66, 72, 98–99, 117, 126–132, 182
Phillips, Phillip, 67–70, 73
Piney Woods physiographic province, 19, 183
Pinola phase, 137
Pipes, 17
Plant remains, 106–115, 123, 125
Plaquemine Brushed, 29
Plaquemine Brushed, *var. Plaquemine*, 29, 31, 32, 34, 37, 41, 43, 45, 48–50, 54, 57, 61, 78, 79, 87, 88, 90, 96–98, 128, 129, 159, 166, 173, 178, 181
Plaquemine culture, 16–17, 21, 68–71, 83, 92, 94, 99, 121, 125, 137, 138, 141–142
Plaza, 20, 31, 68, 101, 183
Pocahontas site and polity, 1, 9–11, 122, 137, 140, 143, 145, 147–149, 153
Polity: Anna polity, 144, 147; Blaine polity, 144, 147, 149; Bottle Creek polity, 137–138, 144, 147, 149; Coosa polity, 15, 146; definition of, 6; interpolity interaction, 1–18, 135–153; Kincaid polity, 62; Lake George polity, 10, 144, 147; large-polity strategy, 14; Lubbub Creek polity, 10, 62, 139, 147, 149; Lyon's Bluff polity, 144, 147; mapping polities, 143–144; Moundville polity, 144, 147; Old Hoover polity, 112, 139–140, 144, 147, 149; Moundville polity, 9–10; paramount polity, 15; Pevey polity, 131, 133, 135–137, 147, 149; Pocahontas polity, 144, 147, 149; size of Mississippian polities, 5, 150, 152; study of interpolity relationship, 14, 124, 144; tribute, 7, 8; unit of analysis, 6; Winterville polity, 144, 147
Posts. *See* features
Pottery, paste. *See* Addis Plain; Baytown Plain; Bell Plain; Mississippi Plain; Pottery, temper
Pottery, rim and lip forms: carination, 39, 92, 98, 99, 102; Flaring-rim, 99, 102; neckless, 92, 99, 103; outslanting, 99; restricted, 30, 92, 99, 102
Pottery, temper: Addis, 58, 75; ceramic ecology, 71; clay-tempered, 70; comparison of temper choice, 64, 65, 90–93, 95; grog, 60, 68–71, 76, 80, 82–84, 86, 93, 137; microscopic analysis, 76–89; mixed temper, 70; sand, 69; shell, 21, 22, 50, 54, 57, 62, 64, 66, 68, 69, 71, 74, 75, 92, 93, 129, 132, 136, 137; significance in Lower Mississippi Valley, 67–71, 94; term, 4
Pottery, Vessel forms: bottle, 92, 99, 100, 104, 105; bowl, 29, 30, 31, 39, 88, 90, 92, 98–102, 104, 105; bowl, carinated, 39, 92, 98, 99, 102; bowl, deep, 98, 99, 102; bowl, flaring-rim, 99, 102; bowl, outslanting, 99, 102; bowl, restricted, 30, 92, 99, 102; bowl, simple, 92, 99, 102; jar, 29, 40, 68, 69, 92, 99, 101–105; jar, generic, 99; jar, globular, 92, 99, 103; jar, Mississippian, 69; jar, neckless, 92, 99, 103; jar, standard, 92, 99, 103; plate, 92, 99, 104, 105
Poverty Point site, 4
Prestige goods, 2, 9–12, 14, 15, 18, 41, 125, 140, 145, 152
Preston phase, 69

Quigualtam, 8
Quimby, George I., 68, 70, 88

Radiocarbon, 54, 98, 127–131, 136
Ramey Incised, 142
Red River, 68, 70
Rees, Mark A., 7
Reindeer Graphics, 80
Ross Barnett Reservoir, 22
Routh phase, 111
Rowe, Simone, 115, 183

Scallorn point, 121
Scarry, C. Margaret, 110
Scarry, John F., 152
Settlement pattern: hierarchical, 8, 145, 146; Lawrence County Mississippian, 55–66, 132, 134, 148; Mississippian model, 62; study of, 2, 55–56, 139, 141, 145, 146; use of, 5–6, 11
Shephard, Anna O., 80
Shipibo-Conibo of eastern Peru, 76
shovel tests, 28, 51, 60–62
Sims, Doug, 136
Sims site, 132
Sixtowns band, 22, 131–133
Smith, Marvin T., 7
Smith Estate No. 1 (22Lw549), 55, 57, 62
Smith phase, 10
Soto, Hernando de, 6–8
Southeastern Ceremonial Complex, 17, 122
Southern Appalachians, 122, 131
Spanish, 6–8, 145, 149
Spencer, Charles S., 5
Steinen, Karl T., 11
Steponaitis, Laurie, 55
Steponaitis, Vincas P., 1, 9, 10, 12, 22, 70, 73, 98, 110, 138, 140, 143, 145
Stoltman, James P., 80
Structure 1, 22Lw593, 126
Structures, 30, 31, 34, 36, 39, 40, 43, 45, 50–52, 54, 100, 125. *See also* architecture; features
Summerville phases (I, II/III, IV), 10, 11, 111–115, 129, 139

Sumptuary goods. *See* prestige goods
Survey, 51, 55–66, 132

Takacs, Jeff, 106
Tascalusa, 6, 8
Tensas Basin, 17, 69, 94, 141, 143, 148
Tobler, Waldo, 5
Tombigbee River, 10, 18, 139, 147
Toqua site, 7, 149
Trade, 5, 9–17, 22, 41, 67, 106, 118, 123, 135, 139, 140, 142, 145, 147, 152, 153
Transylvania site, 142
Travel: canoe, 151; organization, 152; travel time, 5, 143, 149–153
Tristan de Luna, 7
Troyville period, 68

U.S. Army Corps of Engineers, 22
U.S. Geological Survey, 24, 46, 52

Village, 6, 62, 101, 103, 111, 138

Warfare, 8, 11, 12, 121, 123, 151, 153
Wasp Lake phase, 97
Watson Brake site, 141
Wells, Douglas C., 99
Wentworth scale, 82
West Jefferson phase, 138
Willey, Gordon R., 68
Williams, Stephen, 69, 70, 73
Winstead phase, 95–98, 115, 121, 123, 127–129, 131–132, 137, 138, 142, 143, 190
Winterville Incised, 137
Winterville Incised, *var. unspecified*, 160, 167, 174, 178
Winterville phase, 21, 95, 98, 105, 126, 127, 129
Winterville site, 1, 11, 126, 142, 145, 148
Woodland period, 51, 59, 61, 118, 121, 135, 137

XTENT algorithm, 152

Yazoo Basin, 17, 67–71, 76, 126, 127, 142–143, 148